Praise for *Sisters of the Resistance*

"A powerful story of seldom-sung heroines in humanity's darkest days and a vivid reminder of the power of conscience. Using first-hand accounts, Turner crafts an inspiring narrative of courage and sacrifice in the face of terror."
— EDGARDO DAVID HOLZMAN

"Dennis Turner has used some unusual and previously unavailable records to provide a perspective on World War Two that is entirely new: the role played by Catholic nuns in anti-Nazi activities and the Belgian Resistance movement... an engaging account of World War Two as told through the voice of a fictional Belgian nun. Readers interested in World War Two, as well as those who are fascinated by accounts of the remarkable courage exhibited in the lives of ordinary people, will find this book a fascinating and valuable experience."
— DONALD LYSTRA

"...a generous recounting of the deeds of marvelous nuns living in the midst of mortal danger. It's also a great read!"
— FATHER JAMES HEFT, SOCIETY OF MARY

SISTERS
OF THE
RESISTANCE

DENNIS TURNER

AD LIB

First published in 2022 by Ad Lib Publishers Ltd
15 Church Road,
London, SW13 9HE
www.adlibpublishers.com

Text © 2022 Dennis J. Turner

Paperback ISBN 978-1-913543-11-2
eBook ISBN 978-1-802470-27-7

A CIP catalogue record for this book is available
from the British Library.

Every reasonable effort has been made to trace copyright-holders
of material reproduced in this book, but if any have been
inadvertently overlooked the publishers would be
glad to hear from them.

Printed in the UK
10 9 8 7 6 5 4 3 2 1

CONTENTS

Dedicated to the courageous Sisters of Notre Dame De Namur who provided the inspiration for this book.

In Memory of Christine Spoon.

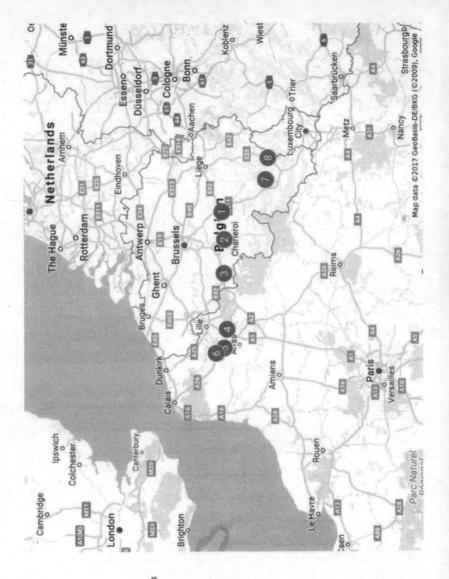

BELGIUM

Untitled layer

1 Namur
2 Jumet
3 Jemappes
4 Courcelles-lès-Lens
5 Bully-les-Mines
6 Béthune
7 Saint-Hubert
8 Bastogne

TIMELINE

1932–1945

1932
General Paul von Hindenburg is elected President in Germany, defeating Nazi Party candidate Adolf Hitler.
November 8: Franklin Delano Roosevelt (FDR) is elected President of the United States.

1933
January 30: President Hindenburg appoints Adolf Hitler chancellor of Germany.
March 25: Adolf Hitler seizes power in Germany. Hindenburg is reduced to a igurehead.
April 7: In Germany, Jews and non-Aryans are banned from practising law and working in the civil services. Later they will be banned from a variety of professions including farming, art, literature, journalism, music, and theatre. Hundreds of anti-Jewish laws are enacted in Germany.

1934
August 2: Hitler assumes the presidency of Germany and gains full control of the government when Hindenburg dies.

1935
September 5: In Germany, the first Nuremberg Laws are passed revoking citizenship of Jews and prohibiting them from marrying non-Jews.
October: Italy invades Ethiopia.

1936
July 17: Spanish Civil War begins.

1937
August: Japan invades China.
November 25: Germany signs military agreement with Japan.

1938
March 12: Anschluss (Austria annexed by Germany).
July 6–14: International conference in France that FDR initiated to discuss the Jewish refugees. Thirty-two nations refused to admit large numbers of Jews.
September: France and Britain adopted a policy of appeasement, agreeing to the German annexation of Sudetenland, Czechoslovakia.
November 9–19: Kristallnacht (Night of the Broken Glass). Nazis violently attack Jews and destroy Jewish property; 91 Jews are killed, and others are beaten.

1939
March: Germany annexes the rest of Czechoslovakia. British government pledges to aid Poland "at once ... with all the support in their power" in the event that Poland is attacked by Germany.
June 17: The Jewish refugee ship the St. Louis arrives in Belgium after being denied access to Cuba and the United States. Most of the passengers are eventually murdered by the Nazis.

August 23: Nazi-Soviet Non-Aggression Pact announced in Moscow.

September 1: Germany invades Poland from the West.

September 3: Britain declares war on Germany at 11 a.m.; France declares war on Germany six hours later.

September 5: The United States declares its neutrality.

September 21: FDR calls for a special session of Congress to repeal the Neutrality Acts. He argues that the United States could preserve neutrality and provide Great Britain and France with arms by adopting a "cash and carry" plan.

October 16: First German air raid on the British Isles.

November 4: The United States Congress amends the Neutrality Acts to favour Britain and France, lifting the embargo and authorising "cash and carry."

November 30: Soviet troops invade Finland.

1940

January: Rationing is introduced in Britain.

April 9: German troops invade Denmark and Norway.

April 14: British forces land in Norway.

May 10: Holland, Belgium, and Luxembourg are invaded by Germany. British troops enter Belgium. British Prime Minister Neville Chamberlain resigns; Winston Churchill becomes new prime minister.

May 15: Holland surrenders to Germany.

May 28: Belgium surrenders to Germany.

June 3: Norway surrenders to Germany.

June 10: Italy declares war on Britain and France.

June 14: Germans enter Paris.

June 22: France signs armistice with Germany.

June 24: France signs armistice with Italy.

August 8: The Battle of Britain begins.

August 26: First all-night air raid on London.

October 28: Italy invades Greece.
December 29: During a Fireside Chat, FDR declares that the US should become an "arsenal of democracy" against the Axis threat.

1941
April 6: Germany invades Greece and Yugoslavia.
June 22: Germany attacks the Soviet Union.
July 12: Anglo-Russian treaty signed.
August 11: Churchill and FDR form Atlantic Charter, establishing the war aims of both nations.
December 7: Britain declares war on Finland, Hungary, and Romania. Japanese bomb the United States leet at Pearl Harbor.
December 8: Britain and the United States declare war on Japan. Japan invades Malaya.
December 11: Germany and Italy declare war on United States.

1942
January 20: Fourteen Nazi leaders attend a short meeting to discuss the elimination of the remaining European Jews. The genocidal plan is dubbed "The Final Solution."
August 5–31: Germans advance in Russia and start the Leningrad offensive on the 28th.
November 8: United States and British forces land in French North Africa.
November 11: Germans enter unoccupied zone of Vichy France.
December: Fighting between German and Soviet forces in Stalingrad in the Soviet Union.

1943
January 31: Seventeen German generals surrender to the Soviets at Stalingrad.
April 7–30: Allied offensive in Northern Tunisia.

May 13: Germans surrender in Tunisia.

July 10: Allies invade Sicily.

July 25: Benito Mussolini is dismissed by King Victor Emmanuel in Italy and is arrested.

August 2: The end of eight days of intensive bombing of Hamburg, Germany, by the Allies.

August 17: Allies complete conquest of Sicily.

September 3: Italy forms armistice with Allies.

September 8: Italy surrenders.

October 13: Italy declares war on Germany.

1944

January 22: Allied landings south of Rome in Anzio.

June 4: Allies occupy Rome.

June 6: D-Day, Allied invasion of Normandy.

June 23: Russians start offensive on Central Front.

July 20: Bomb hidden in Hitler's bunker fails to kill him.

July 27: Americans break out of Normandy.

August 12: Germans in full retreat from France.

August 15: Allied forces land in southern France.

August 25: Paris liberated by the Allies. Romania declares war on Germany.

September 3: Brussels liberated by Allied forces.

November 28–29: First American night air attack on Tokyo.

December 16: Battle of the Bulge begins, the last German offensive in the west.

1945

February 13: Dresden raid. Allied firebombing kills 135,000 Germans, mostly civilians, and destroys 80 per cent of the city.

March 7: Americans find intact bridge across Rhine at Remagen, set up bridgehead on east bank.

March 23: Allies cross the Rhine.

April 1: Germans surrounded in Ruhr Valley.

April 12: FDR dies, Harry S. Truman assumes the presidency of the United States.

April 20: Americans capture Nuremberg.

April 28: Mussolini captured by Italian partisans and executed.

April 29: Dachau concentration camp is overrun by United States soldiers.

May 1: Hitler commits suicide.

May 2: Berlin surrenders to Russian forces.

May 4: German forces in Holland, Northwest Germany, and Denmark surrender.

May 7: Unconditional surrender of all German forces to Britain, Russia, and the United States.

May 8: V-E Day: German surrender confirmed.

June 26: United Nations charter is signed.

August 5: Atomic bomb is dropped on Hiroshima.

August 9: Atomic bomb is dropped on Nagasaki.

August 14: Japan accepts Allied terms of unconditional surrender.

August 15: V-J Day.

PREFACE

In December of 2016, my wife and I shared a meal with Sister Kim Dalgarn, a member of the Sisters of Notre Dame de Namur. The good sister casually mentioned that she'd recently discovered a cache of letters—letters that had not been seen for 70 years.

The letters and other documents had been written by Sisters of Notre Dame de Namur during the Nazi occupation of Belgium and Italy in World War II.

In great detail, these letters document the lives of the sisters and convents under the Nazi regime, detailing the hardships of bombings, hunger, and the executions of innocents.

Moreover, these letters tell the story of how these brave and faithful women worked to defeat the Nazis.

Throughout the occupied territories, the Sisters were active members of The Resistance. From running contraband to hiding resisters and Jews, from spying for the allies to small acts of sabotage, these courageous women risked their lives to save others and to end the war.

This is a story that needs to be told.

Using these precious letters, historical records, and contemporary sources, I have done my best to present these stories through the eyes of Sister Christina, a young American nun of my own invention. By necessity, I have taken literary liberties—but the stories are true. Where I have deviated from the strict historical record, it is noted in the endnotes.

I believe, at the end of this modest fictionalised biography, you will share my sincere gratitude and unending admiration for these unsung heroines of the Second World War.

CHAPTER ONE

A BRUSH WITH DEATH

Saint-Hubert, Belgium, December 22, 1944

THE GERMAN ARMY IS HERE—AGAIN.

When American soldiers marched into Saint-Hubert in September, we believed the war was over. The departing German soldiers told us, "We will be back," but no one believed them. American troops came in such numbers, with hundreds of tanks, trucks and jeeps. The soldiers were so fit and robust, bursting with confidence. What army in the world could resist such a force? Certainly not the dirty, exhausted German soldiers we saw slipping out of town in the dead of the night.

And yet, German shells are now raining down on our town and many of the jaunty American soldiers we saw streaming to the front in September are straggling back into Saint-Hubert with weary, vacant faces, suffering from wounds and frostbite. There is another bad sign. Americans are pouring out on the ground all the gasoline they had stored in their fuel depots. They want to keep it from falling into the hands of the advancing Germans. Engineers are dynamiting large trees to block the roads. Apparently, the Americans are going to abandon Saint-Hubert and they are hoping to slow down the German tanks. Once again, the citizens of Saint-Hubert will be living in a Nazi occupied town. Again, they will be dying from American bombs and shells when they try to retake Saint-Hubert. We cannot flee. There is no transportation. The roads are snow covered, and temperatures are hovering around zero. We cannot abandon our sick Sisters or the homeless children we have sheltered in our school.

I am ashamed to admit that I fear death. All my training as a Sister of Our Lady was meant to prepare me for death. Blessed Mother Julie, our Foundress, tells us:

The surest means of arriving speedily at perfection is to work at becoming indifferent, that is, to desire nothing and to fear nothing, even death. From the moment that a Sister of Our Lady has bound herself to God by her religious consecration, she must accept with indifference whatever obedience demands of her. Let us sacrifice our self-love, our personal views, our very life for the sake of peace. Peace is so precious, that it cannot be bought too dearly.

A hypothetical acceptance of one's death, however, provides only some comfort when faced with the prospect of imminent death. My near-death experience at the start of the German shelling yesterday shattered my philosophical beliefs. I had endured the first German invasion in 1940 and four years of German occupation without dwelling on the prospect of my own death. I may have unconsciously adopted a soldier's mindset about facing death. An American sergeant told me most frontline soldiers endure the unendurable by assuming they are already dead and that there is little or no chance they will survive the ordeal of war. With the fear of death in abeyance, they can emerge from their foxholes and attack machine guns and tanks; keeping the respect of their comrades means more to them than the likelihood they would be killed. Similarly, my love for my fellow sisters trumped my fears and enabled me to carry out my duties with a certain calmness. Thinking of myself as already dead had the ironic effect of enhancing the joy I felt from the small day-to-day pleasures of life, like the laughter of a small child or a rose-tinted sunset. When there is no prospect of a tomorrow, today is the only thing that matters. I squeezed happiness from the mundane. I was contented, even happy, with my life.

Fear can be kept at bay by this psychological trick as long as hope does not begin to creep into one's subconscious. The soldier who begins to believe he may actually survive the war may be haunted by fear.

The dread induces more caution and a reluctance to take risks, which sometimes increases the risk of death to his comrades. No soldier wants to be the last casualty of the war. Hope arrived for me with the liberation of Saint-Hubert. The arrival of legions of jaunty American soldiers distributing salutes, winks, whistles, and candy bars to the welcoming villagers. The town's walls were festooned with the word "Welcome!" I knew the war was over for me, and life could return to normal. Fear was banished. Hope flourished.

I was wrong. An overwhelming fear of death took hold of me with the explosions of German artillery shells and the rumours that the German army had broken through the American army's defences. The dreaded Panzer tanks were on their way. For a while, my anxiety was allayed by the labour of preparing the convent and the school for the inevitable attack on Saint-Hubert, which sits astride major roads the Germans would need to get to Antwerp. There were children in the school along with many other residents of the town who depended on the relative security of our deep cellars. The numbers increased when the American military hospital was partially destroyed by the German bombardment. Space was made for dozens of wounded soldiers and some medical personnel. A day was spent manoeuvring mattresses, cots, food, and medicine down steep, narrow stairs. People were sleeping everywhere—on floors, in chairs, and even in bathtubs. Many doors had been blown off their hinges by the force of the blasts. The church was destroyed, so a temporary chapel was created in a small room near the laundry and the coal cellar. The Blessed Sacrament was displayed in a gold ciborium shrouded in fine bobbin lace and placed in a sturdy oak tabernacle. Half a dozen *prie-dieus* were crowded into the "cave-chapel." Fortunately, the large and well-equipped kitchen was intact, and with great risks to their lives the sisters worked in shifts preparing food for the hundreds of children, soldiers, and refugees sheltering in the damp, cold cellars.

Sister Ursula, Sister Superior of the Saint-Hubert convent, suggested we comfort the children by having them sing Christmas carols, especially during the periodic shelling. The joyful music helped me, too. With so many of us squeezed into the cellars, we were no more secure from the shells and bombs, but sharing a common danger with a crowd of people creates a comfortable illusion of safety.

My sense of safety was totally shattered the next day, December 21st. I went with Sister Ursula and several other sisters to the cellar chapel to pray. I happened to be using the more comfortable padded *prie-dieu*. Sister Ursula said she was having great difficulty with her arthritic knees and asked me if I would change places with her. I did, and then Sister Ursula began a prayer. Before her prayer could be completed, a German artillery shell exploded just outside in the street and the room was filled with dust and smoke. Sister Ursula stood up from the *prie-dieu* and turned to face us. She had a beautiful and calm expression. She never said a word. She clutched her heart and then collapsed. I was so mesmerised by this scene seeming to take place in slow motion, I did not realise I had been hit in the leg by a piece of shrapnel. Then excruciating, searing pain—like I had been branded by a hot poker—coursed through my calf muscle. My habit was torn, and blood was pouring out on the cellar floor. I don't remember screaming. I passed out.

When I regained consciousness, I was lying in a corner of the cellar on a mattress that had been set aside for wounded American soldiers. Sister Angela, my dear friend, was sitting next to me on an apple crate. She told me I was with the other wounded because it was easier for the American doctor to tend to my wound. The soldier who had been occupying the mattress was moved to another part of the cellar so that I might have a bit more privacy. A blanket was hung from a rafter, screening me from the other wounded. I did not feel much pain. Sister Angela told me the doctor had given me a shot of morphine.

The effects of the trauma and the narcotics made me very sleepy, but I insisted Sister Angela tell me the whole story of what had happened. She said the exploding German shell hurled small pieces of shrapnel through a tiny opening in the outside wall of the coal cellar. The red-hot metal passed across the coal cellar and through its open door. One piece struck the oaken tabernacle, made two large holes in the ciborium, and struck Sister Ursula in the heart. She managed to stand, but almost immediately collapsed and died.

With all the smoke and confusion, they had not noticed I was also wounded by shrapnel. When I screamed and fainted, they saw the blood and called for the American doctor, who was already on his way to the chapel. Without the doctor, I might have died from loss of blood. There was a gash in my right calf muscle. The doctor applied a tourniquet to stanch the bleeding and stitched up the wound. It was several days before I could walk without a crutch. Even walking, I was more of a burden than a help to my fellow sisters, who were already exhausted from caring for so many people crammed into our cellars.[1]

CHAPTER TWO

MY JOURNEY FROM A FARM TO A BELGIAN CONVENT

Ohio, 1913–1938

SISTER URSULA'S DEATH AND MY OWN BRUSH WITH MORTALITY GAVE me doubts as to whether we sisters would survive the ordeal. My own terror was consuming my waking hours. I was also cast adrift without my anchor and mentor, Sister Ursula, who had been short on praise and long on critique. She would rarely, if ever, praise me—or anyone—with a "Well done." At the same time, I knew she had confidence in me and trusted me to tackle any task she assigned. That knowledge meant more to me than any laudatory words. Sister Ursula pushed and challenged me to go beyond my self-imposed insecurities. As my confidence grew, so did her expectations. I also knew she "had my back," and I could count on her total support whenever I needed it. She had supplied a nurturing recipe for my personal growth, and now she was dead. I would have been dead if Sister Ursula had not asked to change places with me. I was filled with a sense of dread and guilt. I had inadvertently traded her life for mine.

Prayer did not help. I told myself it was all part of God's plan, but that mantra did not alleviate my depression. I needed to contribute in some way. I had to do something to sublimate the fear. I hoped to lift my veil of melancholy by writing an account of how the Sisters of Our Lady in Belgium, especially the Sisters in Saint-Hubert, coped with the invasion and occupation of Belgium by the Germans. I wanted to ensure that what the Sisters of Our Lady did here in Saint-Hubert under impossible conditions would not be forgotten. Finally, I had another very personal reason for writing this narrative. If I did not survive this second German invasion, I wanted my family back in Ohio to understand why I chose to stay in Belgium, even though as an American I could have returned to the United States before the Japanese attack on Pearl Harbor on December 7, 1941.

I had always kept a detailed diary so my task of chronicling the events from the beginning of the war to the present was easier. Although my history about the Sisters of Our Lady in Belgium during the war begins in 1939, I must first explain how a farm girl from a small town in western Ohio ended up in a convent- school in Saint-Hubert, Belgium.[1]

My name before I became a sister was Sophia Pansing. I was born on a farm near the village of Fort Loramie, Ohio. (We Ohioans pronounce it as "Lor-mc.") It was the year of the flood, the Great Dayton Flood of 1913. I had two older brothers and one younger. My grandparents lived with us on the farm. Oma and Opa had emigrated from Hanover, Germany, in 1880. They never learned much more than rudimentary English, so my brothers and I grew up speaking German whenever we spoke with them. Oma would tell us wonderful stories about her life in Germany, and she was well versed in German history, too. I remember her being a great admirer of Chancellor Otto von Bismarck.

When it came to farm chores, I was expected to pull my weight the same as my brothers. I milked cows, drove the tractor, and operated farm machinery. I did not enjoy killing and plucking chickens, but had no choice. Oddly, killing and butchering hogs did not bother me as much.

My three brothers and I went to school in Fort Loramie. Although it was a public school, many of the classes were taught by Sisters of Our Lady of Namur. There were crucifixes in every classroom. I was a better-than-average student, but my best subjects were literature and French. In high school, boys seemed attracted to me despite that at five feet eight inches, I was taller than many of them. My blonde hair and blue eyes probably came from my German heritage. I was not that interested in boys. They were rather dull and easily manipulated. A slight flutter of an eyelash or a feigned pout, followed by a whimsical smile, was all I needed to induce a boy to carry my books the two miles to our farm or to get an offer of help with my math homework.

I cannot remember a specific event that turned my thoughts to becoming a Sister of Our Lady. Unlike Saint Paul, I experienced no fall on the road to Damascus. When I was a junior in high school, however, I fell under the spell of Sister Bernadette. There was always a sense of joy about her. Nothing we did could shake her calm aura. She smiled with her eyes, not just with her lips, and behind her smile was peace and stability. She made us want to learn. I read all the books she assigned from cover to cover. I did not want to disappoint her.

Most intriguing for me, though, was that Sister Bernadette seemed to have her own private channel to God. If I spoke to her about God, she seemed bemused, like she knew some things about God I didn't. They were good things, but things that could not be expressed in words, only experienced. I wanted that. I believed the only way I could achieve such a noble state of mind would be to join a religious order like the Sisters of Our Lady of Namur.

When I told my parents of my intention to become a Sister of Our Lady of Namur after I finished high school, they were surprised, but not shocked. We were not a particularly religious family, and I was not the most eager one of my siblings when it was time to dress for Sunday mass. In the end my parents, and Oma and Opa, were supportive of my decision, especially after they spoke to Sister Bernadette. She described the process for entering the order and told them how my personality, temperament, and intelligence were well suited for the rigours of religious life.

After I graduated from high school in 1930, I entered the order as a postulant at Our Lady of the Summit Convent in Cincinnati. For six months, I wore a sombre black dress with a little white veil and was introduced to the routines and discipline of community life. It was a time of probation and testing to determine if I was able to adjust to the demands of religious life. The vows of poverty, chastity, and obedience are not taken lightly. Many of the young women entering as postulants left before the end of six months. Those of us who remained became novices, were dressed in traditional habits, and were given names. My name was Sister Christina.

Our postulant probation period seemed benign when compared to the challenges and stresses during the novitiate. We were told by older nuns that if we did not find some aspects of our novice lives agonising, we must be slacking off. The rigour of my life on a farm was good preparation for my life in the convent. Although farmers do not take a vow to be poor, as a practical matter farming is often a life of poverty. As for obedience, there was no sister during my novitiate more demanding than my father on the farm. The commitment to chastity was not burdensome since I was cloistered twenty-four hours a day with women. We took our first vows at the end of our novitiate.

I continued to live in the convent at Our Lady of the Summit, but I finished my education at Cincinnati Normal School. My degree was in secondary education with a focus on teaching German and French. After graduation in 1935, I began teaching at Cuvilly High School in Dayton, Ohio. I took my final vows in 1938. Much to my surprise, I was soon on my way to our Motherhouse in Namur, Belgium. I had never been outside of

Ohio. I could not help feeling scared about the drastic change in my life, especially with all the turmoil in Europe and talk of war. I did not question the decision, of course. The words of our founder, Sister Julie, provided the necessary guidance:

A Sister of Our Lady, who is truly simple, is not always saying 'I have no talent for this, no aptitude for that.' That would be self-occupation. But, addressing her Heavenly Father, she says to Him: 'My God, my Superiors require such a thing of me; You must give me the ability necessary to do this work, since You want me to be obedient.' Then, strong in the faith of obedience and confiding in God, she goes straight forward; and if God should work miracles through her, she would not be astonished because He has promised everything to blind obedience. Thus truth and humility are in accord with holy simplicity.

To some, the vow of unquestioning obedience seems oppressive, but it actually removes so much angst from our lives. What makes us anxious and fearful? Often, we are consumed with worrying about decisions to be made, implementing those decisions, and then agonising about whether we made the right decisions. Practising the vow of obedience removes those anxieties from our lives, replaced with calm acceptance of our future as determined by a loving God. Sister Julie said it perfectly:

At the Day of Judgement, a Sister who has lived by obedience will be found fully justified in all that she has done. If God should ask of her: 'Why did you do such a thing? Why did you not do such another?' she need only answer, 'Lord, I did Thy Will, since I did that of my Superiors!'

CHAPTER THREE

AN AMERICAN NUN IN BELGIUM

Namur, February 1938

SISTER CLARE AND I LEFT DAYTON ON THE CAPITAL LIMITED. IT WAS an overnight train, so we shared a Pullman cabin. When the train arrived in Washington, DC, two Belgian sisters, Louise and Agatha, who were staying at Trinity College, joined us.[1]

They were returning to the convent in Namur, Belgium, and would help us navigate the transportation and immigration challenges we faced. In New York City, we did not see much more than the city's intimidating skyline as we boarded the *USS Manhattan*, operated by the United States Line. The ship was like a huge floating city with highways, byways, and back alleys. After visiting with some Franciscan sisters who were also sailing on the *Manhattan*, we got quite lost, going up and down stairways, and inevitably ending up someplace entirely unfamiliar or back where we started. Fortunately, a friendly steward guided us back to our cabins.

Our vows of poverty were stretched a little by the lovely cabins we were assigned, and they were further challenged when we were invited by Captain Albert Randall to sit at the captain's table for dinner. My life on a Fort Loramie farm and seven years in a convent had not prepared me for a dinner table weighed down with silver utensils and heavy crystal glasses. Before I picked up a fork or a spoon, I peeked to see what other, more sophisticated guests did. I never did develop a taste for caviar.

While sisters in habits may have been off-putting to some of the passengers, they did not deter an Evangelical Christian passenger. He handed us several religious pamphlets and urged us to "mend our ways and get on the path of righteousness." We told him we did not have time for a theological discussion because we were in a hurry to get our laundry to the steward.

It was a beautiful but unexciting sea voyage, and I am happy to say that this flatlander, whose only cruising was in a rowboat on Lake Loramie, did not experience any seasickness.

The ship docked in Hamburg, Germany. There was an army of immigration officials and soldiers who were rigorously interrogating disembarking passengers and thoroughly examining their luggage. The whole atmosphere was intimidating. Curiously, their questioning of us was perfunctory and our luggage was not opened. Was there something about our black habits that deterred them? A vestige of the respect they had for sisters who taught them as children?

We had a short train ride to Namur. It was one of the larger cities in Belgium, but it still retained most of its medieval character. The Sisters of Our Lady of Namur property is like its own village within the larger town. The complex was surrounded by tall buildings, high walls, and extensive gardens. The head of the entire Sisters of Our Lady of Namur order is "Mother General." She usually lives at the Motherhouse in Namur. Most sisters refer to her as "dear Mother" or "my Mother."

The worldwide Sisters of Our Lady organisation is divided into large provinces. A Sister Superior Provincial heads each Province. Within a province there may be dozens of convent-schools, each headed by a Sister Superior Local. In Namur, there was also Sister

Superior Local who was responsible for the Motherhouse's day-to-day operations. A sister who is the head of a school attached to a convent may be called "Principal or Headmistress," but she would be under the authority of Sister Superior Local.

As I discovered, this self-contained village was an island of peace and serenity for the next two years, floating in a sea of European political upheavals and finally, war. German bombs abruptly shattered our bucolic island's calm in May 1940.

In 1938 and 1939, the world was in chaos, and yet a sense of normalcy reigned within our convent's walls. Our strict, unchanging routine and a conviction that whatever happens is God's will made us feel removed from the events of the outside world. Every day we rose with the bell at 5:00 a.m. Our prayers began immediately while we were dressing in our habits; they were meant to help us to direct our intentions for the day.

Jesus, Mary, Joseph and all the Holy angels, I renew my holy engagements; continue, I beg of you, your loving care of me. I unite myself to the Church with all my heart, with all my soul, with all my strength to glorify God, the Blessed Virgin, the Angels and Saints; to provide for all the spiritual and temporal necessities of the children of the Church militant; to procure the deliverance of the Souls who suffer in Purgatory, to obtain abundant graces for all those to whom I am in justice bound, and for all that may be pleasing to your Hearts, O Jesus and Mary!

Those prayers are followed by the *Examen of Foresight*, in which we resolve to avoid a particular fault or to demonstrate a specific virtue. All the sisters then gather in the chapel for communal morning prayers and personal meditation. Meditation is a form of mental prayer whereby a sister endeavors to subdue her will so that virtue can find space to flourish. Holy Mass immediately follows, a ritual that unites the Sisters in worship, song, adoration, thanksgiving, satisfaction, and supplication. Breakfast is served in the large dining hall. Although it is a time when all the sisters are sitting together at long tables, it is not a time for conversation;

silence usually reigns. Only the most necessary words are spoken, and sisters use simple hand signals to request more coffee or that the bread plate be passed. Sisters are instructed to keep "custody of their eyes" so there is little actual eye contact during meals. Any discussion of current events occurring outside the convent walls would be considered a violation of the rule of silence.

Immediately after breakfast the school day begins. The Namur Establishment is a boarding school for young girls who are:

To pursue-under the watch of God and the constant influence of His grace, according to the orders of the Catholic Church and in applying the pedagogical ideals of the Foundress Blessed Julie Billiart—the complete education of young girls: from her body, her intelligence, and her heart.

There is a normal primary school that prepares students to teach in Belgian primary schools and a normal nursery school in which students train to work in children centres and infant care homes. I taught in the normal primary school. The students are between fifteen and eighteen years old.

The atmosphere and the restrictions imposed on the boarding students fostered the isolation of the convent and school from events occurring outside the tall iron gates. Even contact with parents is limited. Students can write to their parents every Sunday, but no other letters are permitted unless special permission is granted by a student's parents and approved by Sister Superior. Classes are held six days a week. Visiting day is Sunday between 10:00 a.m. and 7:00 p.m. Students ordinarily could not leave the grounds, but two-hour outings with parents, twice a month, are permitted. Radios are forbidden, and current newspapers are available only in the library. There is a strict dress code requiring simple black outfits and a hat. Students had to supply their own linen and mattress, 1.9 metres long and .8 metres wide.

Most of the time our students are well-behaved. Slight deviations can quickly be quashed with a marvellous device all the teaching Sisters carry. It is called a "clicker." The handle is made of a hard wood and another thin piece of wood, like a Popsicle® stick, is attached to the handle by a strong rubber band. When the thin stick is pressed by the thumb, it rises from the handle. When the thumb is released, the stick smacks against the handle and produces a sound like someone loudly snapping their fingers. So, instead of raising one's voice, or trying to snap one's fingers and point at the miscreant, a Sister can point the clicker at the culprit at the same time the clicker emits a loud snap. It works almost every time. The clicker is also handy for directing traffic into and out of the classroom, in the halls, and in the chapel without the need for verbal instructions. Point and snap at the first row of students, and the row immediately stands up. The next click prompts them to march quietly out the door. In chapel, it is remarkable to see how with one "snap" all the children genuflect or kneel with the precision of a military unit.

At midday, every sister engages in the *Particular Examination*, or the self-examination of conscience. She reviews the failing or virtue she identified during her morning *Examen* and calculates how often she committed that fault or practised that virtue during the day thus far. The rule of silence applies to the midday meal, but after the meal there is a half hour set aside before the resumption of classes for conversation. The rules governing the conversation, however, do not foster dialogue between individual sisters. Questions must first be addressed to Sister Superior and then, after her response, other sisters are free to comment. After afternoon classes and before the evening meal, every sister performs a *General Examination*. The Sister reviews the day, noting what faults she may have committed in deed, word, thought, or omission, asks God's pardon, and promises to do better tomorrow. Usually, the *General Examination* is performed privately, but occasionally each sister is asked to confess her faults and failings before the entire community and to ask for the community's forgiveness.

The sisters generally observe the rule of silence during the evening meal. There is little opportunity for sisters to converse among themselves, because during most of the meal a designated sister will read from the Bible or other sacred writing. It is only after the meal, during Recreation, that the restriction on conversation is waived. It is also a time for sisters to catch up on their sewing, grade students' assignments, or prepare for the next day's classes.

The final ritual for the day is evening prayer, or *Vespers*, in the chapel, followed by another *Particular Examination*. At 9:00 p.m. the bell rings to mark the beginning of the *Grand Silence*. Sisters retire to their cells and do not speak again until the 5:00 a.m. bell the next morning when we start a new day, nearly duplicating the previous one.

Every Saturday evening, we put our washing into a laundry bag. Each week I could send one cap, one hood, and one collar. Every sister has four pairs of knickers and four tunics. I can send one tunic to the laundry and two pairs of knickers. On Sunday, there is some variation in the routine. There are no classes, so there are a few hours in the day for us to walk and converse with each other.

Spare moments are few during most days, but we did find time to sew and clean. We were responsible for mending our own clothes. All sisters are skilled enough with a sewing machine to make new clothes if needed. We were responsible for cleaning our cells and were regularly assigned to clean and polish the halls and other rooms. Spotless, shiny floors were particularly important. Sisters were assigned to kitchen duties, but for good reasons only a few of us were designated as cooks.

CHAPTER FOUR

WISHFUL THINKING

Namur, September 1938

OUR REGIMEN FILLED ALMOST EVERY MINUTE OF THE DAY. WE WERE to accomplish all our tasks, every day, without giving the impression of hurrying. The outside world rarely intruded on our lives. It was not that we were oblivious to what was happening outside our walls, but it was like looking at the world through a lightly frosted pane of glass. Events could be perceived, yet they appeared indistinct, distant, and a bit unreal. Our perspective was also coloured by wishful thinking. Few people in America or Europe wanted to believe that Adolf Hitler was as dangerous as he seemed. Surely, he did not really believe his own rhetoric. It was just posturing and most believed that ultimately he could be persuaded by reason. Besides, there was also some admiration for the fascist leaders because they "made the trains run on time."

Shortly after my arrival in Belgium in March 1938, Germany annexed Austria, the "*Anschluss.*" Was this such a bad thing? The Austrians were ethnically Germans, so shouldn't they be able to become part of the German nation-state? Some of the Flemish, Dutch-speaking citizens of Belgium might have been happy if Germany annexed the Flemish part of Belgium. I learned the country of Belgium was cobbled together after the 1830 revolution. The French-speaking Walloons in the south and the Dutch/German-speaking Flemish in the north were joined in a union that neither group liked. French became the official language of Belgium, which increased Flemish hostility. Might the Flemish be better off being part of Germany than being dominated by the French-speaking Walloons?

The reaction to the Munich Pact negotiated by Hitler and Britain's Prime Minister Neville Chamberlin in September 1938 was also muted. Hitler was threatening to go to war unless the Sudetenland, the western half of Czechoslovakia, was incorporated into greater Germany. The argument was again that a majority of Sudetenland's population was ethnic Germans. Hitler argued Germans could only be safe when in the protective arms of the Fatherland. Two weeks later German armies marched in to provide that protection. Everyone except the Czechs gave a sigh of relief. War was avoided, and Britain's Prime Minister Neville Chamberlin announced, "Peace in our time."

Peace, however, did not come to the Jews of Germany. November 9 and 10, 1938, became known as *"Kristallnacht,"* the night of the broken glass. Rampaging Germans vandalised thousands of Jewish homes, stores, and synagogues. Almost every pane of glass was broken in Jewish-owned buildings. Characterising the rampage as the "night of the broken glass," however, gave the impression the whole event was little more than exuberant teenagers acting out. The description belies the fact that amidst the shattered panes of glass were hundreds of Jews who were beaten and scores who were killed. In Belgium, the rampage was viewed as a deviation from typical punctilious German behaviour. It was also viewed as a German internal matter, not something that affected the tranquillity of our lives.

The ink was barely dry on the Munich Pact when in March of 1939, the German army, in violation of the Pact's terms, seized what was left of Czechoslovakia. It was much more difficult for Belgians to rationalise this blatant aggression. The excuse of needing to protect ethnic Germans had no credibility. Hardly any ethnic Germans were living in Slovakia. Hitler seemed intent on expanding the German Reich as far as the other European nations would allow him. But what could little Belgium do about it? In the 1925 Locarno Treaty, Belgium had agreed to stay neutral in any future wars. In return, Germany, Britain, and France guaranteed the integrity of Belgium's borders, pledging to defend them if Belgium was attacked. This promise was renewed every few years, and it included a pledge by Hitler in 1939 to respect Belgium neutrality.

Even in our protected world of the convent, the saga of the ship *M.S. St. Louis* was a topic of discussion during evening recreation time.

From May to June 1939, the ship was captained by Gustav Schröder. On the ship there were more than 900 Jewish passengers escaping Germany. Determined to find a country willing to accept the Jewish refugees, Captain Schröder sailed over 10,000 miles without success. The ship's first stop was Cuba, which refused entry to all but 29 refugees. Sadly, my country, America, which prides itself on being a refuge for the downtrodden and oppressed, slammed its doors shut. Canada followed America's lead. Finally, England, France, Netherlands, and Belgium agreed to each take a portion of the remaining passengers.

In August 1939, Hitler once again tried to use the tactic for Poland that had worked in Czechoslovakia. He demanded that ethnic Germans living near Danzig be incorporated into greater Germany. The Poles refused Hitler's ultimatum. Unlike in the Czechoslovakia crisis, England and France backed up Poland's refusal, and on September 1, 1939, the German army invaded Poland. England and France immediately declared war on Germany.

Belgium was in a precarious position. If Belgium threw in its lot with England and France, Germany would have an excuse to invade. If Belgium backed Germany, France might attack Belgium. With Belgium lodged between two warring states, King Leopold tried to walk the tightrope of neutrality. He labelled it an "Independent Policy." He could not even appear to be asking for military help from England and France without triggering the threat of a German invasion. The Belgian army was mobilised in August 1939, and, as part of that mobilisation, hundreds of Belgian troops took over one of our largest school buildings. They dubbed it "Sisters of Our Lady Barracks." Hundreds of sisters from all over the world were participating in a retreat at the time. They made a quick exodus and returned to their home countries.

For a while, the King's balancing act seemed to work. Germany finished up conquering half of Poland while the Russians, with Hitler's blessing, gobbled up the other half. There was then a curious lull in the fighting, like boxers retiring to their respective corners waiting for the next round to begin. When German planes began flying over Belgium doing reconnaissance, however, King Leopold decided it was necessary to send a stronger message to Germany. He declared that if German troops set one foot on the territory of Holland or Belgium, he would throw open the French–Belgium border and allow the French army into Belgium.

The King's warning did not deter the Germans. They increased the number of reconnaissance flights so that almost every day the air-raid warning was sounded. The alarms were immediately followed by the sound of the anti-aircraft guns firing. The citizens of Namur soon adjusted to the booming of the guns. They considered the sound as the equivalent of extra loud church bells. Only the little rat terrier that lived in our convent was disturbed by the racket. He would bark until the firing stopped. Instead of taking shelter, many people would go to their rooftops to watch the fireworks display. They ignored the warnings in the daily papers that they were in danger of being hit by falling shrapnel, and a few were hit in the face by bits of shell casing.

The aerial display was augmented when Belgian pursuit planes were scrambled to challenge the German intruders. On January 13, 1940, a German plane was hit by shellfire and caught fire. The pilot managed to land the plane in a nearby field. He built a little pile of the papers he was carrying and tried to burn them. Before they could be destroyed, however, a Belgian police officer reached into the flames with his bare hand to save them. The contents of the papers were disturbing: they indicated that a surprise attack was planned for January 15.

A national alert was sent out over the radio. All soldiers were ordered to report to their units. Villages along the frontier were evacuated. Over three hundred Catholic sisters, brothers, and priests were told to leave Bastogne. Arrangements were made for the evacuation of Sisters of Our Lady from Bastogne, but it was not mandatory that they leave. Those sisters who wanted to remain could do so at their own risk and could not count on food supplies or any other help. Every private vehicle in Brussels, along with its driver, was commandeered to help with the evacuation of civilians from Liege. Ammunition and weapons were distributed to soldiers, police, and firemen. All the barbed wire and other obstacles along our border with France were removed in one night. Just across the border French troops, tanks, and artillery pieces were poised to enter Belgium to fight the Germans the moment the border was breached.

It was a false alarm. There was some speculation that the whole crash, capture of the pilot, and his rather inept attempt to burn the documents was staged. According to the rumour, the German military wanted to discover how quickly the Belgian army could mobilise and where it would be deployed. There were no German stormtroopers, but the following day there was a huge snowstorm, followed by arctic temperatures. The mercury in our thermometer would sullenly not leave the bulb to register any temperature, which meant the temperature was at least two degrees Fahrenheit below zero. Some of our older sisters jokingly said they might have preferred the heat of a battle to the bitter cold.

An uneasy calm settled on Namur. A semblance of normal life began again. The convent and the school were running as usual. There were three masses every morning and three benedictions given through the day. The routine of personal meditation and *Examens* was scrupulously followed. Sunday was *Sexagesima*, the second Sunday before Ash Wednesday, and we recited the traditional prayer for the conversion of the Jews and added a special prayer asking God to protect them. Three Flemish novices arrived to prepare for taking their final vows on Easter Sunday. The return to ritual was comforting.

I was surprised when two weeks later Mother General, Monica de la Passion, called me to her office and suggested that as an American it might be advisable for me to return to the United States. She was convinced war was coming to Belgium and the country would become the battleground it was during the 1914–1918 war. As the chosen head of Sisters of Our Lady of Namur's worldwide organisation, she could have ordered me to leave Belgium and return to Ohio. She did not insist, however, that I leave. Without hesitation, I asked to stay in Namur. It was my home, and the sisters were my family. I could not desert them. Dear Mother acquiesced in my decision.

Denmark and Norway took the next German punch in April, with German troops quickly over-running and occupying those countries. It was inevitable that Belgium would be next. We hoped that the chain of border fortresses would hold off the Germans long enough for French and British troops to arrive. They didn't.

CHAPTER FIVE

BELGIUM INVADED AND ESCAPE
TO FRANCE

Namur, May 1940

BEFORE DAWN ON MAY 10, 1940, WE WERE JOLTED
AWAKE BY THE roar of dozens of low-flying planes barely
clearing the steeple of the chapel. There were large swastikas
painted on their wings. They did not drop any bombs, but it was
clear they signalled the beginning of the invasion. People rushed
into the streets shouting, "The Germans are dropping parachutists
all over Belgium! The Jemelle fort has been bombed, Holland
invaded!"

Our meagre phone line was overwhelmed with parents of our
boarding students demanding they be sent home immediately. We
began escorting the children to the train station.[1] I was responsible
for a group of twenty girls. There was complete pandemonium.
Every schoolboy or schoolgirl in town was trying to get on a train
before they stopped running. Trains arriving at the station were
already packed with children whose terrified faces looked out
through windows of broken glass. Before I could get any of my
group aboard, a German plane flew over low, firing its machine
guns at the locomotive. I ordered my girls to dive into the ditch
beside the tracks. Their uniforms were covered with mud, and

my habit changed from black to brown. I took the students to the nearest train car. It was full of other students who were refusing to squeeze any tighter to make room for my girls. I began yelling at them in French, German, and English to let my girls in the car. They had probably never in their lives encountered a mud-spattered screaming nun before and thought it wiser to jam themselves together tighter than to challenge a crazy sister.

All twenty of my girls managed to squeeze into the car. Sadly, not all our other children were able to board a train before they ceased running. The remainder returned to the convent. We hoped that their parents would find some way to get them home.

Plans for this emergency had been formulated months before by dear Mother and Sister Superior Local, Head of the Namur Motherhouse. Namur is a strategic spot where the Sambre River joins with the Meuse, and there are bridges across both rivers. Our convent was located on the north side of the Meuse, close to the Pont d'Ardennes. We knew the Germans would bomb the bridges, putting the convent in the middle of the target zone. Germany would also want its soldiers to occupy the town as quickly as possible.

Therefore, a month before the war began, the ill and older sisters were evacuated to convents in Brussels. That still left over a hundred sisters at the convent. Unfortunately, when the bombing of Namur began, Mother General, dear Mother, was trapped in Antwerp. She could not get back to the Motherhouse. Similarly, Sister Superior Local of the Namur convent was resting in our convent in Salzinnes for health reasons and could not return to Namur. The burden of deciding on a course of action fell on Sister Superior Provincial. She decided to evacuate almost all the sisters and disperse them among other Sisters of Our Lady convents, including our convent in Jumet, Belgium. Sister Superior Provincial and ten sisters who were neither too young nor too old would remain at Namur to guard the Motherhouse. I was to go with the group destined for Jumet.

If transportation could be arranged, we planned to leave the following day, but in the meantime, evacuees were pouring into Namur from villages further east. The refugees were desperate for food and a safe place to sleep. Six sisters from a nearby convent and our chaplain added to the numbers. They were given the "best" corner in the sturdiest cellar. Mattresses, a couple of chairs, and a table were carried down from a dormitory. The Blessed Sacrament was moved from the altar of the chapel to a temporary chapel near our wing of the cellar. We placed the box that contained the relics of our foundress, Blessed Julie, under the table that was serving as an altar.

The decision was made to evacuate most of the sisters the next day. Everyone else in Namur was trying to leave, too. The rumour was that Namur would be completely destroyed. Bags were quickly packed.

Our chaplain said it would be risky to take all the consecrated hosts with us, so he suggested we consume all of them before leaving. We paraded to the makeshift chapel and each of us received communion twenty to twenty-five times.

The first group of novices, postulants, and pupils who had not been able to get to their homes left for Ixelles. A later group of sisters only managed to get to the nearby town of Charleroi, where a bombardment forced them to take shelter in the cellar of the Sisters of the Rue de Marcinelle's convent. I was in the last group of sisters who were to leave Namur. However, the truck that was supposed to transport us to Jumet did not arrive. We returned to our cellar home for the night. Were we going to be trapped in Namur?

After midnight, the truck arrived. The brave driver had stopped in Salzinnes and picked up Sister Superior of the Namur convent and four other sisters. They had spent the entire day on the road trying to get to Namur. They were exhausted. Sister Superior of Namur decided it would be safer if everyone, including the children, spent the remainder of the night in the cellar and continue the journey at first light. Heavy bombing arrived before the sun and thwarted the plan. We were jolted awake when a tremendous blast rocked the cellar like an earthquake. The bomb took off part of the roof of the *pensionnat*—the boarding school. Worse followed. Buildings adjoining the convent on the Rue Lombard were on fire. The fire department was called, but the firemen were already overwhelmed. They had been fighting fires all night long; their spirits and energy were shattered. There was little water for the hoses, the town's water supply being shut off. When German planes dropped more bombs and sprayed the streets with bullets, the firemen had to seek shelter in the nearest cellars.

The fires spread rapidly along the houses on Rue Lombard. Flames burst through the windows and the roofs of the houses, and sparks ignited the roof of our dormitories. Firemen finally arrived. They had two hoses that they connected to our cisterns, which quickly ran dry. A bucket brigade formed of sisters had the effect of throwing glasses of water on a forest fire. The bombers returned and as our last dormitory went up in flames, the firemen rushed for the protection of our cellar. Curtains, beds, and partitions all crashed into the conflagration. Building after building was consumed by the flames. The inferno raged without pity. We could feel the heat from the flames in our cellar. It was just a matter of time before they began eating away at our sanctuary. If we remained in the cellar too long the fire would trap us, but outside bombs were still falling.

I shouted, "We have to get out of the cellar, now!"[2] Once again, the spectacle of a nun yelling got everyone moving. We quickly gathered provisions and blankets and left through the door to the garden. Sister Superior Provincial was holding the box with the relics of Blessed Julie. Where to seek shelter? Buildings were on fire everywhere. Streets were filled with rubble. Sister Superior

Provincial told us to go to the convent of the Dames de St. Julienne. We tried to avoid the streets where the fires were worse, but there were no safe streets. Some flaming gauntlets had to be run. Our coifs, veils, scapulars and tunics provided some protection from the heat and the sparks. We tried to shield the children by covering them with blankets. We supplied additional protection for them by wrapping our arms around their shoulders. The excess fabric in our tunics acted as a heat barrier.

The Dames of St. Julienne convent was not located near the bridges or the train station, so it avoided most of the bombing. Although dozens of refugees were already being cared for by the Sisters of St. Julienne, we were graciously taken in and provided with a space in their cellar. Our presence required some of the refugees to move and make room for us. Nevertheless, we were enthusiastically welcomed: "Oh, here come some sisters who will pray for us!"

Late in the afternoon, there was a lull in the bombing. Several of us ventured to return to the Motherhouse. It was still burning, but we managed to fill suitcases and wheelbarrows with foodstuffs that had been stored in the cellar. Just as we were leaving there was a huge crash as the roof of our church collapsed and sent sheets of flames and debris into the sky. When evening fell, I climbed to the roof of the Dames of St. Julienne convent, and I could see off in the distance all the Motherhouse buildings still in flames. Nothing remained of our home.

We barely had time to settle in when Sister Superior Provincial told the group of us who were to be evacuated to Jumet that we had to leave immediately. There was a lull in the bombing, and miraculously, the truck that had brought the sisters from Salzinnes escaped damage. We gathered what few possessions we had and began packing ourselves into the truck.

Before I boarded the truck, Sister Superior Provincial took me aside and told me I was to be responsible for getting the twenty sisters and ten students to Jumet[3]. Essentially, I was to lead the exodus. I was bewildered by her decision, pointing out that Sister Superior of the Namur convent was a member of the group and that she was the logical choice. I also mentioned that over the years I had never managed to suppress my outspokenness and struggled to keep the rule of silence.

Before speaking, Sister Superior Provincial raised her index finger, which we all knew indicated what she said next was not subject to debate—that our vow of obedience obligated us to submit to her instructions. She said that my fluency in German, French, and English might prove to be very important. Furthermore, we were going to be in the middle of a war and Belgium might become the battleground or be occupied by the Germans. The ability to make oneself heard and listened to could be the difference between life and death; the rule of silence would be of little help in the coming conflict. In this war, she said, my weaknesses may prove to be strengths. Sister Superior Provincial then walked to the back of the truck and informed the huddled sisters of her decision. She said I was in charge of getting them to Jumet safely and they were to follow my guidance without question. As the truck pulled away, we said our goodbyes to Sister Superior Provincial and the ten sisters who remained in Namur.

Twenty sisters and ten students were wedged into the truck. There was no room to sit, so everyone stood for the entire journey.[4] Being packed like sardines in a tin had the advantage of there being no room for us to be tossed around by the bouncing and jerking of the truck. Our route took us by the Charleroi convent, where we managed to squeeze five more sisters into the truck. I rode in the truck cab with the driver and two other sisters.

Once past Charleroi, the road to Jumet was choked with refugees fleeing west and soldiers, mostly French, marching east. Our progress proceeded at a crawl when we were moving at all. Frequently, all movement was halted when a German plane appeared. Their bullets and bombs did not distinguish between soldiers and refugees. I knew a truck was an inviting target, so I ordered the driver to get off the road and under the nearest tree whenever we heard the sound of an airplane.

It was heartbreaking to see the thousands of Belgians struggling to escape the fighting that was destroying their country. There were families carrying wailing babies and dragging young children, encouraging them to take just a few more steps. The elderly refugees were clearly on their last legs, with many of them dropping out of the procession to lie in the ditches, awaiting whatever fate had in store for them. The truck was surrounded with men and women clinging to the windows of the truck pleading for us to take them or their children. We just could not squeeze another person into the back of the truck. Even if space could be made for one more, how would we pick the person to rescue?

I was charged by Mother Superior to get these young postulants, novices, and students, some only thirteen years old, to safety. Do I order them to leave the truck and take their chances on the road? Should I risk their lives for the lives of the other refugees? My entire life as a Sister of Our Lady did not prepare me for what had now been thrust upon me. I was trained to unquestioningly follow the decisions and orders of my superiors, knowing that they were being guided by God. Now I was compelled to make life-and-death decisions for others, and I had no sense that God was telling me what to do. Sister Superior Provincial, who was guided by God, had given me a clear mission: to escort my charges to Jumet as safely as possible.

Our Foundress, Blessed Julie, clearly said in her "Little Treatise of Perfection" that unquestioning obedience was essential:

Let us run, nay, let us fly in the way of perfection, above all by the practice of renunciation of our own will and our own judgement, by a blind obedience to all that is commanded by our Superiors, who hold the place of God in our regard. We must be models of obedience. No reasonings, no criticisms, such as 'Why am I told to do such a thing?' My good daughters, we must be able to say at the hour of death: 'My God, I have always done what At the Day of Judgement a Sister who has lived by obedience will be found fully justified in all that she has done.' If God should ask of her: 'Why did you do such a thing? Why did you not do such another?' she need only answer, 'Lord, I did Thy Will, since I did that of my Superiors!'

I agonised over my choices. My vow of absolute obedience would not allow me to challenge or change the mission. In that respect, I was not much different from an officer in the army who is ordered to undertake a dangerous assignment. For myself, I would have gladly given up my place on the truck to a desperate refugee who had reached the limit of endurance. To do so, of course, would mean abandoning the very people Sister Superior had directed me to protect. Alternatively, I could have required every young girl to leave the truck and have refugees take their places. Would that decision contravene my duty to them and Sister Superior by exposing the young women to a much higher risk of death and injury? Finally, I could allow the young girls to make their own decisions about surrendering their places in the truck. Would that be an abdication of the responsibility Sister Superior Provincial gave me? I would be asking young women who were not even allowed to decide what dresses they could wear to choose the lives of the refugees over their own lives. How could they assess the risks of being captured by German soldiers?

May God forgive me, but I refused to allow any refugees onto the truck. I feared refusing to help might incite some of the more desperate refugees to take matters into their own hands and forcibly remove us from the truck, but that did not happen. Was it again the power of our black habits? From their decades of training were Belgians so in awe of sisters that they would never consider challenging their decisions?

After many hours on the road, we arrived at the Sisters of Our Lady convent in Jumet. I was thankful that God and Blessed

Sister Julie had protected us on our dangerous journey. It was a great relief to have the Sister Superior of Jumet take over the responsibility for the sisters and students as soon as the truck drove through the convent's iron gates. Over eighty evacuees from Namur were now in Jumet. Sadly, they were no safer in Jumet than they had been in Namur.[5]

French and Belgian soldiers were flooding into Jumet. They were setting up their camps, digging trenches, and constructing bunkers for their cannon and anti-aircraft batteries. They took over a large portion of the convent's grounds. Troops occupied parts of the boarding school. The presence of large numbers of troops nearby did not make the convent safer; it was now more likely to be in the middle of a battleground.

The French General warned us that the cellars of the convent would not protect us from the inevitable bombardment. He said he did not have the authority to order us — or any of the town residents — to leave Jumet, but he would do nothing to protect them or us. Neither did he suggest any plan for evacuating the town or offer any form of transportation.

Belgian soldiers had commandeered our one truck; we were on our own. Sister Superior of Jumet made the decision. The younger sisters would join the stream of other refugees walking west. Many refugees had no idea where they could go to find a safe haven or even places to rest during their flight. They wandered aimlessly east, west, and south. Our sisters at least had a destination and a direction, west. We knew we would be welcomed at our convent and the convents of other religious orders in Jemappes, Belgium.

Everything was done with feverish haste, and the sisters were ready to begin their trek within an hour. We adopted the travelling mode we had seen used by many other refugees on the road. Everything we took was wrapped in a blanket that was tied on both ends, forming a cloth tube six feet long. The blanket was slung over a shoulder, around the back and tied in front. This left both hands free and less encumbered for taking cover in a ditch when forced to do so by the bullets and bombs of marauding German planes. Sister Superior also gave us permission to pin up our tunics to make walking easier.

Sister Superior of Jumet divided us into four groups, each with an older sister designated as a leader. She believed it would be too difficult to keep together and to keep track of eighty people during the exodus, especially since each group would ultimately be housed in separate convents. Once again, I was selected to be responsible for the thirty-two sisters who were going to the Sisters of Our Lady convent in Jemappes. Sister Superior of Jumet said I had proven myself by bringing the sisters from Namur safely to Jumet, and my English skills would be particularly useful because we were likely to encounter British troops on the way.

The distance between Jumet and Jemappes was forty-five kilometres—more than twenty miles. On the first day we were fresh and made good progress, about thirty kilometres. We slept on the pews of a village church in Thieu. The parish priest, Father DuBois, persuaded a few of his parishioners to feed us soup, bread, and cheese. The next day we arrived at the Jemappes convent, only to discover all the sisters had departed less than an hour before. Apparently, Jemappes was no more secure than Jumet. During the Great War it had been the site of a huge battle, and it seemed destined to be a killing ground again. Some of our sisters were exhausted and could go no further that night, so we scavenged some food and slept in recently vacated student cots. Before dawn we joined the throng of panic-stricken people with their carts, bicycles, and bags, all of them pushing south to France. One family with six children had ridden their bikes across Belgium from Leuven. Mimi, nine years old, was the youngest. She asked me if we were running from the Germans, too. She said she was so tired.[6]

All day we walked, but not everyone could keep the pace—some began to fall farther and farther behind the faster walkers.

I was desperate to keep us all together; they were my family. We settled on a staggered walking pattern. The stronger walkers could continue at their quicker pace and carry the most weight, especially food. After several kilometres, they would stop at a church or other site and wait for the other sisters to catch up. Before the lagging sisters would arrive, the first group would find fresh water and prepare a meagre meal from the food they were carrying or could find nearby. After eating, everyone would rest for thirty minutes and then begin the next leg of the journey. By nightfall of the first day, we had crossed the frontier into France.

On the second day, we walked with no idea where we were heading. French and British officers kept giving us directions, but they often seemed contradictory. It was Saturday when we first began to hear the rumours about German parachutists. Warnings had been issued about watching for parachutists and that anyone seeing a suspected parachutist was to immediately inform the army or police. The frightening part of the rumour was that some of the parachutists might be disguised as priests or nuns. Other refugees apparently believed the rumour, and they began avoiding us sisters.

By mid-afternoon, Sister Paula Marie was at the point of collapse and could walk no farther. She begged the rest of us to go on and leave her to rest by the bridge over a small stream. Sister Maria Joseph insisted on staying with Sister Paula Marie, and assured me that they would catch up.

As I learned later, the two sisters were nearly shot as spies. Sister Maria Joseph is a large woman and Sister Paula Marie can only be described as petite. A panicky French woman who lived near the bridge began shouting that the two sisters were German parachutists, a man and a boy, disguised as nuns who were going to blow up the bridge. The sisters were quickly surrounded by French soldiers with revolvers and bayonets and ordered to put their hands above their heads. They were marched to a small house through a gauntlet of French men and women shouting, "Shoot, shoot." The sisters were terrified and subjected to a barrage of confusing questions. Fortunately, a Red Cross nurse was nearby, and she confirmed for the soldiers that the sisters were not men. The soldiers apologised to Sister Maria Joseph and Sister Paula Marie and allowed them to continue their journey. Their travails were not over. Before they were able to rejoin us, they were detained and interrogated four more times.

All of our sisters were detained and interrogated multiple times by French police and French soldiers during their journey. In the early evening on the same day that Sister Maria Joseph and Sister Paula Marie were accused of being parachutists, we were searching for a farm owned by Sister Marie Julie's uncle. We hoped to rest and spend the night in his barn. As we approached the village, the cry of "parachutists" began spreading through the village. The villagers came out of their houses and surrounded us. Some of them carried clubs, hoes, or shovels. Messengers hurried off on bicycles to alert the local police about the "capture" of German parachutists. A swarm of officers on bicycles descended on the village square. Suddenly, Sister Marie Julie began jumping up and down and waving her arms, crying "Uncle Louis! Uncle Louis!" Uncle Louis was one of the bicyclists. He recognised Sister Marie Julie immediately, and all the talk of parachutists was quickly stifled. If the villagers were disappointed, they had not captured German spies, they did not show it. Instead, their suspicions and fears were transformed into genuine warmth. The bicyclists picked up our rolled-up blankets and escorted us to the uncle's farmhouse. Then Uncle Louis and several of his neighbours went off on their bicycles to search for our two missing sisters, Sister Maria Joseph and Sister Paula Marie. God and Blessed Julie were still watching over us. Uncle Louis found the sisters being interrogated by French soldiers, but he quickly organised their release and brought them back to his farm. My family was all together again. Sleeping in the uncle's barn with sheep, cows, and horses could not diminish our joy.

We could not stay in the village, for it, too, was being evacuated. On we went to the Bernadine convent ten kilometres farther into France, where we slept only until one o'clock in the morning. The Bernadine sisters woke us and said they were leaving that minute—that the whole town was being evacuated. We hurriedly rolled up our blankets and once again joined the hundreds of other refugees on the road. British officers first directed us toward Douai and later changed their minds, telling us it would be safer to go to Bethune. The reason for the change became obvious when huge plumes of smoke arose from what I presumed to be the town of Douai. The officers also told us that it would be better if we walked at night to avoid the heat of the day, German planes, and the mass of refugees who were filling the narrow roadways.

On May 20, we walked until two o'clock in the afternoon and then took refuge in an abandoned house in the village of Courcelles. Near midnight, we continued our journey, with the full moon to light our way. Sister Paula was exhausted after two hours and entreated us to leave her behind, saying she would rather die than continue. Sister Marie Thomas relieved her of her blanket roll. Sister Andre declared she would not leave Sister Paula alone and would stay with her. With that encouragement Sister Paula stood up and said she would try to continue with Sister Andre's help. Another sister offered to carry Sister Andre's blanket roll. We resumed our flight, but Sister Paula and Sister Andre lagged behind and were soon lost in the crowd of refugees.

Once again, the cry of "parachutists" arose, and we were surrounded by French soldiers. The soldiers separated us from the other refugees and told them to move on. They took us into the large kitchen of a nearby cottage. Outside, people were shouting, "Shoot them!" A young French captain demanded to see our Belgian identification cards, which we produced. The cards did not seem to satisfy him. He guided me to a corner of the kitchen and began to ask me questions.

The captain said he was a devout Catholic and he had been taught by Dominican sisters, adding that he had great respect for nuns. He described his experience with the Dominicans, interspersed with questions about life in a convent. It was clear to me that he was trying to trip me up with my answers, hoping to show I was not really a sister from a convent. He was not a skilled interrogator, however. He mixed up the hours of prayer, calling the Morning Prayer Compline, which is the evening prayer. Then he threw around some Latin phrases from the Mass that any first-year Latin student would know were wrong. After a few minutes of this charade, I put on my best intimidating frown I used on my misbehaving students, fixed him with my eyes, and put an angry edge in my voice. I spoke slowly and deliberately, emphasising each word to ensure he knew I meant every syllable.

I said it was ludicrous to believe the German army had battalions of women parachuting into France. He must believe, therefore, that these spies who were supposedly dressed as nuns and priests were actually men. As I had hoped, he nodded his head in agreement. I decided at that moment to take a very big gamble. I said to him in a voice only he could hear, "If you are willing to risk your immortal soul by ordering a nun to undress, I am willing to step in the back room and show you I am not a man."

His faced blanched. He did not call what may well have been a bluff on my part. At the time, I really was not sure what I would have done if he had agreed to my offer. The captain did not answer me. Instead, he announced to the room that he was satisfied we were Sisters of Our Lady, and if I were willing to vouch that every sister in the kitchen was a member of our order, we would be free to go. I happily obliged. We picked up our blanket rolls and left the cottage.[7]

As we were leaving, we heard back down the road, in the distance, a burst of shooting. When we rejoined the refugees on the road, they told us a couple of parachutists had been shot and that the men had deserved their fate. At the next crossroad, we sat down to wait for Sister Paula, Sister Andre, and Sister Jeanne to catch up. When they did not appear, we asked other refugees resting at the crossroad if they had seen any sisters pass by. They said they spoke with a Sister Jeanne. She was riding in a farm cart that took the right fork in the road, just south of where we were standing. We hurried down the same road, too, but a British soldier told us the road was closed. After waiting another half-hour, hoping to be reunited with our dear sisters, we sadly continued on to Bully, France, praying all three sisters had escaped down the other road.

A generous Dr. Millard in Bully took the rest of us into his home. We slept in the cellar, the attic, and the hallways. Dr. Millard never complained about the burden we were imposing on him and his family. He allowed us to stay in his home from late May until late June.

Belgium surrendered to the Germans on May 28, 1940, but that did not mean we sisters who had fled to France could return to Namur. The French were still at war, and it was not until June 22, 1940, that France signed an armistice with Germany. Only then were we permitted by the Germans to re-enter occupied Belgium. In just a few weeks the Belgium I knew was transformed into a German province, swarming with German soldiers and German bureaucrats. They were quickly followed by German businessmen looking to make fast money by acquiring cheap property and goods from desperate Belgian merchants. To our surprise, trains were operating normally, almost like the war never happened. We travelled to Ghent, Belgium, where many of our sick and invalid sisters were sent before the beginning of the invasion. Since those sisters were not able to endure the rigours of a train trip, the German military authorities provided automobiles and drivers to return the sisters to our convent in Berchem. German soldiers who only a few days before were killing Belgian, British, and French soldiers were gently and respectfully carrying our afflicted sisters to the automobiles. Blessed Julie tells us that there is a reservoir of goodness in everyone. Did this prove the truth of her words?

Our group of thirty sisters reached Namur on June 26. Forty other sisters were not so fortunate. They had been steadily pushed south by the fighting in France to the foothills of the Pyrenees Mountains near the Spanish border. They were not able to get to Namur until the end of August, but that was soon enough for our schools to open on September 2. The destruction of our Motherhouse, of course, meant that we would not be able to reopen our boarding school in Namur.

It was not until we returned to the Motherhouse in Namur that we learned the fate of Sister Jeanne. We were shocked and joyous to find that Sister Jeanne had returned to Namur two weeks before us. She said that near Douai her feet were so sore she could not walk any further. She just sat down by the edge of the road. A farm family came by and offered to take her up the road in their farm cart. She thought that being in the cart she would quickly catch up to us, but when we were detained by the soldiers the cart must have passed us. Being totally alone, the family took pity on her and made her a temporary member of the family. When Sister Jeanne returned to Namur, she had a hundred francs in her tunic pocket that her adopted family gave her for travel expenses.

Nothing was heard about the fate of Sister Paula and Sister Andre until dear Mother, Superior General, received a brief letter from Sister Louise, Sister Superior of the Congregation of Soeurs de la Misericorde in Hainaut. Sister Louise said she had received information that two sisters of Our Lady of Namur had been killed near the town of Douai. She possessed no other details, but she would make inquiries to find out if there was any truth to the story. Within a week another letter arrived from a Trappist priest, Father John. In the letter, he described that near the town of Douai he found the bodies of two nuns by the side of the road. They had been shot several times in the chest. He was able to identify the sisters from their books and other papers as Sisters of Our Lady of Namur. He quickly buried the sisters in shallow graves and prayed for the repose of their souls. The Germans were only a few kilometres away.

He did not know if he would soon join the sisters in death, so he only had time to write a cryptic note to Sister Superior of the Congregation of Soeurs de la Misericorde describing what he had found. He put the note in a pocket of his cassock, hoping that if he were killed that someone would take the note to our Motherhouse in Namur. By the grace of God, he survived his ordeal and thought it best to communicate directly with dear Mother about the deaths of Sister Paula and Sister Andre.

Subsequent to the letter from Father John, a Benedictine priest, Father Andrew, was visiting at our convent in Charleroi. He had taught for several years in Charleroi and, while there, he had become friends with the missing sisters, Sister Paula and Sister Andre. Father Andrew promised that when he returned to France, he would do everything in his power to learn why the two sisters were shot on the road to Douai. He posted a notice in the Douai newspaper asking if anyone had any information about the death of the two sisters. He received several responses. He also talked to several eyewitnesses. An elderly French woman had Sister Paula's and Sister Andre's prayer books and other documents, confirming the identity of the two murdered sisters. All the witnesses told the same tragic story. Sister Paula and Sister Andre came to the door of the first house in the village. It was owned by a kind, elderly man. One of the sisters could hardly walk and had to be supported by the other larger sister. They rang the bell, but before the good man could open the door someone was yelling "parachutists!"

Two French soldiers stormed out of the tavern next door. They grabbed the sisters, threw them up against the wall, and shot them before anyone could stop them. Their duty to protect France done, they calmly returned to the tavern.

Dear Mother was determined every effort should be made to retrieve the bodies of Sister Paula and Sister Andre for burial in the consecrated earth of our cemetery at Namur. The father of Sister Andre was adamant about going to Douai to find their graves and bring back their bodies. His journey was delayed for several months until he could acquire the required travel documents. When he eventually reached Douai and located the crossroad described by the Father John, he could see it had been the site of a major battle between the French and the Germans. The land was like a moonscape. There were craters from bombs and artillery. Foxholes and trenches had been dug in the fields and woods. The ground had been churned up by hundreds of tanks. He searched and searched but was unable to find his daughter's and Sister Paula's graves.

Our inability to provide our sisters with a proper burial added to my distress. I felt responsible for their deaths. I had been charged with getting them safely to France, and I failed in that duty. Their bodies will remain forever in unmarked, unblessed graves. Telling myself their deaths must have been part of God's plan did not assuage the guilt. I was forced to make decisions, and I have learned that having the ability to choose may ultimately trigger deep remorse for the choices we make.

CHAPTER SIX

COPING WITH GERMAN OCCUPATION AND PASSIVE RESISTANCE

Namur And Saint-Hubert, June 1940

WE FERVENTLY PRAYED THAT LIFE WOULD RETURN TO NORMAL. Many of our schools were starting classes. Sisters were preparing to take their final vows. Postulants and novices were returning to their convents. Eight new postulants were admitted to the order, willing to give their lives to God in such troubled times.

Nearly all the Sisters of Our Lady houses had held retreats by August 1940. Trams were running in cities, and most towns were accessible by train. Church services were held as usual, accompanied by the ringing of bells, although only for a shortened time. We soon learned, however, "normality" is a delusion when a country is in the middle of a war, especially with the people of Belgium being even more divided politically after the end of the fighting than they had been before the invasion began.

King Leopold believed that Belgium had satisfied its treaty with France and England by defending the country to the best of its limited ability. With his army defeated and his people at the mercy of German soldiers, he believed it was his duty to seek the most favourable outcome for Belgium. Unlike Queen Wilhelmina of the Netherlands, he chose not to flee to England with the remnants of his army to form a government in exile.[1] Many of the Belgian government ministers, however, considered the king a coward for not continuing the fight, and their view was shared by a large proportion of the population, particularly the French-speaking Walloons.

Many Flemish, however, were happy to end what they saw as useless slaughter. Some of our Flemish neighbours rejoiced openly about the defeat of the Belgian army and displayed the German flag in their windows. They hoped that the Germans would restore Flemish rights and perhaps join the Flemish part of Belgium with the German Reich. The towns of Eupen and Malmedy were re-annexed to Germany, and German became their only official language. The enthusiasm of young males of Flemish Belgium to join the Third Reich may have been tempered upon learning they could be drafted into the German army.

Our Walloon neighbours often repeated the rumour that Flemish soldiers surrendered and laid down their arms as quickly as possible. At the same time, reports about the bravery of Flemish soldiers were common.

One story, regularly repeated, was about a Flemish soldier in Bastogne who had been told by his mother, "Never surrender." He single-handedly faced a German tank with just his rifle, trying to put bullets into the tank's sighting slits until he was cut down by the tank's machine gun.

At first, the occupation overseen by the German Military Administration under General Alexander von Falkenhausen might be described as benign. The general told the Bishop of Namur, Monseigneur Heylen, no harm would be done by his troops, and the occupation would secure peace and protection for people and property.

The German army marched into Namur in silence. There was no cheering or singing of German patriotic songs. No tanks or other tracked vehicles. The only sound was that of their hobnailed boots on the cobblestone. Civilians were not mistreated. Although most of the public buildings were taken over, the Germans interfered little with the life of the city.

Within weeks, however, "regulations" began to be issued. Signs bearing warnings were posted around the city. One of the first to appear banned listening to the BBC, the British Broadcasting Company. A violation of the BBC regulation could result in a sentence of twelve years at hard labour, and the threat of immediate execution was implicit.

Rationing was soon imposed. Meat, butter, eggs, milk, coffee, and white bread rapidly disappeared from the shelves. All such basic foodstuffs were allocated to the German army. If people were suspected of hiding rationed food under their coats, they could be stopped and searched. An egg cost 20 francs (75 cents) and children's shoes could not be purchased for under 460 francs ($9). Even thread was rationed. A ton of coal that could be purchased for 200 francs ($2) before the occupation cost 1200 francs ($25) per ton, if you could get it at all.

At the beginning of each month, each resident was issued a sheet of dated ration stamps. On the top of the sheet was the name of the person who was entitled to use the card. The cards were good for only one month, making it impossible to stockpile them. Nor could they be easily transferred or sold. If a person's photo identification card did not match the name on the ration sheet, immediate arrest was possible.

Mother General worried about having enough potatoes. Each sister was allotted fifteen kilos of potatoes a month, essentially a pound of potatoes per day. If one ate the well-scrubbed skins too, the allotted amount was sufficient. The total absence of milk was the most difficult challenge. Sometimes weeks would go by without any milk, although from time to time an unknown benefactor would leave a pail of milk on our doorstep. Almost all the milk was given to the children under thirteen years old.

The sisters working in the kitchen were challenged in preparing meals. They developed recipes for wild plants like nettles, rutabaga, and a type of Jerusalem artichoke that was easy to find or grow. Acorns were crushed to brew a kind of coffee. Its bitter taste was the only similarity. Any stimulation from caffeine had to be imagined. Tea was fashioned by steeping mint or lavender leaves for ten minutes. Even crushed cilantro seeds produced a credible tea. Sugar was saved for use as a preservative in canning fruit. Honey, when available, and saccharine were used to sweeten our tea and coffee. Saccharine had been banned before the war, perhaps to protect the sugar beet industry, but German officials lifted the ban.

The one food staple we were awash in was tinned sardines. Boxes of them arrived with the mail on Wednesdays. The postman suggested we open a fish market. There were shelves filled with stacks of sardine cans. Although the packages' return address was a street in Lisbon, Portugal, and the postmark said the packages were sent from Portugal, we assumed the sardines were being sent by our generous Sisters of Our Lady in America. *"Elles viennent Amerique!"* we shouted when the first package was opened. Tinned sardines travel well and last forever, so they were the perfect foodstuffs for shipping over a long distance. We also assumed that to disguise their American connection, there were collaborators in Portugal who purchased and packaged the sardines, then sent them on to us in Belgium. The Germans would never have permitted us to sell the sardines, so Sister Agnes volunteered to make some discreet inquiries in the developing black market about exchanging some of the tins for bars of soap. She kept her vow of silence as to whom she met, but she did return to the convent with fifty bars.

As if the rationing of food and clothing was not oppressive enough for the Belgians, the German authorities set an exchange rate between the Reichsmark and the Belgian franc. The artificial rate rewarded anyone paid in *Reichsmarks*, namely German soldiers and German bureaucrats. The rate penalised Belgian citizens, who only received francs. Prior to the war, one Reichsmark was worth ten Belgian francs. After July 1940, it took fourteen francs to equal one Reichsmark. So, every time a German officer came into a bakery to buy bread, he was automatically entitled to a thirty per cent discount. The artificial exchange rate drove up prices and added fuel to the inflationary firestorm sweeping Belgium. Belgians working for Germans could not insist on being paid in *Riechsmarks*. They were paid less for their labour while being forced to pay more for their food and clothing.

An eleven o'clock curfew was instituted and a complete blackout, "occultation," was ordered. Very few people were on the streets after dark, it being almost impossible to find your way even in your own neighbourhood. If a street warden or passing patrol saw any light escaping from a blackout curtain, there would be a shout of *"Licht aus!"* — lights out. Should the shout prove ineffective, it could be followed by a rifle shot through the offending window. Every pane of glass from which the slightest ray of light could escape had to be "occulted" by dark paint or black cloth. The electric lights were draped with eerie millinery creating a Halloween haunted house atmosphere. The dear Lord alone lit our way to morning and evening prayers. We blindly stumbled through the passageways, sometimes holding the hand of another sister to keep from falling on the worn stone steps.

Another concern for the people of Belgium was what would happen to all the Belgian soldiers who surrendered. They had been marched off to temporary camps in Germany. Sister Monica's brother, Albert, had been one of those soldiers, a pilot. Three months after Belgium's surrender, he came to the Saint-Hubert convent. He told us that most of the Flemish soldiers were immediately released and allowed to return home. The French-speaking Walloon soldiers, however, were put in permanent prisoner-of-war camps. Albert assumed it was part of a German strategy to drive a wedge between the Flemish Belgians and the Walloon Belgians.

Although Albert was a Walloon, he managed to pass as Flemish due to being relatively fluent in the Dutch language. Flemish officers from the Belgian army who often sat on the "language examination juries" may have abetted his ruse. The juries determined those who were true Flemish and who were Walloons masquerading as Flemish. Many of those officers were not eager to condemn fellow soldiers to POW camps, so they often told the Germans a soldier's Dutch was excellent when in fact the soldier's accent and grammar were faulty. Albert believed it was the Flemish officer on his jury panel who kept him out of a POW camp.

Albert was out of the war, but he was adamant about continuing to fight the Germans. He was determined to get to Britain by way of Spain and Portugal. Sister Monica argued against Albert's plan, but to no avail. He left Saint-Hubert the next day. One month later, Sister Monica was relieved to receive an unsigned postcard of a Portuguese Beach with just one written line, "The sea is bluer than I ever imagined." Three weeks after the postcard a phone call was received at the convent. It was an anonymous caller, who said, "Thank Sister Monica. The package has arrived." We knew then Albert had reached England.[2]

In our attempt to achieve a kind of normality, dear Mother, Mother General, decreed that we would continue to celebrate the religious holidays with prayers of thanksgiving and songs of praise. Often the sisters in the kitchen would create a special treat to be eaten during Recreation. Dear Mother did not forget that our sisters in America would be celebrating the 100th anniversary of the arrival of Sisters of Our Lady of Namur in America. Flowers were put on the table, and a tiny American flag was placed in the middle of the bouquet. The flag had been found in a storage cabinet. One could only guess what the German authorities would have done if they had seen our patriotic display. Perhaps nothing, since Germany was not yet at war with the United States. Seeing the flag of my homeland, however, did send a slight shiver down my spine and gave me a momentary bout of homesickness.

Germany was locked in a war with Britain and Sister Madeline, who was a British citizen, suffered the consequences. She was ordered to report to the *"Komandantur"* with one suitcase containing what she would require for a journey. Mother General, dear Mother, went with Sister Madeline to ask the *Komandatur* to rescind his order. He refused to even speak with Mother General, and no one would tell her where Sister Madeline was being sent. They bundled her into a black Mercedes and drove off.

A month later we received a long letter from Sister Madeline. It was postmarked Wurttemberg, Germany. She described that she was at a "charming" camp near the Swiss border. The scenery was beautiful. There were 369 "guests" in the camp; forty-six of them were religious. There were two former SND pupils, but she was the only SND sister. She did not have any information about other British SND sisters. Sister Madeline then described her life in the camp. She received three meals of nourishing food every day: breakfast, dinner, and supper. She did have to provide her own tea. There was Mass and communion every morning. Each afternoon they could walk for up to two hours, but could not to go too near the fencing erected for their protection. Since what Sister Madeline described was more like an alpine spa than a concentration camp, we assumed the letter was written in language that would not be censored. We were grateful that Sister Madeline was alive.

We were not aware of it at the beginning of the occupation, but the Germans also had a strategy for stealing Belgium's cultural heritage. The plan was to loot our museums and private art collections of their most valuable works of art and ship them to Germany. Our special art collection, *"Tresor d'Hugo d'Oignies,"* was probably high on their looting list.

Half the items of the *Tresor* are reliquaries that contain the bones, teeth, and fragments of clothing from saints. Their original purpose was to make the relics available to the faithful who believed that contact with the relics would enlist the saint's help on their journey to heaven. The *Trésor* reliquaries were crafted in the twelfth and thirteenth centuries and were adorned with gold, silver, and jewels. A second part of the *Tresor* included sacred objects used in liturgical ceremonies such as gold and silver patens, chalices, and crosses. The third part of the collection contained bejewelled miters, rings, and a Byzantine cross and triptych that were likely stolen by Crusaders from a Constantinople orthodox church in the twelfth century. The entire collection was entrusted to the sisters of Our Lady of Namur for safekeeping in 1818. Although Mother General did not consider the Sisters of Our Lady to be owners of the *Tresor*, she did believe the order had an obligation to preserve and protect the collection.

Less than a month after my return to Namur, and before I moved to our Saint-Hubert house, a German general arrived in a black Horch convertible at the front gate of the Dames of St. Julienne convent, where we were living after the destruction of the Motherhouse. His driver informed Sister Bernice that General Steiner wished to speak with Mother General. The general's unannounced arrival was a complete surprise. Mother General could not guess the purpose for the visit of such a high-ranking German officer, but she was suspicious. Mother General asked me to be present at the meeting and serve as a translator. Although Mother General spoke excellent German, using me as a translator to repeat the questions of the general provided her with a few more seconds to carefully weigh her responses. More time could be gained if she feigned misunderstanding of a question and I politely had to ask the general to repeat it. I could also be a witness to what was said and what wasn't.

I was worried about saying or doing something that would put the convent in jeopardy, but Mother General appeared calm and composed. She told me to use the disciplines I learned when I was a postulant and a novice. We put on our inscrutable praying faces; alert, aware, with no emotional facial clues. As we entered the parlour where the general was waiting, our light tread with a slow, deliberate pace and erect posture expressed calmness and serenity. Our custom of inserting our hands in the sleeves of our tunics when speaking eliminated nervous and unnecessary hand movements. I was grateful for this tradition because my hands were shaking as I entered the room.

The general stood and introduced himself as General Steiner. He said he was a member of the "Commission for the Preservation of Belgium Art." He asked Mother General if she spoke German. Without answering his question, she told him I would do the translating and followed up with a question of her own. "Do you believe Belgian works of art are in danger?"

General Steiner responded, "Not at the present time." Then he immediately asked about the whereabouts of our "Treasure," presumably referring to the convent's beautiful collection of reliquaries.

Mother General told him, "I do not know exactly where it is; it is probably under the rubble of the Motherhouse."

I was amazed the General seemed to accept this response at face value without any follow-up questions like, "Who would know?" It was very early in the occupation, and perhaps the German authorities did not want to alienate potential collaborators by resorting to oppressive measures. Or perhaps it was the "power of the robe" again, and a centuries-old culture of not challenging religious authority.

The General may have been testing the "buried beneath the rubble" explanation when he asked to be given a tour of the ruins. We rode to the destroyed convent in the General's car. Mother General and I walked him around the property. He took careful note of the devastation, exclaiming all the while, "What a disaster! This is frightful!" His apparent distress was ironic, if not hypocritical, considering it was German bombs that destroyed the Sisters of Our Lady of Namur convent. While examining the ruins, the General was gloating about how Britain would be invaded and defeated in three weeks. Mother General reminded him that in war, defeat is always a possibility. General Steiner bristled, saying, "Germany never loses!" Mother General sighed. "Well, God works in mysterious ways."

After General Steiner drove away, Mother General told me she had lied about not knowing the location of the *Tresor d'Hugo d'Oignies*. After war began in September of 1939, the *Tresor* and other works of art were removed to a safe location. Mother General was convinced the only "danger" the Commission for the Preservation of Belgium Art feared was that the Belgian masterpieces would be hidden before the Germans could start stealing them. Now that she understood the German intentions, she directed the Sisters of Our Lady's "treasure" to stay hidden, with only a few sisters knowing its location. Three or four times during the four-year occupation a German official would make inquiries about our "treasure," only to be told it had not been found and must still be buried underneath the bricks and stone of our Motherhouse.[3]

Shortly after the General's inspection, Mother General, dear Mother, sent me to teach at our convent and school in Saint-Hubert, Belgium. The town of Saint-Hubert is in the Ardennes, just west of Bastogne, in the eastern part of Belgium. Our buildings in Saint-Hubert escaped serious damage during the invasion so it was a logical place to restart one of our schools and begin preparing our postulants and novices for taking their final vows. Dear Mother thought I would be more useful there since one of Saint-Hubert's programs offered a diploma in Agricultural Household Management. The program instructed young country girls on the "rational running of a farm household." The course work included classes in anatomy, zoology, botany, milk and cheese making, horticulture, animal husbandry, and poultry farming, subjects in which I was well versed.

Saint-Hubert also had another advantage beyond being largely intact. The convent owned a nearby farm. My life as a farm girl proved helpful beyond lecturing about the theory of good farming practices. I showed the novice gardeners how they could plant beans, peas, carrots, lettuces, and potatoes much closer in rows without hurting the harvest. They were surprised to learn that a fall crop like squash could be planted in the same plot as a spring crop like peas. By the time the squash vines were covering every inch of ground, the peas had long been harvested. We also raised rabbits and chickens in cages. For some of the sisters raised in cities, I had to explain why the rooster had to be kept absolutely isolated from the hens. It also startled the students to see a sister down on her hands and knees digging in the soil and getting quite grimy.

Although the Germans never raided our farm, we took no chances. We kept enough produce out and available to allay any suspicions that we were hoarding food (which we were). Produce was hidden in every nook and cranny, including behind the altar in the chapel. Sister Agnes kept a detailed list of all the hiding places lest we forget the location of our caches. Sister Ursula, Sister Superior of Saint-Hubert, had been through the occupation of Belgium in the Great War. She anticipated strict rationing would eventually be imposed by the German occupiers. Soon after Belgium's surrender, she sent out a troop of sisters to buy or scavenge all the sugar, flour, salt, and coffee they could find. They did such a thorough job of accumulating the provisions that false walls in the rectory had to be constructed to hide all of it.[4]

Our plan for enduring the occupation was to avoid conflict with the Germans as much as possible, yet not be seen as collaborators. The German occupation authority aided our strategy by taking a more *laissez faire* approach, allowing Belgians to resume ordinary lives. Occasionally army officials would visit the convent with offers to help if we needed it. One officer in particular, with a chest covered in medals, told Sister Ursula his wife had suggested he visit the convent. She had a sister who was in a convent in Mulhausen, Germany. He offered to render us any service within his power. It was a tempting offer. Sister Ursula knew from her experience in the Great War, however, that favours from an occupier usually came with strings attached. Accepting them could put the Sisters of Our Lady on the slippery slope to collaboration.

Sister Ursula did permit several German priests in the German army to say Mass in the convent chapel. The Masses were open to the public. The hours of the Masses varied depending on whether the priests were off duty, sometime being as late as seven o'clock in the evening. One priest told me he had been a professor at the University of Bonn, but was now spending his days washing army trucks. Another recently ordained priest, Father Louis, said he was a stretcher-bearer for the ambulance corps. Often a dozen or so soldiers came with the priests to attend mass. Father Louis was not a zealous soldier. One evening I saw him kneeling in the back of the chapel. His belt and pistol were on the pew beside him. He was sobbing. When I approached him, he quickly picked up his pistol and belt and hurried out.

In the early stages of the occupation there was not much resistance to the German presence. Most people just wanted to resume the lives they had before the war began. If anyone felt guilt from their passivity, slight acts of disobedience seemed to suffice at easing their consciences. For a while it was a popular activity to paint, chalk, or etch the letter '*V*' on walls, buildings, trams, public bathrooms, and, for the braver mischief-maker, on German military vehicles. A member of the Belgian parliamentary office in London, Victor de Laveleye, wrote a little jingle to the tune of the first three notes of Beethoven's Fifth Symphony. The letter V in Morse Code, dit-dit-

dit-dah, duplicates those opening notes. The letter V is also the first letter in the French word for victory (*victoire*) and the first letter of the Dutch word for freedom (*vrijheid*). The jingle was played nearly every hour on the Belgian broadcasts of the BBC.

The Germans at first tried to suppress the V craze. Perpetrators were rarely caught since it only took the V-artist a second to paint the letter on a wall. Cleaning the walls or painting over the Vs only seemed to multiply their number. Although it was tempting for us sisters to grab a paintbrush and join in, Sister Ursula, Sister Superior, forbade us from doing it.[5]

Eventually, the Germans found a strategy that worked. They adopted the letter V for their own propaganda purposes. The German-controlled radio stations began claiming that all the Vs appearing around the country stood for the Victory that German armies would soon achieve. German soldiers painted beautifully designed Vs on tanks, trucks and buildings, including our convent wall. Painting Vs ceased to be a sign of protest once it could also be interpreted as popular support for the German occupation of Belgium.[6]

Another way Belgians could assert their discontent with the occupation regime without too much risk was to read some of the clandestine newspapers being published. Many of them were only published a few times before disappearing. The penalty for publishing an underground newspaper was very severe. The newspapers were usually one page printed on thin mimeograph paper and published in French and German. *Le Soir* was allowed to continue publishing, but it was obvious to everyone that its owners were collaborating with the Germans. It was rarely read and largely ignored. *La Libre Belgique* was the most successful underground paper and was widely disseminated. Anonymous distributors would stuff them into letterboxes or under doors. Somehow a copy of *La Libre Belgique* mysteriously appeared from time to time on the altar of the Saint-Hubert chapel.

A central purpose of the underground press was to foster resentment toward the German occupiers by repeating stories about German oppression and brutality. Early in the occupation, the Germans seemed to be acting with restraint. Tales of German cruelty told by the clandestine press, whether or not actually true, were designed to show that German restraint was only a facade. I read in one publication how a Belgian man was summarily executed for having picked up a spent cartridge. According to the paper, he had to dig his own grave, then kneel down on the edge of the hole before being shot in the back of the head. There was no way to confirm the stories in the underground papers, but they contributed to the hostile narrative that the German occupiers were capable of anything.

Listening to BBC broadcasts was a major offence, but catching anyone actually listening was nearly impossible, if he or she were discreet. Just tuning in the "News from Belgium" portion of the BBC broadcast was another way for Belgians to defy in a small way the occupation regime, again with little risk. The Germans tried to jam the BBC signal, but the underground press published detailed instructions on how to make a simple device that filtered out the jamming static. It consisted of wire wrapped tightly around a cardboard cylinder like those found inside a roll of toilet paper. As long as you detached the filter from the radio and did not leave your radio tuned to the BBC wavelength, it was impossible for German police making a surprise visit to conclude you were illegally listening to the BBC. I suspect many Germans themselves actually listened to the BBC.

Our convent owned a French-built radio called a *Melodiaphone*. We sisters huddled around the radio every evening during the time set aside for evening prayers to listen to the latest BBC "News from Belgium." The irony was not lost on us that we depended on a British radio station to tell us what was happening in our own country. The BBC also gave us hope. The German press and news reports crowed about how the bombing of England was reducing its cities to rubble and that it was just a matter of time before England gave up the fight. The BBC newscasts made it clear that England still had plenty of fight left in her. As an American, I was gratified when I heard on the radio that America was lending its support to England by giving the country massive amounts of weapons under a program called "Lend-Lease."

The German authorities never lifted the restrictions on listening to the BBC, but eventually they must have realised it was impossible to enforce without expending an enormous amount of time and energy trying to catch those tuning in to the BBC. If the German police had actually been successful in rounding up all of the Belgian BBC audience, there would not have been enough prison cells to house them. Many German soldiers turned a deaf ear toward BBC broadcasts.

This casual attitude was illustrated by a story told to Sister Agnes by Madam Varley, who lived near the convent.[7]

A German officer came to Madame Varley's home and handed her an official order that said he would be billeted in her home. She was outraged. She refused his outstretched hand and spent the next three months ignoring him. The officer had his own key and could come and go as he pleased. While in the house he kept mostly to his room. When the officer was transferred to another unit, he left a vase of flowers on his dressing table with a note addressed to Madam Varley. He thanked her for the use of her house and suggested that in the future she turn down the volume on her radio when listening to the BBC. He said the next officer assigned to her house might be a troublemaker.

One strategy adopted by many Belgians to annoy the German authorities was the playing of jazz music. The Nazis shunned jazz as being music of black people, and obviously not fit for their superior race. On the other hand, the Nazis approved of "swing" music played by the Big Bands. A kind of cat-and-mouse game developed between musicians and the German censors. The dance bands tried to slip in as much jazz as they could under the guise of swing music. One high-level officer of the "music police" attempted to set out clear regulations as to when acceptable music crossed the line into the forbidden jazz genre. For example:

Compositions in Major keys are given preference as well as lyrics expressing joy in life.

On no account will Negroid excess in tempo (so-called hot Jazz) or in solo performances (so-called breaks) be tolerated.

So-called Jazz compositions may contain at most ten per cent syncopation.

The double bass must be played solely with the bow. Plucking of the strings is prohibited.

Musicians are forbidden to make vocal improvisations (so-called scat).

The use of saxophones of all keys should be limited.

Many bands took on these regulations as an exciting challenge. Classical jazz pieces and swing music were reworked to ostensibly satisfy the regulations and still sound very much like the prohibited jazz. The restrictions on the playing of jazz may have had the effect of actually increasing the amount of jazz being played. Musicians and audiences could relish the delightful sound of creative jazz and at the same time be thumbing their noses at the Nazis.[8]

In October 1940, the first regulations were issued by the German Military Administration in Belgium imposing restrictions on Jews. All Jews were required to register with the police. Other regulations followed in later months resulting in Jews losing their jobs and having their shops and businesses boycotted. The Belgian underground newspaper *La Libre Belgique* was quick to react. It urged Belgians to express their rejection of the regulations and demonstrate their solidarity with Belgian Jews by small gestures. The paper urged Belgians to make a conscious effort to greet Jews in the street, offer elderly Jews your seat on the tram, and patronise their shops and businesses. The goal was to "Make the *Boches* furious." Many Belgian citizens eagerly adopted the suggestions. The sisters at Saint-Hubert were more than ready to show their discontent with the occupation regime. I liked to think when I walked into a Jewish shop in my nun's habit that I was sending a strong message that the regime's anti-Jewish regulations were anathema to all practising Catholics. Of course, my nun's habit also protected me from retaliation.

CHAPTER SEVEN

ACTIVE RESISTANCE TO OCCUPATION

Saint-Hubert, January 1941

IN 1941, IT WAS BECOMING INCREASINGLY CLEAR THAT PASSIVE, annoying resistance was not going to be enough to deter the Germans from implementing harsher and more draconian laws. Perhaps the German Military Administration interpreted the passivity of many Belgians as a sign that more restrictions, especially more oppressive measures against Jews, would be tolerated. The Germans miscalculated. Cardinal Jozef-Ernest van Roey began protesting to the German authorities, criticising the anti-Jewish German policies and legislation.

I later learned from Sister Ursula, Sister Superior of Saint-Hubert, that unbeknownst to the Germans, however, Cardinal van Roey was quietly communicating to Belgian priests, bishops, and the heads of all the religious orders that they should be doing whatever they could to help the Jews. Sister Ursula said the Cardinal also gave permission to tap into Church resources to foster the campaign of resistance. The Cardinal had been ready to launch a public campaign, using the church pulpits to condemn the treatment of the Jews. That did not happen. Sister Ursula believed Cardinal van Roey was dissuaded from the campaign by fellow bishops, who feared it would be used as an excuse by the Germans to repress the Catholic Church.

On June 22, 1941, the German army invaded Russia in a surprise attack. The invasion of the Communist country had grave ramifications for the people of Belgium. It initially had the effect of dividing the country more. Belgian Catholics were staunchly anti-communist, so many of them initially cheered the invasion of the godless country. The German army took advantage of this anti-communist enthusiasm to launch a recruiting campaign aimed at young Belgian men. They were exhorted to enlist in Belgian Waffen SS units. The recruiting propaganda promised that the units would only fight against the Russians and would not be used against the British who were still holding out. Many young men were seduced by this appeal. The recruitment campaign had serious repercussions in Belgium. Many Belgians who had previously been engaged in only passive resistance to the occupation realised active resistance was the only way Belgium could free itself from German rule. Recruiting young men into the Waffen SS strengthened the Resistance movement.

Late in 1941, German authorities ordered unemployed persons of both sexes, between the ages of 18–50, to leave their homes and report for work in German factories for slave wages. The extradition policy reopened old wounds from the Great War, when German occupiers transported thousands of Belgians to Germany to work in its mines and factories. Thousands of Belgians refused and were forced "underground" to avoid being transported to Germany. Many of them joined the increasing number of organised Resistance units. More and more Belgians realised Christians were not immune to the constraints the Nazis imposed on Belgian Jews.

In the fall of 1941, Mother General undertook a tour of all the Sisters of Our Lady of Namur convents and schools in

Belgium. The ostensible purpose was to assess the progress the schools had made in restoring their educational programs for young Belgian girls and to develop a strategy for increasing the number of girls entering the order as postulants. We learned her true intent when she visited our school in Saint-Hubert. We were like a company of soldiers when we gathered around her in the refectory as she gave us our "marching orders." She recounted the increasingly oppressive nature of the occupation, especially with respect to the onerous restrictions on the Jews of Belgium. She was distraught that increasing numbers of Belgians were being forced to live "underground" to avoid persecution by the Germans. Dear Mother's message was not all pessimistic, however. She predicted that the German invasion of Russia and the continued survival of Britain would ultimately lead to the defeat of the German military juggernaut. She also foresaw the entry of America into the war against the Germans. She expected it was just a matter of time before Belgium would be liberated. She said it was imperative for everyone who cherished Belgium and her people to direct all their efforts to frustrating the Nazi attempt to use Belgium, her citizens, and resources to further their evil plans. She added that there should be no question about the character of Nazism. It was evil. She said that as of that moment the Sisters of Our Lady of Namur were part of the Resistance movement, and we would cooperate with Resistance groups.

We could not, however, assist in any Resistance activity that could take lives, even the lives of German soldiers and officials, but we should be ready to risk our own lives trying to save others. I was surprised by this pronouncement, a feeling that was immediately superseded by one of amazement.

Mother General had already been in communication with a Resistance group, the "*Front de l'Independence*." She told us the code name of our contact person with the Front and made arrangements for us to meet him. Dear Mother's last instructions described the relationship between the Motherhouse in Namur and the other convents with respect to our resistance efforts. She said there would be few, if any, instructions emanating from her about how we should participate in Resistance activities. Saint-Hubert's Sister Superior would make those decisions. Directives coming from Namur would only increase the risk of discovery by the Germans and future Resistance efforts would be more effective if developed around local attitudes and conditions.[1]

After dear Mother left Saint-Hubert, we were at a loss on how to transform our religious order dedicated to a life of teaching, prayer, and meditation into an underground resistance organisation. What skills did we possess that would make us effective spies, able to conduct clandestine operations? The more we considered the mission given to us, however, we began to realise that perhaps we were uniquely qualified for the world of undercover operations.

By keeping the rule of silence through much of the day, using a minimum of words the rest of the time, and having our own special sign language, we sisters know how to keep secrets. Sisters spend years honing the discipline of self-control, always presenting an aura of serenity and calm to the world. Sisters are unlikely to appear anxious when questioned by police or the Gestapo or display agitation when undertaking dangerous missions. In an odd way, sisters are masters of disguise without being disguised. Our habits make us obvious in a crowd and at the same time give us anonymity. To the average observer sisters all look alike. Was it Sister Agnes, Sister Maria, or Sister Christina who was waiting at the railway station? Large pockets sewn inside our flowing habits allow us to transport documents, food, and radio parts without raising a hint of suspicion or suggesting further inquiry might be necessary.

Of course, inquiry is even less likely because of our status as nuns. So many German soldiers and police were raised as good Catholic boys that they, like many Belgians, would step off the sidewalk to make room for a passing sister. For them, the thought of interrogating a nun could be unnerving, while the prospect of actually searching a nun would be truly intimidating.

Many resistance groups are a loose conglomeration of members who share a common goal of undermining the occupying regime. Beyond that one objective, they are bundles of conflicting desires and interests. Personality conflicts often threaten the survival of the organisation. Such divisiveness is not likely when an organization like the Sisters of Our Lady decides to operate as a Resistance group. There already exists a culture of absolute obedience to orders. The vow of obedience taken by a sister at the time of her induction into the order is sacred. Years of practising that vow keeps her on an unwavering course, never being distracted by her own whims and desires. If Sister Superior orders a sister to take contraband through a police roadblock, she will do it.

Other resistance organisations are often hampered by the creation of rogue splinter groups. The split could be caused by a conflict of personalities or political philosophies. For example, Catholics in a Communist Resistance group would be like mixing oil and water. Sisters, on the other hand, have spent years building collaborative relationships, creating bonds that have been forged in a crucible of love for each other and the love of God.

It seems ironic, but black-robed nuns can also be accomplished at gathering intelligence. Almost all the sisters at Saint-Hubert speak several languages, including German. We often overhear German officers talking about the war on the street or sitting in sidewalk cafes. I suspect they believe we speak only Dutch and cannot understand High German. I am amazed how many tidbits of information one can casually pick up strolling down the Rue De La Converserie.

I wonder if anyone notices how many Sisters of Our Lady there are running errands on the street? On our walks, we make a special effort to speak to other Belgians on the street, trying to make friends. This extroverted behaviour of sisters who had rarely been outside of their convent walls before the war must also seem strange. Sisters have a natural empathy for people, and empathy is the basis for establishing trust. Soon our new acquaintances are passing on useful morsels of information they have overheard.[2]

Two days after we were told about our new role in the Resistance, Sister Superior informed me I would be meeting our contact with the Front de l'Independence. I assumed she intentionally did not tell me what the meeting was about or why and how it was arranged. The less I knew, the less I could divulge if questioned. We were all new to the espionage game and were feeling our way.[3]

I followed Sister Superior's instructions. I walked to the public square in front of the *Basilique*, arriving at eleven o'clock in the morning, and I sat on the end of a bench near the park's entrance on Rue Saint Gilles. A man sat down on the other end of the bench and took out a newspaper, *Le Soir*. When no one was watching, he handed me a slip of paper containing a list of addresses. I memorised the addresses and returned the paper to him. Everything went as planned. My initial anxiety gave way to a sense of euphoria. I had successfully played the spy game. It was a thrilling experience, not unlike what I imagine it feels like after taking some kind of drug.

Sister Ursula was not pleased with my obviously elated state. She said in the future I would need to have more control over my emotions, and added that spies who succumb to hubris do not live long lives. I learned why I had to memorise the addresses. They were locations where people who had to go underground were hiding.

There were more challenges to disappearing than just finding a secure place to hide. One had to eat. Covert people were not eligible for ration cards. The large underground population could only be fed if other people reduced their already scanty diets. *Unless.* Unless they could get forged ration cards or be given food by fellow citizens, such as farmers who had more than they needed.

The next challenge for the Resistance was how to get the forged ration cards and farm produce to those in hiding. Sister Superior had a solution. The sisters of Saint-Hubert would begin a campaign of raising alms for the poor. They would periodically go door-to-door soliciting money. Behind some of those doors would be hidden refugees. At those homes the soliciting sister would extract from secret compartments sewn in her habit forged ration cards, half a dozen eggs, or even half a head of cabbage. The pockets were so well designed, a sister could carry two kilos of food across the middle of the town square and no one would be the wiser.[4]

One of the addresses I was given was in Vesqueville, a small village south of Saint-Hubert. Sister Superior told me to take two forged ration cards to the family hiding at that location.

When I arrived at the cottage, I was surprised to be met at the door by the very person who was to receive the ration cards. This type of exchange rarely happened. Usually, some third person would accept the ration cards and the documents would then be given to the persons who had gone underground.

Madam Mariette Van Daelen-Speckaert introduced herself and said she was Jewish. She explained how her family—her husband and two children—had come to Vesqueville. They had been passengers on the *S.S. St. Louis* when it docked in Antwerp in June 1939.

They were part of the small group of Jewish passengers who were allowed by Belgium authorities to disembark and take up residence in Belgium.

They came to the Village of Vesqueville less than two months after their arrival in Antwerp. The villagers welcomed them from the very beginning. Then, after the German invasion and the anti-Jewish regulations that followed, all their neighbours began treating them as just another Catholic family in the village, and no one even uttered the word "Jewish." Of course, they had to change their name, Rosenfeld, and obtain false identity cards through a clerk who worked in the Brussels Town Hall. They became Pierre, Mariette, Jean-Michel, and Louisa Van Daelen-Speckaert.

The rationing regime made life hard even with false ID papers. The Van Daelen-Speckaerts could not easily get ration cards without risking being identified as Jewish. They tried to eke out a living by barter. Mariette would spin wool and trade a kilo of spun wool for a kilo of flour. The village people were generous and seemed intent on ensuring that they got the better side of the bargain. The town butcher would always slip some extra bone marrow into their packages to use for soup. Farmers would sell them milk at a discount. Their firewood ration was the same as that of other villagers. Jean-Michel and Louisa attended the local school and made good Catholic friends. Mariette believed that most of the people in the village knew who they really were. They actually managed to go underground in the open.[5]

I decided that I could do more than bring them forged ration cards. I could foster their disguise as a Catholic family by making their "Catholicism" even more open. The next time I came to the village, I brought them rosaries and a statue of the Blessed Virgin Mary to prominently display in their cottage. I also taught them the words to common Catholic prayers.[6]

I was never sure how Sister Ursula communicated with members of the Front; she never told me. Clearly there was regular contact. On any given day, she would call us one by one into her office and tell us where and when we were to meet Front agents for the exchange of ration cards and addresses. The sisters receiving the forged ration cards were never given the addresses of the recipients at the same time; other sisters were told where to deliver the ration cards. After a couple of months of this undercover work, my spy-craft skills were honed. All my senses were on high alert. Was that man across the square pretending not to watch me? Were those footsteps a bit too slow for a woman on her way to the market?[7]

As we soon discovered, it is not possible to just dabble in Resistance clandestine activities by delivering forged ration cards. It was inevitable the Front de l'Independence would expect the Sisters of Our Lady to do more to help the cause. Sister Superior Ursula was asked to hide Belgians who had gone underground and were on the run from the Nazis. Sister Superior knew sheltering resisters would put the order at much greater risk, yet she agreed to turn the convent into a haven.

Before the refugees could be sheltered, however, secret rooms and hiding places had to be constructed. The Front provided masons and carpenters to do the work. Some came at night, and others attended mass in the chapel, staying behind to build false walls and doors. The biggest room, able to accommodate six people, was carved out of the cellar. One end of the cellar was bricked in, and no access was available through the cellar itself. The only way into the cellar was through a trapdoor cut in the refectory floor. A large piece of slate covered the hole, and a small stove was placed on top of the slate. Two sisters could move the stove off the slate using two thick boards that were concealed under one of the dining room tables. The stove could be moved even while a fire was burning in it. Unfortunately for the occupants of the cellar, no heat from the stove leaked into their cold, damp refuge.

Another location, less damp but cold, and often hot, room was created in a corner of the attic. The original trapdoor giving access to the space was removed. The hole was covered with wood and plastered to match the rest of the ceiling. The only way into the attic was through a removable panel in a toilette. The panel was next to the commode and held the toilette paper dispenser. The panel was unlatched by lifting up on the dispenser. Behind the hidden door was a ladder to the attic. As an additional security precaution, if German police searched the building, two sisters were assigned to make sure the secret door was properly closed after the refugees had climbed the ladder. Then one sister was to sit on the commode, creating an embarrassing diversion to any officer bursting into the room.

In searching for other locations to hide refugees, the Resistance workmen discovered that behind the pipes of the chapel organ was a small alcove that allowed access to the organ pipes for purposes of repair and tuning. It was large enough to accommodate two people. The alcove was entered through a false, carved wood door on the right side of the organ. The door was a duplicate of the wood panel on the left side of the organ. It was a simple matter for the carpenter to add a set of locks on the inside of the door that could be secured by whoever was hiding in the room. Assuming a policeman even tried to move the door, it would seem as solid as the duplicate panel on the left side of the organ.

When considering places for people to hide, we had to provide for the possibility of the police invading our convent so quickly that all the refugees would not have time to get back to their secret rooms. Tiny contingency hidey-holes were created around the convent. The thick walls of the buildings were ideal for carving out a niche where a person could wedge himself in for a short period of time. The wainscot panelling in many of the rooms was perfect for concealing the niches. One particularly clever hideout was behind a stairwell. Two of the steps swung out, allowing one person to squeeze in behind the stairs. Like the organ access door, the fugitive could bolt the steps from the inside, preventing anyone on the outside from moving them.[8]

There were no hiding places in the school building or the dormitory for our residential students. Sister Ursula insisted on building a virtual wall between the activities of the convent and the school. The less the students knew about the refugees hiding on the property, the safer both the students and the refugees would be. We assumed no student would intentionally disclose the location of the safe havens, but a student could inadvertently tell the wrong person about what was happening in the convent. The students themselves were also safer not knowing the truth. They could truthfully say they were totally ignorant of the convent's clandestine activities.

It was not long before men on the run from the Germans began showing up at our convent door.

CHAPTER EIGHT

CONCEALING FUGITIVE

Saint-Hubert, October 1941

IN OCTOBER 1941, A FEW DAYS AFTER THE COMPLETION OF THE convent's secret rooms, three men came to our gate and rang the bell. I was on door duty. I slid open the small speakeasy-style door and asked them what they wanted. They told me they were sent by Father Cryil.

Father Cryil meant nothing to me. I did not unlock the door. One of the men asked to see Sister Superior. They seemed nervous and kept looking around. Thinking they might be avoiding the German police, I opened the door and led them into the small parlour just inside the door.

I asked Sister Agnes to tell Sister Superior about the visitors. When Sister Superior entered the room, the men repeated that they had been sent by Father Cryil. Sister Superior asked if they had anything to give her. They each handed her a one-franc French coin. The exchange of the coin confirmed they had, indeed, been sent by Father Cryil. It was only then that I learned Father Cryil was one of Sister Superior's main contacts with the Front.

The men were anxious to get undercover. Sister Ursula was concerned, however; if the men walked across the courtyard in the daytime to the refectory and the cellar where they would be living, they might be seen by curious neighbours whose apartments in adjoining buildings overlooked the courtyard. It would also be awkward for them to stay in the parlour until dark. Sister Agnes devised the solution. She went to the chapel and borrowed cassocks from the chaplain's wardrobe. Disguised as priests, they crossed the open courtyard to the chapel from which they could enter the refectory building and climb down into the secret cellar where they would be living.

The men were so grateful for finding sanctuary with us that they vowed to receive Holy Communion every day of their internment in honour of the Immaculate Heart of Mary. This seemed to me at the time the kind of pledge we would call in Ohio a "pie crust" promise, easily made and easily broken. Sister Ursula did not appear to share my scepticism, and she welcomed their devotional promises.

The men's proposal, however, created a dilemma. Having men traipsing around a convent courtyard, going to and from the chapel every morning, could easily raise the suspicion of neighbours. The solution, of course, was another raid on our absent chaplain's closet.

Each of them was given a clergyman's cloak and hat to wear whenever they were outside. The cassock worn by the tall man, whom we called The Count, was twelve inches too short, but it sufficed. One of the men added to his disguise by carrying a large Bible under his arm.

More resisters arrived during the next several weeks. Not all of them stayed. Some joined the active Resistance after a day or two. They moved to safe houses run by the Front and other organisations. Others found family or friends who would house them. The few who became more or less permanent residents created an additional challenge Sister Ursula had not anticipated; some of them had wives who wanted visitation privileges. Several of them showed up at our front gate almost every day, often carrying bags full of food. This created a huge security risk. How could Sister Ursula explain to the German police why the same women brought food to the convent so often? Neither could Sister Ursula risk a public scene by shutting the door in their faces. Ultimately, Sister Ursula had to say, with her index finger ominously raised, the men would have to leave their sanctuary unless they could convince their wives to visit them no more than once a week. The daily visits ceased.

In the autumn of 1941, persecution of the Jews increased. As a result, Sister Ursula quickly agreed with Cryil's request to give refuge to Jews. The first to arrive was an elderly Jewish couple, Rachel and David Liebermann. The husband was very old and ill. He was not likely to survive the winter if forced to stay in the cellar where they had been hiding. Sister Ursula moved them into the warmest secret room in the convent, the space behind the chapel organ. The fact that both husband and wife were partially deaf meant that the thundering of the organ would be less painful to their ears. A warm relationship quickly blossomed between the Liebermanns and the sisters. It might have violated our vow to show charity and kindness to all equally, but Rachel and David became favourites. They never complained and were grateful for the meagre accommodations and food they received. They especially appreciated Sister Mary Helen, who filled up their hot water bottles every few hours. They slid the bottles under their blankets for warmth.

The next Jewish refugee to arrive was a young woman, Leah Rosenberg. She was allocated space in the attic room. Leah was the only woman among six men, which made her uncomfortable, but it could not be helped. A sheet was hung from the rafter that provided her a modicum of privacy. Leah was consumed by her fear that one of our neighbours in the adjoining buildings would identify her as being Jewish if they saw her in the courtyard or garden.

Again, it was Sister Agnes who suggested the solution. Leah would dress as a Sister of Our Lady when she was outside of her room. At first, Leah struggled with the ordeal of putting on a habit, but being disguised as a nun eliminated her anxiety. Wearing the habit also gave her freedom to move around the buildings and grounds. As her confidence level rose, she began wearing her habit all day long. She went to prayers with us and took her meals with us. In the evening, she sat with us during Recreation listening to the BBC broadcast. She became a virtual member of our community, taking the name Sister Lucy. Sister Lucy stayed with the Sisters of Our Lady until the American Army liberated Saint-Hubert in September of 1944.

It is rare to find anything humorous about thousands of innocent people hunted by Nazis and being forced to hide in dismal attics and dank cold cellars. Life, however, does sometimes resemble a Shakespearean tragedy, inserting a comic scene in the midst of deceit, death, and oppression.

Our bit of comedy arrived at our front gate in the form of a highly agitated man with a shaved head. He poured out his tale of woe to Sister Ursula. He said he had gone underground to avoid being sent to work in German factories. He took refuge in a nearby Trappist monastery. Although he had been given his own cell, he was obliged to assume all the obligations of a Trappist monk. He participated in all the monastery prayer services while kneeling on a stone floor. At other times, he alternated between scrubbing floors and working in the garden. The cruellest requirement, he said, was keeping the absolute vow of silence. He moaned that only men with a true vocation could endure the Trappist life. Finally, the distraught man pleaded with Sister Ursula to let him take sanctuary in our convent. Sister Ursula smiled infrequently, but I detected a slight twinkle in her eye when she asked me to escort the man to his accommodations in the cellar. Two days later he left us and returned to the Trappists. A cell of his very own and rigours of a monastic order were apparently preferable to being crammed into a cold, damp subterranean vault with seven other men.

On December 8, 1941, the crackling BBC broadcast reported that on the previous day Japan had launched a sneak attack on the American fleet stationed at Pearl Harbor, Hawaii. The United States and Britain immediately declared war on Japan. The BBC announcer said the United States had not declared war on Germany. We had always expected the United States would eventually enter the war against Germany on the side of Britain. Would this development, however, mean the United States would divert its vast resources to a war against Japan, letting Britain and Russia fight Germany on their own?

As an American, I had mixed feelings. I was outraged by the sneak attack on our homeland and was eager for America to strike back against Japan. At the same time, I was concerned Belgium would never be able to be free of the Nazi yoke without America entering the war in Europe. Did America have the resources to fight a two-front war with those fronts on the opposite sides of the world? America's dilemma was resolved on December 11, 1941, when Hitler declared war on the United States. Once again, within less than twenty-five years, the United States was coming to the aid of Europe occupied by the German army.

Sister Ursula had no doubts that after Pearl Harbor the United States would enter the war against Germany. She told me the next day she was going to immediately apply for exit visas for Sister Clare and me.

Without thinking, I said, "I would prefer to stay."

Instead of reminding me I had just violated my vow of obedience, Sister Ursula uncharacteristically explained her reason for our having to leave Belgium as soon as possible. She said once a state of war existed between Germany and the United States, I would be considered an enemy non-combatant. In that event, it was highly unlikely the German authorities would allow us to remain at the convent in Saint-Hubert. More likely, they would send us to a concentration camp, like they did to our British Sister Madeline when Britain declared war on Germany. I begged Sister Ursula's forgiveness for forgetting my vow of obedience and thanked her for kindly explaining her decision.

The plan was to get us to Lisbon, Portugal, where we could fly to the United States on Pan American Airways. The money for the flight, $625 plus a 5% defence tax, would be paid by Sister Rosalia, Sister Superior for the sisters of Our Lady Convent in Ilchester, Maryland. However, it was too late. As difficult as exit visas were for Americans to get even before the outbreak of the war, they were impossible to get after Germany declared war on the United States. I wrote a letter to Pan American Airways describing our situation:

It does not seem probable that Sister Clare and I will be able to travel to Lisbon as we hoped. We were told exit visas would not be given to any citizens of the United States. It seems, therefore, that the only thing for us to do is to cancel any arrangements made for our return to America.

I am not sure how Sister Clare felt about not being able to leave Belgium. For me, there was a sense of relief. I would not be forced to abandon my convent family in its time of need. I realised, of course, the Germans might have had other plans for Sister Clare and me, like sending us to a concentration camp in Germany.

We did not have long to wait. Sister Clare and I were ordered to report to the *Kommandantur* in Namur. Ominously, we were advised to bring one suitcase, each filled with essential items. We assumed our fate was to be similar to that of Sister Madeline.

The train to Namur took a couple of hours. A sergeant ushered us into the office of Major Gormann. After examining our passports, the Major asked me in French how I came to be in Belgium.

I answered in English that my name before joining the Sisters of Our Lady was Sophia Pansing, and I grew up in a small town in Ohio, adding that my grandparents had emigrated from Hanover, Germany, in 1880.

That was the first time the Major's face registered any emotion, saying he had grown up in a small village not far from Hanover. I described how Sisters of Our Lady take a vow of absolute obedience, and that Mother General sent Sister Clare and me to teach in the Namur convent school in March 1938. After the destruction of the Namur Motherhouse during the invasion, we were reassigned to teach in the Sisters of Our Lady School in Saint-Hubert. My particular subjects in the Agricultural Household Management program included horticulture, animal husbandry, and poultry farming.

Major Gormann seemed to get more and more agitated as the interview went on. As his tension increased, mine subsided. The reason for his discomfort became clear when he whispered to us that he had been ordained a priest before being drafted into the army. Perhaps catching himself in an unmilitary moment of weakness, he then adopted a more formal tone. He informed us that he had the power to send us to a camp in Germany for the duration of the war, but in light of our charitable work teaching Belgian children he was granting us the privilege of remaining at Saint-Hubert, assuming good behaviour, of course. He then added another condition: Under the terms of our probationary status, we would have to report to him twice a month.

Sister Clare and I thanked Major Gormann. We managed to maintain a calm countenance, but once out of the building my joy was expressed by briefly taking Sister Clare's hand and squeezing it (an intimacy discouraged by our vows).[1]

For the next two years, Sister Clare and I were the epitome of good behaviour. As long as the trains were running, we reported to the *Kommandantur's* office every two weeks.

After a few months, Major Gormann was replaced by a Captain Hess. We always arrived at least half an hour early for our appointment and quietly waited in the hallway outside of his office. Whenever we spoke to each other, we used American English, never German. When we spoke with Captain Hess, we used French. I doubt anyone working in the *Kommandantur's* office suspected we were fluent in the German language. Soon we became invisible in plain sight, helped by the fact that our habits hid most of our features.

All kinds of information useful to the Resistance, the British, and the Americans could be gleaned from the casual conversations taking place all around us. The morale of the army could be judged from the frequency and tenor of grousing by the staff or from officers passing in the hallway. Did they believe the war was going well or not?

Soldiers actually have a good sense if their side is losing. We learned how to identify uniforms and insignias of rank so we could report what troops were stationed in Belgium. Whether there were SS Divisions or Panzer Divisions was especially important. When allied bombing attacks became more frequent, we would take some minor detours on the way back to the train station to assess bomb damage. We once reported that a bombing raid on the railroad marshalling yards had been totally ineffective, and the only damage was to a residential neighbourhood.

We would never write down the tidbits of information we gathered from our visit to Namur, but on the train back to Saint-Hubert we would try and recall as much as we could remember, speaking in English, naturally. Once back to the relative security of the convent, we transcribed our information in the margins of a newspaper, and the paper was left on a park bench.[2]

I assumed the information we provided was eventually passed on to the Allied command either by smuggled documents through France and Spain, or more often by radio transmitter. It was rumoured that even carrier pigeons were used. The British were regularly smuggling radio transmitters into Belgium by sea in small boats or by parachute drops from small planes.

Although possessing our own transmitter would have shortened the time for sending messages, we did not have a radio transmitter at the convent. There were several ways the Germans could have easily detected a transmitter located in the convent.

First, there was the *Funkabwehr*, or radio defence. Trucks were equipped with radio direction-finding devices. It was obvious which trucks had the devices. A large antenna was mounted on the top of the truck. It looked like four metal clothes hangers welded together, and the whole contraption could swivel 360 degrees. Two or three of the trucks working together could determine from which direction a radio signal was emanating to within an area of 100 square metres. The operators needed time, however, to pinpoint the origin of the signal. The longer a clandestine transmission lasted, the more accurate the operators could be in determining its location. Consequently, transmissions were kept short and sent at random hours. In an urban area, narrowing down the range to a three- or four-block area meant the haystack was just smaller when trying to find the needle. The radio transmitters could be hidden in a hundred different apartments or shops.

The Saint-Hubert convent and school, however, was larger than 200 square metres. Any signal coming from anywhere within our extensive compound meant the Germans only had one place to search. They would also know the transmissions could only have been sent with our full knowledge and consent.

A second technique used by the Germans to find radio transmitters would also quickly determine if our convent was the location of an underground radio station. Once one of their detectors picked up a radio signal, they would shut off the electricity in a small section of the city or town. If the signal stopped, they would know the transmitter was somewhere in that neighbourhood. They would still have to search a great number of buildings, however. If we sisters were sending radio transmissions from a room in the convent, and the local electrical power was cut off, it would be obvious to the Germans they should be pounding on the convent's front door.

A third tactic was for German security officers to go rapidly through a neighbourhood, knocking on every door, one after another. If the radio transmission signal abruptly ceased after the knock, it was clear the radio signal was emanating from that location. Our convent would have also been vulnerable to this knocking strategy.[3]

As the number of people hiding in the convent increased, so did our concerns about security. It was unreasonable and cruel to compel all the refugees to stay in their cubbyholes most of the day, so refugees could often be found in the library, the dinner hall, and the chapel. The more confident they felt about our convent being a safe haven from the German police, the more they spread out, some even venturing into the garden.

Sister Ursula was not so sanguine. She knew how the German secret police operated. They liked to organise surprise raids, pounding on doors and demanding immediate entry. If a raid were made on our convent, it would be impossible to quickly shepherd all the refugees into their secret rooms unless some kind of early warning system was devised.

A civil engineer hiding in the cellar was determined to solve the problem. He proposed installing a warning bell system. A request was made to our Resistance agent, and within a couple of days the engineer had a truck battery, five doorbells, and two hundred yards of wire. The battery was hidden beneath a false bottom in a kitchen cabinet and was connected to a light switch. Another concealed wire ran from the switch to doorbells hidden behind wood panelling in the library, refectory, and the chapel. Flipping the switch sent an electrical current down the wire, ringing the hidden doorbells. After some testing, the bells in all the rooms would ring when the switch was thrown.[4]

After all the electrical pieces were in place and working, Sister Ursula had all of us, including the refugees, gather in the refectory. She complimented the civil engineer on his handiwork, but added that it was not enough to have an alarm system in place.

Being forewarned about an imminent German intrusion onto the convent's grounds would not make the refugees safer unless there was also a definite plan for what should happen after the alarm sounded. Without a strategy, everyone would be running helter-skelter, not knowing what to do or where to go, bumping into each other and getting in each other's way.

Sister Ursula laid out a detailed plan of action, assigning a role for each sister and each refugee.

Refugees living in the cellar had to go immediately to the trap door in the refectory. The stove and the slate plate would be removed, opening up access to the cellar. After all the cellar refugees were accounted for, two sisters were given the task of replacing the plate and the stove over the trapdoor.

Similarly, the group that was hidden in the attic had to hurry to the toilette room, where the access panel to the ladder was located. When that group was safely up in the attic, two sisters would replace the panel and one of the sisters would then sit on the commode.

If the alarm sounded again, that would mean the Germans had entered the convent grounds and that all trapdoors had to be immediately hidden. If there were any refugees who had not gotten back to their hiding places, they were to squeeze themselves into the contingency niches, such as the one behind the staircase.

Sister Ursula assigned responsibilities to every sister and refugee except for two sisters, Sister Angela and me. After going back to her office with her, Sister Ursula said we were to go to the locked front door when its bell rang. My assignment was to speak to the callers, while Sister Angela was to peep out a window and determine the nationality of the visitors and assess their intent. If there was any doubt, Sister Angela was to rush back to the kitchen and flip the switch, sounding the alarm. Sister Ursula said my task was to stall the Germans without appearing to be stalling. I asked how I was supposed to do that.

She answered my question with her own question. "Did you ever flirt with boys in high school?"

I was stunned by what Sister Ursula seemed to be asking. "Do you want me — a nun — to pretend I am attracted to a German soldier?"

The calm tone of Sister Ursula's response, "Yes," confirmed the seriousness of her request. At the same time, it was clear she was asking me to freely choose the role of temptress, and I was not obligated by my vow of strict obedience to comply with her plan.

Uncharacteristically, Sister Ursula did not stop me when I questioned the wisdom of her scheme. I was confused. Questions burst out of me. Why me? Wouldn't I be committing a serious sin and violating my vow of chastity? Why would a German soldier be attracted to a nun in a habit? Wouldn't he be even more suspicious?

Sister Ursula patiently waited until my spate of queries ebbed before responding. She said I was best suited for the assignment. I was fluent in German. I had a German heritage. I was an attractive woman. And I was a risk-taker.

As for the sin issue, Sister Ursula was sanguine. She doubted flirting would constitute a sin since I would not be doing it with an immoral intent. Even if my acts did pass the threshold for sinfulness, they would be readily forgiven because the sins would be committed for the much more important purpose of saving lives. Then, with a wry smile, Sister Ursula said that it may seem impossible for a man to be attracted to a nun, but like Adam and

Eve in the Garden of Eden, the forbidden often becomes more appealing.

Sister Ursula shared my apprehension that if a nun played coy with a German soldier, he might suspect we had something to hide. Sister Ursula was willing to take that risk and said she trusted me to not over-play the part. The hope was for me to offer just enough ambiguous hints to distract the German officer. To delay his mission by thirty-seconds could mean the difference between life and death for the refugees. Offering refreshments might also gain a few seconds, even if refused. Sister Ursula told me at no time was I to display any reluctance in allowing the intruders access to all our buildings. In fact, she said I should be the congenial guide who was only too happy to show the Germans anything they wanted to see, including our modest sleeping chambers.[5]

Sister Ursula knew that the effectiveness of our electronic alarm system and our plan for quickly hiding the refugees was dependent on everyone, refugees and sisters, knowing exactly what they should do when the alarm sounded. Drills were staged every day. At first, we knew in advance when the alarm would sound, but later on, the alarm would be given at random times of the day.

It reminded me of the lifeboat drills conducted onboard the *S.S. Manhattan*. Within two weeks everyone knew their stations and what they had to do. Sister Ursula insisted we practise until all the refugees could gain their secure hiding places in less than two minutes.

I had to practise flirting without looking like I was flirting. I had to achieve that effect using only facial expressions and my voice. I spent hours in front of the mirror trying out looks that might intrigue a man, but not too much.

I quickly decided a woman's hair was important in creating an attractive aura, but all my blonde hair was hidden under my wimple. I partially solved the problem by pulling out one strand of hair. The wisp looked like it had accidentally escaped from its confinement. I was surprised when I looked in the mirror and saw how it softened my features and complemented my blue eyes. Since I could not be showing a strand of my hair all the time, I contrived a way to quickly pull it out from under the wimple.

I experimented with nibbling on my lower lip, which I had heard was a trick for showing a man you are interested. When I tried it in the mirror, however, the ploy was too obvious. If I moistened my lips, however, the sheen subtly highlighted the lips and conveyed a more ambiguous message. My eyelashes are naturally long, and I remembered from high school that boys were supposedly charmed when girls looked at them with rapidly blinking eyes. The mirror told me I looked ridiculous. I remembered the women in the movies I watched in high school. Those who were the most successful in attracting a man usually spoke in deeper tones. My voice had always been in the alto range, so I only had to slightly lower the pitch.

What to do with my eyes was the biggest and most crucial challenge. Gazing directly and long into a German officer's eyes was obviously out, yet there had to be some eye contact. I could not keep my eyes constantly focused on the floor and convey the message I was not a typical shy nun. After many disappointing experiments, I decided the best strategy was not to face the officer directly. Instead, I would tilt my head down and to the side. Slowly I would raise my eyes, glancing at the officer's face until we made eye contact. Then I would quickly look away like I had been caught doing something improper. Once I decided on tactics, I was surprised how instinctive they felt.

CHAPTER NINE

GERMAN RAIDS AND THE NEW NORMAL

Saint-Hubert, January 1942

WITHIN THE MONTH OUR ALARM SYSTEM AND CONCEALING DRILLS had their first real test. Late in the afternoon, a captain with five soldiers came to the convent's gate. Sister Justina had seen them approaching the gate and forewarned us.[1]

Sister Angela and I were already on our way to the gate when the bell rang. We did not need to guess their intent. I told Sister Angela to return to the kitchen and sound the alarm. I quickly pulled out my strand of hair, licked my lips, and pinched my cheeks before turning the corner and slowly but deliberately walking to the gate. Once again, my nun's habit hid my shaking hands and legs. My face, after years of training, displayed no hint of the emotional turmoil inside me.

I greeted the captain in German and asked how we might be of service. I could see by the captain's insignia he was a Wehrmacht officer and not a member of the SD. This had a calming effect. Wehrmacht officers were usually polite, trying to demonstrate the softer side of the occupation.

He introduced himself as Captain Siegel and asked if he and his men could enter the convent. Of course, I could not refuse this demand disguised as a request, so I unlocked the gate. I could play the politeness game, too, and I said Sister Ursula would be pleased by their visit.

It was then I decided to test my coquettish persona. While making eye contact with a furtive sidewise glance and then quickly looking down, I asked Captain Siegel and his men if they would like to take some refreshments. For a brief moment Captain Siegel looked perplexed, wondering what he had just seen—if he had seen anything. He hesitated a moment in responding to my proposal.

I took advantage of this pause to explain we could not serve coffee, only tea made from lavender. Captain Siegel declined the tea and said he was there to search the convent and its grounds for Belgian men who were refusing to work in German factories. He had heard rumours of such men residing at the convent. He also assured me that if Sister Superior would ask those men to leave the convent with his squad, there would be no consequences for the convent.

As if on cue, Sister Superior Ursula came around the corner with her deliberate measured tread and her calm, enigmatic expression. She asked me if I had offered the men tea and acted disappointed when I told her Captain Siegel had declined my offer.

Captain Siegel was then obliged to describe again his reasons for coming to the convent and to repeat his request that Sister Ursula direct the Belgian men to leave the convent.

Sister Ursula replied that there were no men residing at the convent, but the captain was free to satisfy himself on the matter by searching all the buildings and grounds of the convent, including the sisters' cells and the dormitory rooms of the students.

She told him I would serve as his guide. She instructed me to explain to any sisters and students we met why soldiers were there. Make sure, she added, no room was left unexamined.

Sister Ursula's sphinx-like demeanor gave no hint she was lying, and yet this was a woman who had little or no experience with telling lies.

At the time it seemed less than a minute had elapsed since I opened the door, not enough time for the refugees to get back to their hideaways. I learned later Captain Siegel and his men had actually been delayed by our charade for over four minutes.

The first stop on the tour of the convent was the refectory. It was empty except for the two sisters who were tending the fire in the small stove that sat atop the trapdoor to the hidden room in the cellar.

The only person in the chapel was Sister Agnes. She was practising on the organ next to the removable panel behind which Mr. and Mrs. Liebermann were concealed. The soldiers spread out to inspect the sisters' and students' rooms. I knew they would find nothing in those rooms, so I let them wander on their own. I spent the time talking with Captain Siegel, sharing information about my history. He told me about his family. My flirting distraction may have worked earlier, but there was no need to continue the pretense with all the fugitives safe.

The sergeant checking rooms in the hallway outside the library literally jumped backwards when he opened the door to the toilette and found a sister sitting on the commode. He could not exit quickly enough, trailing a stream of profuse apologies in his wake.

Because there had been sufficient time to get all the refugees to their assigned spaces, the emergency niches spread around the convent were not needed. Sister Ursula, however, was taking no chances a soldier might accidentally discover the hidey-holes.

Sisters were stationed near all the niches, engaged in some activity that would hinder close inspection. For example, Sister Clare just happened to be on her knees polishing the stairway with its swinging steps.

The last stop on the tour was the cellar underneath the refectory and kitchen. I was most worried about the room constructed behind a fake wall on one end of the cellar.

Its only access was the trapdoor under the stove in the floor above. Sister Ursula devised a clever ruse to prevent discovery of the phony wall. She hoped the Germans would not do precise measurements of the cellar and compare those measurements to the length of the rooms on the floor above the cellar. Those measurements may have alerted them to the shorter length of the cellar.

The first floor was broken up into so many different size rooms, however, that getting accurate measurements was a challenge. The lighting in the cellar was also kept especially dim. Even beams from flashlights seemed to be absorbed by the darkness. Finally, Sister Ursula had us create a tempting distraction for anyone inspecting the cellar.

Thirty feet from the fake wall she had piled a cache of rationed food. Included in the hoard were cartons of cigarettes, something more valuable than beefsteaks.

Captain Siegel's orders did not include searching for contraband food, and he seemed disinclined to enlarge his assignment. He only hesitated a moment when I urged him and his soldiers to take the cigarettes, adding how they were absolutely useless to nuns. The eager gathering-up of the cigarette treasure trove by the soldiers quickly ended their desultory inspection of the cellar.

We had passed our first test. The hidden rooms were not detected. No refugees had been discovered. All the drills and rehearsing produced a superb performance.

We were also fortunate in that Captain Siegel and his men were not eager to conduct a diligent search for secret rooms. They did not tap on walls, have tape measures to calculate the size of rooms, or employ sensitive listening devices.

Sister Ursula told us in the future we must be prepared to face those techniques. In the meantime, we were to think of new strategies to thwart them.

We did not have long to wait. Within a month, three black Mercedes 260 automobiles drove up to the convent's garden gate. We knew from the Resistance paper, *La Libre Belgique*, that these menacing-looking vehicles were the favourites of the Gestapo, the German secret police.

There was no need to guess the intent of the man in the black trench coat and the six soldiers in gray SS uniforms. The alarm was immediately sounded. As I approached the gate, I knew my flirting act would have no effect on the grim man facing me. He was not the benign Captain Siegel.

His first words were, "Open the gate." His second words were, "I want to see Sister Superior immediately."

Surprisingly, although his words and conduct were meant to be intimidating, they had the opposite effect on me. I now knew they were not at the convent to launch a surprise raid and search. By the time Sister Superior Ursula was sent for and she came to welcome our visitors, the refugees would have time to be securely hidden. The agent did not introduce himself. He merely flashed his warrant disc at Sister Ursula and me, which identified him as Gestapo, but did not include his name.

He ordered Sisters Rose, Germaine, Winifride, and Louise Marie to be summoned. I went off in search of the sisters and told them what had happened so far, and that they were to hurry with me to the garden gate. I did not want the Gestapo to have any reason to search the convent for themselves.

When we arrived, the Gestapo officer immediately verified they were the four sisters he wanted. His next words were chilling. He told the sisters he was placing them in "protective custody."

Sister Ursula did not know what "protective custody" meant. She adopted her firmest tone and demeanor, demanding an explanation for the detention of the sisters. None was forthcoming. The agent ordered the SS officers to put the sisters in the waiting Mercedes automobiles and they drove off.

The next day, Sister Ursula received a message from the Gestapo. It ordered that clothes and other personal items of the four detained sisters be delivered to Gestapo headquarters in Charleroi. This was ominous news.

Sister Ursula and three other sisters carried the four suitcases by train to Charleroi. She tried to discover why the sisters were put into "protective custody" and where they were being held. The sergeant at the front desk refused to answer her questions and rejected her request to see the Standartenführer.

When dear Mother in Namur was told about the detention of the four sisters, she was determined to do all in her power to get the sisters released. We were particularly concerned about the health of Sister Winifride, who was more than seventy years old.

Mother General pestered the military administration in Belgium and travelled to Brussels several times to protest the sisters' detention with the Wehrmacht High Command. She wrote dozens of letters and asked Cardinal Van Roey to intervene.

All this effort was met by cold silence and seemed fruitless. Then, one month after the Gestapo took the sisters, Sister Ursula received a brief letter, censored, of course, from Sister Rose. Sister Rose said all four of the sisters were in prison at Liege. She added that each sister had her own cell and they were being well treated, the food being similar to the fare they received at Saint- Hubert.

The receipt of the letter brought a great sense of relief. The fact that they were able to tell Sister Ursula where they were being held meant there was less chance they would just vanish like so many people who fell into the hands of the Gestapo. Liege prison was controlled by the Wehrmacht, which meant they were no longer under the control of the ruthless Gestapo.

Also, at that stage of the war, the Germans were still hopeful of reconciling the Catholic Church to their occupation of Belgium. The disappearance of four sisters of Our Lady while in their custody would certainly alienate the Church hierarchy and thousands of lay Catholics. Finally, knowing where the sisters were imprisoned gave dear Mother and the Cardinal a focus for their efforts to free them.

Silence from the German authorities reigned for two more months, but the efforts of Mother General and Cardinal Van Roey may have had some effect on the German authorities. Three months after the sisters had been suddenly whisked away in the black Mercedes, they just as suddenly reappeared in an identical black Mercedes outside the gates of the Saint-Hubert convent, where they were casually dropped off.

There was such rejoicing among us to have our sisters back. The chapel echoed with prayers and songs of thanksgiving. We naturally assumed our founder, Blessed Sister Julie, had intervened and secured their release from prison. Sister Ursula was especially anxious to hear about the sisters' detention and interrogation to determine if the convent could be in jeopardy for its clandestine activities. She asked Sister Rose to tell her and me about what happened after they were taken by the Gestapo.

Sister Rose said the first thing the agent had them do was to sign an official-looking document saying they had asked for protection. On paper, at least, the four sisters had asked to be taken into protective custody and were therefore not illegally detained.

Sister Ursula said the fabrication was typical German attention to the letter of the law while completely ignoring the law's intent. Sister Rose then described her interrogation, which she assumed was similar to the questioning of the other three sisters. Most of the questions were designed to ascertain if men avoiding transportation to Germany were hiding in the convent.

The interrogator was unrelenting and sometimes threatening, but Sister Rose was never physically harmed. I speculated whether it was another example of the power of a nun's habit providing some invisible barrier men are reluctant to cross. Or was the interrogator under the illusion that nuns would necessarily be inept liars? Hours of questioning did not break Sister Rose. She continued to insist there were no refugees at the convent. Finally, she was told that all four sisters would be put into solitary confinement cells until they agreed to be more cooperative.

The cells were approximately twelve square metres in size, window- less, and had a solid metal door with a slot for a food tray. The only furniture was an iron cot with a thin straw mattress and one blanket. I could not help saying to Sister Rose that she was like Brer Rabbit in his briar patch. Of course, Sister Ursula and Sister Rose had no idea what I was talking about.

I explained that the expression came from an American folk tale. His archenemies, Brer Fox and Brer Bear, had caught Brer Rabbit. They threatened Brer Rabbit with all kinds of torture and abuse. Brer Rabbit told them he was not frightened so much by their threats as he was by the prospect of being thrown into a nearby briar patch. He pleaded with Brer Fox and Brer Bear to do anything they want, but "Please don't throw me in that briar patch."

Inevitably, that is exactly what Brer Fox and Brer Bear did; they heaved Brer Rabbit deep into the briar patch. Instead of the cries of pain they hoped for, however, all they heard was Brer Rabbit's laughter. Then Brer Rabbit shouted how he had been born and raised in a briar patch, and this briar patch felt just like home. Sister Ursula and Sister Rose chuckled. They agreed that requiring a nun to live in a small windowless cell with an iron cot and thin straw mattress with unlimited time for prayer and meditation was not likely to break a nun's spirit.[2]

While the Germans were getting no information from our sisters, they were getting a black eye in the propaganda war. The

Resistance had radioed the British about the four sisters being arrested and held in Liege Prison. Soon the story was widely reported in the British and American press and the phrase "protective custody" was turned into a bad joke.

The bad publicity added even more pressure on the German authorities to free our sisters.

After the release of Sisters Rose, Germaine, Winifide, and Louise Marie, Sister Ursula had no way of imposing any kind of penance on the Gestapo and SS, but the Lord and Blessed Julie work in mysterious ways.

Jean-Michel de Selys Longchamps was a Belgian pilot who fought against the Germans during the 1940 invasion. Jean-Michel grew up in the village of Lorcy, not far from Saint-Hubert. His mother, Elfrida, lived there in the family cottage.

Elfrida sometimes attended mass in our chapel. She told Sister Rose that a few months into the Occupation she had received a letter from Jean-Michel. It was pushed under her door one morning. He wrote about his escape to Britain and joining the Royal Air Force as a fighter pilot.

In the spring of 1942, the BBC broadcasts were describing how the German army's invasion of Russia was floundering and soaking up more and more German military resources. Consequently, the German air defences in Belgium were weakened and more British planes were appearing in our skies. They were bombing bridges and rail yards.

On April 15, 1942, a British fighter flew low over Saint-Hubert dropping small Belgium flags packed in small bundles on the convent grounds. The same plane dropped more flags near Elfrida's cottage.

Two days later, Sister Ursula heard from our Resistance sources that the same plane, after its pass over Saint-Hubert, flew to Chareleroi and strafed Gestapo headquarters where our sisters had been taken, killing several SS officers.

Elfrida was sure the plane was piloted by her son, Jean-Michel. I know it is wrong for me to take any gratification from the death of a fellow human being, but I could not suppress the surge of warm satisfaction I felt when I heard the news. I prayed for the SS officers' souls.[3]

Much of this account of the war is about death, destruction, and tragedy, but even in the midst of war there is happiness, contentment, and love. Our abnormal, chaotic, war-torn world changed over time into what passed as normal.

Memories of what life was like in peacetime were dimmed and our wartime day-to-day lives, even with bombs falling, settled into a kind of comfortable routine. We sisters may be especially predisposed to this phenomenon. Our daily observance of Blessed Julie's rules and prescribed religious devotions remained largely unchanged, imposing order on an anarchic world. We ran our schools with the same firm discipline. Following familiar customs was an attempt to keep the war at bay as much as possible.

Sister Ursula also tried to minimise the impact of the war on the people of Saint-Hubert by insisting that there be three masses offered every Sunday in our chapel, just as we had done before the war. The chapel was nearly full for every Mass. There is something about the well-known repetitive ritual of the Mass with its rhythmic Latin liturgy that created an aura of peace.

Sometimes the worshippers themselves provided a humorous diversion to the wartime tension. One man who regularly attended the 8:30 a.m. Mass would suddenly be absent for weeks at a time. Everyone knew he was spending his Sunday mornings at the Methodist church service.

After a few weeks he would return to our chapel. He would assist at Mass and take Holy Communion. When the *"Domine non sum dignus"* (Lord, I am not worthy) was spoken, he would pound his breast so hard the thump was heard throughout the chapel. If his breast-beating reflected his profound repentance for his apostasy, his regret would not last more than several weeks before he returned to the Methodists. Nevertheless, he always came back to our chapel and resumed the blows to his chest.

There is an American phrase to describe this kind of split devotion between two conflicting beliefs. I think it originates from the world of gambling. It is called "Hedging your bets."

Another man thought he could improve his odds for salvation by mimicking us. First, he cut his hair in the manner of a monk, tonsured. He would then stand behind us sisters at Mass and imitate everything we did. He knelt when we knelt and stood when we stood. During our readings after Mass we sit, so he sat as well. He joined us in reciting the rosary and when we extended our arms during the recitation, he held out his arms, too.

Perhaps one of the most interesting attendees of our Sunday Masses was a ninety-eight-year-old woman, Marie, who would not sit in a pew during mass. Instead, she would squeeze into a less drafty confessional box and sit on the penitent's kneeler. Marie would alternate between praying and sleeping. One minute she could be heard saying, "*Mea culpa, mea culpa, mea maxima culpa*," and the next minute she would be snoring, with only her feet visible under the confessional's door.

We did not disturb her slumbers. Sister Ursula would sometimes speak with Maria while she was in the confessional and often gave her a little gift, such as an egg, a chestnut, a flower, or a few mint leaves tied with a string. Maria loved Sister Ursula. She was ever cheerful with a warm smile radiating from her care-lined face. The wisdom she had acquired during her ninety-eight years on Earth was distilled into one phrase, which she happily bestowed on anyone and everyone: "He who is satisfied is happy."

Another source of diversion for us was the presence of children in our primary school. Children have a way of finding joy in some of the most trying circumstances. Where adults see a street cleared of bombing debris and curbs lined with piles of brick and stone, a

GERMAN RAIDS AND THE NEW NORMAL

boy sees a ready-made football pitch. Soon he and his friends will be kicking a soccer ball amidst the rubble of bombed buildings. Children live in the moment. Their minds are easily diverted from serious matters by the occurrence of the most inconsequential events. Their diversions often prove to be a welcome distraction for adults, too.

Sister Paula could not help but be distracted by some of the well-intentioned antics of her kindergarten class. She told her children about an imminent visit by Sister Ursula to their classroom to wish them happy Christmas. One child coughed, so Sister Paula told the children they should try not to cough while Sister Ursula was speaking to them. If they felt the need to cough, they should do so now before Sister Ursula arrived.

The room erupted in a cacophony of coughing and hacking, each child trying to demonstrate a first-rate cough. Before Sister Paula was able to quell the din, made more difficult by her own suppressed laughter, Sister Ursula entered the classroom, and, like a miracle, all the coughs were suddenly cured. She wished all the children a happy Christmas, gave them her blessing, and said she would pray for a quick recovery from their colds.

The young children were given religious instruction every day. A child is never too young to learn about the love of God and how He watches over all of us.

Theological lessons, however, sometime elicit comments and questions from young boys and girls that may be both profound and humorous. They remind us that some things, like the curiosity and innocence of children, never really change, providing a breath of normality in an abnormal world.

Sister Paula welcomed questions posed by her first-grade class, like "Does God watch over German soldiers, too?"

She was bemused by the answer to her question, "What was there before God created the world?"

"Antiques!" was one response.

When asked by Sister Paula about the duration of eternal punishment, a young girl of four responded, "It isn't like being sent to sit alone in the chapel. You get out of the chapel some time, but you never get out of hell."

Planning and celebrating Christmas was the best opportunity for us to forget about the war, especially when the celebration was focused on making it a joyful time for children. Sister Ursula was determined to make it a special Christmas, even if it meant depleting our stockpile of rationed goods. She said that sometimes prudence and frugality must give way to spreading a little cheer. The refectory was festooned with strands of holly and boughs of pine branches. A replica of a red-brick Santa Claus chimney was built, complete with a mantle for hanging stockings. The fire was a small light bulb behind a red piece of paper cut to look like flames.

A week before Christmas, Sister Paula thought she had come up with a strategy for keeping the little ones quiet while she distributed their lunch boxes.

She described to them how the Infant Jesus felt so cold because he was poor and did not have many clothes. She told them lovers of Jesus could show him their love and wrap him in warmth by keeping a finger over their lips while she handed out the lunch boxes. Then Sister Paula stepped out of the room to bring in the lunch cart. When she re-entered the room, however, instead of silence she was greeted by a roomful of little voices rising to a crescendo. She was on the verge of giving them a good scolding when she realised what they were doing. Each child had his or her finger tightly pressed to their lips while trying to say in their clearest voice, *"Soeur, j'aime bebe Jesus"* (Sister, I love baby Jesus). At that moment, the war and the Occupation seemed a bit less oppressive to Sister Paula.

On Christmas Eve, our chaplain, Father Xavier, said Mass in the chapel. Some of our little tots recreated the scene of the Nativity by dressing up as the Holy Family, the three Wise Men, and the shepherds. The older girls sang "Silent Night" in French and sang "*Adeste Fidelis*" in Latin. After Mass, everyone gathered in the refectory where Santa Claus and a clown made a surprise visit. Santa gave each child a small piece of chocolate and a tiny bit of soap. The soap excited the children more than the chocolate. Some said they would get up extra early the next day so they could wash themselves with real soap. Sister Ursula did not forget us sisters either. There was a stocking hanging from the fireplace mantle for each sister. Inside the stockings were a spool of thread and a piece of chocolate. We could forget the war for at least one evening.

War does not diminish the attraction between a man and a woman.

Virgil said it best: "*Omnia vincit amor*" – love conquers all. War may actually lend more urgency to falling in love. That was certainly the case with a young man, Henri, who appeared at our gate in February. He said he was sent by Father Joseph, who believed Sister Superior could help him.

Before I could usher him in to see Sister Ursula, however, I needed to know more. He said he wanted to get married as quickly as possible. I was intrigued. I told him I doubted Sister Superior could aid him in that quest.

Henri said all he wanted was a baptismal certificate so he could be married in a church, something on which his fiancé, Parisee, insisted. He had heard we sisters were skilled in procuring those kinds of documents.

I asked if he remembered where he had been baptised. He said he couldn't remember because he was so young. Had he made his First Communion? "Yes, at least fifty times." Have you been confirmed? "I don't know." How old are you? "Twenty."

He was very disappointed when I explained that Sister Superior would probably not want to disrupt the course of true love, but it was highly unlikely she would issue a false baptismal certificate. I told him, however, I had no authority to make a final decision on his plea, and I would ask Sister Superior Ursula for her advice.

I briefly related Henri's story to Sister Ursula, and her response once again proved my total inability to guess what she was thinking. Without hesitation, she proposed a solution to Henri's dilemma: She would ask our chaplain to baptise Henri and to issue a baptismal certificate.

Sister Ursula reasoned that, based on the skimpy evidence, there was serious doubt the man had ever been baptised, so to save his immortal soul he should be baptised. On the other hand, if Henri had been baptised as a baby, no harm would be done. When I saw the glow of happiness on Henri's face, I was pleased that my original opinion had proved wrong.[4]

It is impossible to describe meals as normal during a time of food scarcity. Sister Barbara and her kitchen staff managed to work minor miracles. She could not turn water into wine, but she could transform turnips, dandelions, and stinging nettles into a palatable soup. One evening she surprised us all by featuring corn-on-the-cob for dinner. The corn had come from a small patch of corn grown on the convent's farm. Most of the sisters hadn't a clue on how to eat the corn, so Sister Clare and I demonstrated how Americans do it. We picked up our ear of corn with both hands and held the ends of the cob between our thumbs and index fingers. We then proceeded to gnaw the kernels from the cob.

Our fellow sisters were appalled. None of them were willing to follow our example, so I showed them how the kernels could be eaten with a fork after they were scraped off the cob with a knife. All the corn was consumed, of course.

We did not have the luxury of refusing any kind of food. I could tell, however, the sisters were not fond of the taste and the tough texture. I explained that Sister Barbara had done her best, but that the corn we were growing on our farm was field corn and not sweet corn, which is more tender and considerably sweeter.

Americans, I said, rarely eat field corn unless it is swimming in butter and coated with salt, condiments that were strictly rationed and in short supply. A few sisters noticeably grimaced when I told them field corn is usually fed to pigs and chickens.

Sister Barbara promised that in the future any corn we happened to acquire would be fodder for the chickens and any pigs.[5]

One of Sister Barbara's biggest challenges was finding something to burn in her stoves. A family of four was entitled to only 150 kilos of coal a month. At best, one stove would use that amount in two weeks. More often it lasted even less time because the coal had been mixed with water to create "*schlamm*." The water added weight to the coal, but decreased the heat it produced.

The only available substitute for coal was wood, and the only accessible wood was from the trees growing on the convent's farm and the *allee d'arbres* on our grounds. Sister Ursula decided the 200-year-old oak trees on the farm would be cut down first. The ancient lime trees in the *allee* would only be cut when all the wood from the oaks was burned. In return for a share of the wood, two farmers felled the trees and cut them up into yard-long pieces. Four sisters piled the logs on a farm cart and made many mile-long trips back and forth to the convent delivering the wood.

The logs were too large to go directly into the stoves. I could not count the hours I had spent on the farm in Ohio splitting wood, so Sister Ursula asked me to teach the other sisters how to make kindling. I first assured them splitting wood was not a task that could only be done by burly lumberjacks. Rather, it was a distinct art. The skilled woodsman—or woodswoman—working *with* the grain of the wood, and not against it, could make more kindling in an hour than a muscle-bound oaf trying to club a log to smithereens. Done correctly, splitting a log neatly with a satisfying crack could be enjoyable.

I demonstrated how to use the bucksaw to cut the yard-long logs into three one-foot pieces. I stood the smaller pieces up on their ends and lifted the eight-pound maul above my head. The maul, sometimes called the "Go-Devil," is half sledgehammer and half axe. Barely using any muscles, I let the maul descend on the end of the log. It is important to allow the weight of the maul, rather than your arms, do the work. The art is to make sure your aim is accurate, and the axe side of the maul hits the end of the log squarely.

Sisters who had rarely stepped out of the convent until the war became adept at wielding an axe, a bucksaw, splitting maul, and steel wedges. Kindling piled up until it was moved to the cellar under the kitchen. Sister Monica became so skilled at splitting wood that the older students began calling her "Axe-Sister" (not to her face, of course). Sister Monica told me a few weeks after her first instruction that swinging the maul might be even better than meditation and prayer for controlling anxiety and channelling anger.[6]

In May, an unanticipated surprise arrived in the form of a package from the Sisters of Our Lady's house in Rome. Due to the alliance between Mussolini and Hitler, we could receive mail from Italy. The package contained two kilos of figs that the sisters in Rome had harvested from their garden. The note with the package said they had sent ten kilos of figs. Eight kilos had obviously been stolen by some mail handler along the way.

The missing eight kilos of figs stimulated much debate among us. "Why would the thief take eight kilos of figs and send two kilos on to us?"

"If you are going to commit the sin of stealing, the theft of ten kilos is no greater sin than the theft of eight kilos." I doubted two kilos was the difference between a mortal sin and a venial sin.

Sister Agnes thought it had to do with the amount of guilt a person could live with. She suggested regret for one's actions was on a sliding scale. At some point, one's maximum endurance level for guilt would be reached, and in this case that level was attained at eight kilos. A kilo more would have dulled the pleasure of eating the figs.

We sisters did not suffer from similar guilt pangs; we relished every bite and thanked God for our good fortune.

May turned out to be a banner month for good news. A gentleman, Mr. Bonheur, who owned a small piece of property outside Saint-Hubert, came to the convent to speak with Sister Ursula. She asked me to be part of the conversation.

Mr. Bonheur offered to lend the convent two milk cows and one small piglet. Mr. Bonheur explained that even though his property was small, he had kept four milk cows and a sow. He bought food for the animals from nearby farmers. A week before his visit to the convent, two Holstein cows and the Belgian Landrace sow were stolen. He assumed the meat ended up being sold on the black market. He also assumed it was just a matter of time before the other two cows and the sow's little piglet would be stolen. He said he would lend the animals to the sisters of Our Lady and let us keep the milk rather than enrich black marketers.

Sister Ursula asked me if the convent could accommodate the animals. I said the convent's nearby farm could easily handle the three animals, but they were just as likely to be stolen from our farm as from Mr. Bonheur's. The appeal of having a source of fresh milk, however, was too strong to resist. I proposed the animals be kept within the confines of the convent's walls. Pens could be built to house them. As for food, our farm produced some hay the cows could eat. I pointed out the grass lawns within the convent where the cows could graze. As for the piglet, pigs can eat practically anything. Our farm produced some corn. Although unloved by our sisters, it would be devoured by a pig. Sister Ursula accepted Mr. Bonheur's offer.[7]

The first challenge was getting two cows and one piglet from Mr. Bonheur's property to the convent. I offered to shepherd the animals and volunteered Sister Angela to help. I made two nooses to loop over the cows' heads and commandeered our trusty wheelbarrow. Then Sister Angela and I provided some welcome amusement to the citizens of Saint-Hubert: two nuns parading down the Rue de la Converserie, one leading two milk cows and one transporting a small piglet in a wheelbarrow. Bystanders were even more amused when we took them through the front gate of the convent.

Once we had the piglet installed in his pen, I realised there was another problem. The piglet had not been weaned and was still nursing when his mother was stolen. The piglet would die unless a way was found to give him milk. The solution was essentially the same one we used on the farm when a sow gave birth to thirteen piglets and she only had twelve teats. The runt of the litter would never get a place at the table, so we had to feed it cow's milk from a baby bottle. It was relatively easy to find a mother whose weaned child no longer needed a bottle. It was a little more difficult to explain to the mother why a nun needed a baby bottle.

Finally, cows need to be milked twice a day, or they get very uncomfortable and cranky. I had milked cows on our farm, of course, but I thought teaching the students in the agricultural school how to milk a cow was a learning experience for them not to be missed.

With all the students gathered around me, I demonstrated the proper techniques. I first washed my hands and rubbed them vigorously with a towel to warm them up before sitting on the low stool. Then I calmed the cow by stroking her udder gently. I could tell she was full of milk. The stroking also helps bring down the milk to the teats. You can tell the cow is relaxed when she is standing perfectly still. If she is disturbed, you will also know it. She will try to kick you with her hind foot.

A teat is taken in each hand, and you wrap your pointer finger tightly around the top of the teat. You do not pull on the teat— that is a common mistake, which makes the cow unhappy. The milk is already in the teat so all that is needed is a gentle squeeze and the milk squirts out. The pointer finger is eased for a moment to allow more milk to fill the teat, then another squeeze, and another stream of milk shoots into your bucket. I described how on the farm I often rested my head on the side of the cow to ease the strain on the back. My wimple, of course, made doing that impossible.

Finally, I encouraged the students to talk softly, hum, or sing to the cow while milking her. The sound of the human voice keeps the cow relaxed and helps the hands move at a smooth rhythmic pace. The cow might even respond, turn her head, and look at you with those big, kind, brown eyes.

The young girls took to milking like they had lived their entire lives on dairy farms. They gave the cows names of two Shakespearean characters, Beatrice and Rosamunde. The students did not consider milking Beatrice and Rosamunde to be work, but as a brief respite from the war and occupation.

We drew up a milking rotation list, and they eagerly awaited their turns. One girl told me when she was milking our cows the ever-present war faded into the background. She could only think about the comfort of the cow, her rhythmic milking motion, and hitting the bucket with the stream of milk.

Students were not so enamoured, however, with the backside of keeping animals. Beatrice and Rosamunde produced a lot of manure. It had to be removed from their pens every day to ensure the milk would not be contaminated. Handling manure might be as distracting as milking, but it is definitely less pleasant. Whichever girls were on dung duty had to shovel the manure into a wheelbarrow, take it to the farthest end of the convent property, mix it with tree leaves, add it to the compost heap, and cover the pile with a tarp. Under the tarp the manure produced tremendous heat that killed off most of the bacteria. After cooking under the tarp for several months, the compost could be mixed into the garden soil, a slightly more agreeable task. I was proud of our girls, though. They never shirked their duties. Within a couple of months, they had completely taken over the care, feeding, and milking of Beatrice and Rosamunde, leaving me nothing to do but to periodically check the cows for disease. Thanks be to God and Blessed Julie, Beatrice and Rosamunde remained remarkably healthy, and after the Americans liberated Saint-Hubert, we returned them to Mr. Bonheur.[8]

These interludes of normality were just that—interludes. The growing intensity of the war with increasing death and destruction was the norm.

Three events in September 1942, reminded us of war's reality. Sister Ursula told us the grim news that eighty-two sisters of Our Lady of Namur had died since the German invasion in May 1940. Most of them had died in bombings, both British and German. Food and medicine shortages caused by the occupation shortened the lives of other sisters who were ill or aged. The abstract number of eighty-two became faces when she showed us the list of names. They were friends. They were family. Grief filled the room. Together, we knelt in the chapel to pray for them.

Although we all prayed for the success of the Allies, the intensified bombing by the British and Americans meant increasing numbers of innocent Belgians would be killed and their homes destroyed. Many bombs missed their intended targets, often by miles. A farm family living in a remote cottage might be caught in a barrage of bombs from a disabled bomber, the pilot hoping that by lightening its load he would be able to nurse the plane back to England.

We heard that one group of errant bombs fell on a school and convent in Antwerp. Six sisters and four hundred students died. Ordinarily the Royal Air Force says nothing about their bombs killing civilians, but in this case the Royal Air Force actually issued an apology on the BBC.

The same British bombing attack also killed the parents of Iole, one of our students in the Upper School who was planning to enter the convent. Iole had lived in Antwerp with her parents before the war. They enrolled her in our school in Saint-Hubert once the British began bombing Antwerp, hoping she would be safe. Iole did not learn what happened to her parents until she went to visit them in Antwerp. When she arrived at her home, it was nothing but rubble.

A neighbour told Iole her mother had been pulled from the ruins seriously injured. She was taken away on a stretcher, but no one could tell Iole where. The neighbours assumed her father was still buried under the bricks and stone. Iole went from hospital to hospital searching for her mother, finally finding her at Saint-Elisabeth Hospital. Her mother's back was broken.

The doctors told Iole there was no chance her mother could survive, yet she lived for two weeks in agonising pain, there being no morphine for civilians. Iole visited her mother every day. Not wanting to add to her mother's pain, she did not tell her mother about the death of her father, saying instead that he was being treated in another hospital.

When Iole was not comforting her mother, she was working with her neighbours to clear the wreckage of her home and search for her father's body, which they found after four days. Iole arranged a Catholic burial for her father in the cemetery of Saint-Andrieskerk.

During the next week, Iole spent hours sifting through the ruins trying to find family possessions that may have survived the bombing. She especially hoped to find the trousseau she planned to wear when she took her first vows.

Iole's mother died one week later and was buried next to her father. Now the sisters of Our Lady were Iole's only family. She took her vows as a postulant within the month in her slightly burned trousseau.

The third incident was a vivid reminder of the dangers of living in an occupied country. The German occupiers were especially concerned about the growth of an effective resistance movement. Their strategy was to crush any incipient resistance activity before it had a chance to spread. The German army's response to a suspected act of sabotage was always draconian compared to the damage caused by the sabotage.

If a German soldier or official were targeted, however, their response was swift and brutal, usually imposing collective punishment. When one soldier was injured, dozens of ordinary citizens from the neighbourhood would be rounded up and shot. This ferocious retribution was effective in deterring Resistance groups from attacking Germans.

In September 1942, citizens in the nearby village of Lorcy almost became the victims of German collective punishment.[9]

A family in Lorcy operated a very successful black-market trade from their home. Somehow, they managed to accumulate large amounts of the most sought-after foodstuffs like coffee, beef, beet sugar, coal, and flour. Apparently, they had so much sugar and flour that they made large batches of cookies.

They sold the cookies to townsfolk craving something sweet, which was just about everyone. Perhaps an envious neighbour or an informant tipped off the German police about their business, and a night raid was made on the house. Someone must have warned the family about the raid. By the time the police broke into the house, the family had fled. It was a narrow escape for the family; there was a batch of warm cookies still cooling on the table.

One of the young police officers had been posted in the woods behind the house to cut off a possible escape route. When he did not return after the Sergeant called his name, a search was begun. The young officer was found unconscious in the woods. There was a hefty tree limb lying near him. The Sergeant assumed he had been attacked by one of the fleeing family.

Five minutes after being told of the attack, the SD, German Security Service, arrived on the scene in three trucks and ordered all the neighbours out of their homes. They randomly selected thirty men, women, and children, put them in the trucks, and drove off. The neighbours who were left assumed they would never be seen again alive.

Fortunately, the injured police officer regained consciousness and told the doctor he had tripped in the dark woods, and hit his head on a rock. The innocents who had been rounded up by the SD were released. The sergeant who had led the raid, in what was perhaps a bizarre act of repentance, offered some of the seized cookies to the lucky thirty.

CHAPTER TEN

HIDING AMERICAN PILOTS AND YOUNG JEWISH GIRLS

Saint-Hubert, October 1942

BY THE END OF 1942, IT WAS BECOMING INCREASINGLY CLEAR THAT the nature of the war was changing. More and more Allied planes were appearing in the skies of Belgium.

The consequences of the widening war were brought home to the people of Saint-Hubert on a rare blue-sky day in October.

A German fighter and a British Spitfire were in a battle over the town. I now understood why they were called "dog-fights." The two planes circled around each other, performing loops and rolls just like two angry dogs preparing to fight, each looking to exploit any gap in his opponent's defences. Then suddenly the pilots dispensed with their preliminary tango and flew directly at each other, guns blazing.

I was sure neither pilot was going to flinch, but just as if on cue, both pilots turned away a second before impact. Neither plane was unscathed, though. Both were trailing smoke. The planes were too close to the ground for the pilots to use their parachutes, and their attempt to land their planes in nearby farm fields failed. They crashed and burned on impact.[1]

With thousands of Allied planes passing over Belgium to bomb targets in Germany, and the Germans doing everything in their power to stop them, it was inevitable that thousands of British and American airmen were forced to bail out of their disabled planes over Belgium. Most of the men who parachuted from their planes exchanged a cockpit for a prisoner-of-war camp in Germany. Their big white parachutes were easily spotted by German soldiers, and many were captured the moment they touched ground. Rarely were they shot.

Hundreds of airmen, however, did manage to elude immediate capture and were found by Resistance agents. If they were lucky, they became passengers on the Belgium Underground Railroad. It was called the "Comet Line," and our convent in Saint-Hubert became one of the stops.[2]

Sister Ursula did not tell us much about how the Comet Line worked. I am not sure she knew much about the details herself. It is usually safer in underground organisations if each member only knows the identity of a couple of other members. If any one member is captured by the SD or Gestapo, he or she could only reveal the names of one or two people in the covert group. No one was under the illusion that a person tortured by the Gestapo would not eventually give names. All Sister Ursula told us was we would periodically be hiding British and American airmen until they could be moved to other safe locations. She said it would not be necessary to alter our well-established drill for concealing refugees.

After the first liberation of Saint-Hubert by the American Army in September 1944, I learned how the Comet Line worked. It was the brainchild of Andree de Jongh. She was a wealthy young Belgian woman who joined the Resistance soon after the invasion. In August 1941, de Jongh turned up at the British consulate in Bilbao, Portugal, with two Belgian and one Scottish soldier in tow. She told the military attaché she had a plan for getting British airmen who had been shot down over Belgium back to Britain. At first, she was ignored and then patronised. Eventually her persistence, plus escorting two more Scottish soldiers to Bilbao three weeks later, convinced British Intelligence she was for real. They agreed to finance her operation and gave her the code name "The Postman." De Jongh returned to Belgium, adopted a Belgian code name, "Dédée," and set up her escape network. She named it "Comet Line."

It soon became standard practice for airmen flying missions over Europe to be issued false identification papers with photos. If they were lucky enough to be picked up by members of the Resistance, they were immediately handed over to one of Dédée's Comet Line agents. He or she would guide the airman to the nearest safe house to be delivered to another agent. Like any good clandestine organisation, Dédée's agents only knew the identities of two other agents in the chain, the "deliverer" and the "receiver."

The Comet Line had safe houses and agents stretching from Belgium to the Pyrenees Mountains on the Spanish border. From there, Basque guides took over and led them over the mountains. Once in neutral Spain, the airmen could get to Portugal and ultimately back to Britain to fight another day. Dédée herself was a conductor on the Comet Line and guided over a hundred airmen to the Spanish border.

All we knew in the fall of 1942, however, was what we were supposed to do when our "deliverer" agent, Gabrielle, came to the front gate and introduced the British or American airman. A few days later, our "receiver" agent would appear and take the airman to the next safe house on the Comet Line. Sister Ursula asked me, as a native English speaker, to be the first sister to meet with the agent and the airman. She wanted our well-established concealment drill thoroughly explained to the airman. Sister Ursula did not want any confusion due to a flawed translation.

In the spring of 1943, Sister Ursula told me the *Abwehr* were aware that large numbers of British and American airman who bailed out of their planes over Belgium were not being found by German patrols. The *Abwehr* heard rumours the Allied airmen were not only being hidden by members of the Resistance, they were actually being shepherded to Spain. To shut down the escape route, the *Abwehr* tried to infiltrate the Comet Line organisation by having soldiers who were fluent in English pretend to be downed Allied airmen.

The German soldiers were supplied with captured British and American parachutes, and they were dropped out of German planes at night in an area the *Abwehr* knew would not be patrolled by German army units.

The Germans hoped the infiltrators would be picked up by members of the Resistance, who would pass them on to a Comet Line conductor. Sister Ursula said that several Comet Line agents had fallen for the ruse. They were arrested and executed, breaking some of the links in the underground railroad.

Sister Ursula did not fault the Comet Line agents. She assumed it would not be difficult for a glib, English-speaking German to deceive ordinary Belgians into believing they were Americans. The Belgian agents would know little or nothing about America, so they could not test an infiltrator's story.

After her prologue, I knew why Sister Ursula had asked to speak to me. She told me my responsibilities as "first greeter" were going to change. I was to use my knowledge of America and its culture to expose German infiltrators. If I was sure the airman was an *Abwehr* agent I would very nicely explain to the infiltrator and the Comet Line agent the convent's secure rooms were full and it would be safer for the airman to be taken to another secure location.

My saying the convent lacked safe spaces was the signal to the Comet Line agent that the airman was an imposter. The conductor would then tell the German infiltrator he would be taken to an alternative safe house.

Sister Ursula told me under no circumstances should I hint I knew the airman was a fraud. If the imposter suspected his cover was blown, he would probably try to escape and could put the convent and all the refugees in grave danger. Finally, Sister Ursula informed me that in the future I would be vetting more downed airmen than I had up to that point. The convent would become a regular stop on the Comet Line so infiltrators could be weeded out. Sister Ursula had described the mission. It was up to me to devise the tactics.

I decided to deploy a few of the flirtation skills I had worked so hard to develop, essentially foregoing any signs of shyness. As a fellow American who had been cut off from all information about America, I would feign wide-eyed innocence, someone eager to learn the latest news from home. "Where are you from?" had to be one of the first questions.

His answer would then suggest the tenor of additional questions. I would make sure no trace of cross-examination crept into my queries—just a few questions about American culture, food, movies, and sports that as an American I would want to know about.

I had to be clever, but not too clever. It helped my planning strategy that the next two airmen I interviewed were obviously American. I was suspicious of Sam Niven at first because he claimed he had escaped from a German prisoner-of-war camp. That seemed highly unlikely, but on reflection, it made his story more credible. A German trying to impersonate an American flyer would only invite extra scrutiny by concocting such a tale. Sam said he was from Vermillion, Iowa, so it only took a few questions about winter wheat farming to assure myself he was truly an Iowan. I then took the opportunity to pick Sam's brain about some valuable Americana tidbits that I could use in later interviews.

The next airman brought to the convent by Gabriella aroused my suspicion immediately. He introduced himself as Adam Baker, and before I could ask him one question, he said he was from Boston, Massachusetts.

I was no expert on American accents, and I had never been to New England, but I had heard the Boston accent was distinctive. Adam Baker sounded more like the folks I knew in Ohio. I then went into my act, asking what was happening in America before he was shipped overseas. His answers were vague and sketchy. The one hard fact he threw out was that he had seen the movie *Gone With the Wind*. The problem with his claim, however, was *Gone With the Wind* had been out for years and had won the Academy Award for best film long before the war started.

What convinced me beyond any doubt he was an imposter was when I suggested that, being from Boston, he must be a Yankee fan. He agreed.

I thanked Adam for indulging my curiosity, and I wished we could have had more time to chat, but unfortunately our convent's safe rooms were filled with refugees. I suggested that he would be more secure at another safe house. Gabriella immediately told Adam there was another station on the Comet Line nearby, and she would take him there.

It was not until hearing Gabriella's calm assurances that I fully grasped the enormity of what I had done. I had just condemned Adam to death. I knew he would never leave the "safe house" alive, and it was all based on my belief he was a German spy.

Doubts began to creep in immediately. One part of me wanted to rewind the scene and give Adam a chance to prove he wasn't a German soldier masquerading as an American airman. If he ultimately confessed, he would have condemned himself and I would not carry the crushing guilt of causing his death. The other part of me knew that if Adam were made aware of the trap, there was a good chance he could escape—Gabriella and I would be unable to restrain him. If that happened, the lives of all our hidden refugees, airmen, and the sisters who were hiding them would be in danger.

The convent had not prepared me for these kinds of choices. If any decisions needed to be made, my Sister Superior made them. I naively assumed that if I were somehow given the power of choice, it would simply be a matter of choosing the obvious good and rejecting the obvious evil. The options were black and white, like our habits. Thus, it was a distressing surprise to discover that having freedom of choice drops you into a world of moral ambiguity. Evil may be wrapped in goodness, and good may have evil buried inside.

Then there are the dilemmas of having to choose the lesser of two evils, or choosing the most good for the most people. Coping with ambiguity does not end once a choice is made—there are the agonising, lingering doubts about whether you made the best choice. Of course, I might let Sister Ursula carry the entire moral burden of choice. I could escape responsibility by claiming that when I marked Adam for death, I was just obeying Sister Ursula's orders. I am sure, however, such a rationalisation would not have eased my troubled conscience much. When I decided Adam was a German spy and condemned him to death, it was my choice to make, not Sister Superior's. I had to wrestle with the moral ambiguity and to accept the consequences of my decision.

German soldiers came to the convent two more times trying to infiltrate the Comet Line by pretending to be American airmen. It was not difficult to tell they were imposters; the bigger challenge was to keep them from suspecting my role.

I did have an advantage in the cat and mouse game. The soldier imposter did not know there was a cat in the room and did not understand that he had been cast in the role of the mouse.

It was disconcerting to realise my qualms about rendering death penalties seemed to diminish each time I had to do it. The conscience-appeasing rationale that I was saving more lives by taking one life gained more weight. Was I becoming calloused? Was I on the slippery slope? Would I eventually think the taking of a human life was just part of my duty? Fortunately, I did not have to answer those questions. The *Abwehr* soon stopped trying to pass off German soldiers as American airmen. Perhaps too many of their imposters were disappearing.

Sadly, Dédée herself vanished in December of 1943, presumably caught by the Gestapo. The Comet Line continued its rescue work. Our convent remained a way station on the Comet underground railroad until the successful Allied landing in Normandy. Then it was safer for the airmen to stay hidden until the liberation of Belgium rather than trying to negotiate the dangerous route across German-occupied France.

The *Abwehr* visited our convent only one more time in 1943 for what turned out to be a more serious and thorough inspection of our buildings. Our hiding drill was so efficient, though, I only needed to delay them for a minute or two. The soldiers brought measuring tapes, hammers, and probing poles and fanned out throughout the convent and school. They did not wait for me to act as their guide. Every sister played her part like an accomplished actress and the soldiers found nothing suspicious. The irony was that without my guiding them, the soldiers actually missed some of the rooms.

One of the more frightening events occurred one evening when there was a loud banging on the door. We had never experienced a night raid, and the men at the door sounded particularly violent. The refugees ran for their hiding places, and I went into the small atrium by the door. I opened the speakeasy door, asking them what they wanted. At first, they did not hear me, my voice drowned out by the din they were making. I had to shout, "*Was willst du?*"(What do you want?) before the pounding stopped. One man kept repeating "*Lichter aus*," which literally means "light out."

He pointed to a window in the refectory where a small beam of light had slipped through the blackout curtain. A wave of relief washed over me. It was a problem easily solved. I apologised profusely for our stupidity and promised to seal the window immediately. Their mission accomplished, the police officers moved on.

Simultaneously with the increase of Allied bombing, the *Abwehr* was intensifying its efforts to round up Jews and deport them to camps outside of Belgium. From the beginning of the Occupation, many Belgian civil servants refused to cooperate with the German edicts. When the Germans demanded local registrars to provide lists of Jewish citizens, the registrars cited the clause in the Belgium constitution expressly forbidding discrimination on the basis of race or religion. Furthermore, the registrars pointed out that the registration form did not include a line for designating one's race or religion. Many Belgian police officers refused to arrest Jews who had not complied with the German demand to present themselves at certain specified locations.

The *Abwehr* commanded that all Jews wear a large yellow star on their chests. But, without the full cooperation from Belgium officials, many Jews were able to evade the requirement. The Queen herself intervened and persuaded General von Falkenhausen to exempt Belgian Jews who had served in the armed forces. Many mayors and city fathers would not distribute the yellow stars, so the *Abwehr* local commanders had the daunting task of determining who was Jewish and then pinning stars on them. If Jews wearing the yellow stars were supposed to turn non-Jewish Belgians against the Jews, the policy failed miserably. Non-Jews often went out of their way to be polite and supportive, even encouraging Jews to move up in ration lines or take their seats on the trams.

By the middle of 1942, however, it became clear that German efficiency would ultimately prevail over Belgian passive resistance. If Belgian Jews were to be saved from deportation, more active measures were necessary.

Monsignor Kerkhofs, the Bishop of Liege, signalled the change in strategy when he secretly urged all the religions in his diocese to do whatever they could to save the Jews from deportation. This was all the guidance Sister Ursula needed; she told us we were going to redouble our efforts to make Saint-Hubert Convent and school a place of refuge for Jews.

Father Joseph Peeters came to meet with Sister Ursula in August 1942 to plan how three young Jewish girls could become students in our boarding school.[3] Their parents were afraid the families would soon be arrested and transported. They begged Father Joseph to find safe places for their daughters. Father Joseph had already created forged identity papers for the girls with more Christian-sounding names.

The bigger challenge was how to incorporate the girls into the very Catholic life of the school without revealing their true identity, or at least revealing their identity to as few people as possible.

Saint-Hubert was better prepared to meet this challenge than many convent schools. We already had a sophisticated system for hiding refugees and Allied airmen. All the sisters and the chaplain were integral parts of our Resistance-like organisation and were well-schooled in deception and silence, and everyone could be totally trusted.

The problem was that the Jewish girls had to be hidden in plain sight. The girls would not be kept in hidey-holes but would live in the dormitories, attend school, and go to Mass and prayers with scores of other young girls. They would need to blend in by acting like girls who had been raised Catholic. They could not, under any circumstances, reveal their true identities, even to their best friends. The girls had to make the transition from being Jewish to acting Catholic immediately after entering the school. To help with their rapid conversion, Sister Ursula assigned three sisters to act as mentors to the girls. I was one of them.

Sister Ursula gave us strict instructions on what we should and should not do with the Jewish students. She said our first task was teaching the Jewish girls the essentials of Catholic religious rituals so they could participate in Masses and prayer services. They should be able to make the sign of the cross, genuflect, know when to kneel and stand during Mass, and also know by heart the "Our Father" and "Hail Mary." During religious services, they should imitate whatever the other girls were doing. In addition, at meals, they could complain about the quality of the food, but they must eat the food even if it did not comply with kosher requirements.[4]

Even if the students could speak other languages, especially German, they should always use French and never, never, never let Yiddish phrases slip into conversations. To lessen the risk of inadvertent use of Yiddish, we were not to tell our students the names of other Jewish girls or whether there actually were other Jewish girls in the school.

Sister Ursula emphasised her final instruction by raising her "do not deviate one iota from this order" finger.

She firmly said, "Under no circumstances will you try to convert the young Jewish girls to Catholicism. Should a Jewish student express a desire to be baptised and become a Catholic, you will discourage her. Explain she could only be baptised with the full consent of her parents."

I thought, but dared not ask, if we would remove the prayer for the conversion of the Jews in our liturgy.

Andree was the adopted name for the young Jewish girl I was to advise; I never did discover her real name. She was eleven years old when she and her two-year-old brother, Samuel Aaron, were brought to the convent by Father Joseph in the dead of night.

Andree was small with light brown hair and hazel eyes. Samuel's hair was almost blond, and his eyes were blue. Andree was sleepy and scared while Samuel was alert and sobbing, which was understandable. They had been separated from their parents and family for the first time in their lives and shifted almost every night from safe house to safe house for several weeks.

Despite the trauma she was suffering, Andree was quite attentive when I was giving her a quick primer on how to adapt to life in our boarding school. It was harsh, but I told Andree she might be apprehended and transported if she did not precisely follow my instructions on how to fit in as a Catholic student. I was surprised by how calmly Andree took my implied threat.

Samuel, however, was a typical two-year-old, quick to pretend he did not understand some instruction if he was not inclined to obey. Samuel's stubbornness was a manageable problem. Sisters have experience in encouraging good behaviour in children. A much larger dilemma was keeping a two-year-old boy in a convent without raising German suspicions. [5]

Sister Ursula found a solution to the "Sam problem" after consulting with her good friend Sister Marie Victorine, Superior General for the Daughters of the Cross, in the nearby town of La Louviere. The Daughters of the Cross was a nursing order of nuns, and they operated hospitals and sanitariums throughout Europe and Africa. Sister Marie Victorine proposed sending Sam to the order's *preventorium*, an institution for children infected with tuberculosis, located near the Belgian coastal town of Ostend.

Sister Lucia and I took Sam to the Daughters of the Cross convent in La Louviere without telling his sister, Andree. Sister Ursula said she did not want to risk a tearful tantrum scene, and it was safer for Sam if his sister did not know where he was being hidden. Andree was only told Sam was in a safe place. We later learned Sam's middle name was changed from Aaron to Dede to make it sound less Jewish.

Sam did not stay long at the *preventorium*. The presence of a rambunctious, healthy two-year-old among all the very sick children could not be explained to government inspectors without risking disclosure of his true identity. Furthermore, if Sam remained long at the *preventorium* he could easily contract tuberculosis himself. Sister Camilla, a nurse at the sanitarium, devised a solution. She took Sam back to La Louviere to live with her parents, Henri and Irene Detrys. They were willing to raise him as a young Christian boy alongside their own son, Jean Marie.

Andree and the other Jewish girls were quick learners. I was amazed at how fast they adapted to life in a Catholic boarding school. Within weeks, one could not tell the difference between them and the girls who had been Catholics for their entire lives. A Yiddish word or phrase never slipped out. In fact, I was the one who bent the no-Yiddish rule. At our first meeting, I asked Andree how to say "Sleep well" in Yiddish. She answered, "*Shloof git mein kind.*" She said the phrase meant, "Sleep well, my child." For the next few weeks when I was helping Sister Clare settle the girls down for the night in the dormitory, I would lean close to Andree and whisper, "*Shloof git mein kind.*"[6]

We hoped the Jewish girls would blend in with the other students, but the problems of taking communion and going to confession needed to be solved. When it was time to receive communion, the Catholic girls would stand, approach the altar and receive the host. Andree and the two other Jewish girls would have to remain kneeling in their pews. A similar scene would unfold during the weekly hearing of confessions by the chaplain. The Catholic girls would line up to enter the confessional one-by-one, and the Jewish girls would stay in their pews. The difference in behaviour would naturally raise suspicion, especially to someone who was already inclined to tell the *Abewhr* about possible hidden Jews. The Catholic students would also suspect who among them were Jewish and who were not.

Sister Ursula knew this dilemma needed to be resolved before more Jewish girls were taken into our school. She sought my views and those of the two other sisters who were mentors. The solution of allowing the Jewish girls to receive communion was ruled out immediately. It would be a sacrilege and a mortal sin for the three unbaptised girls to take communion. Sister Ursula warned that the souls of any person who knowingly aided an unbaptised person to receive communion would be in jeopardy.

Sister Monica suggested that the easiest solution would be to baptise the girls so they could go to communion and confession. Sister Ursula quickly rejected Sister Monica's plan. She said the Catholic Church had a regrettable history of forcing baptism on unwilling persons in the past and she was loath to resurrect that practice even for the best of reasons. Sister Ursula also pointed out that baptised Jewish girls might not be accepted back into their families and the Jewish community after the war.

We seemed at an impasse until Sister Monica proposed an ingenious plan. The plan would require the cooperation of the Convent Chaplain, Father Dominic. Sister Ursula said she would speak with him, but she was sure Father Dominic would agree.

Sister Monica proposed that a small partition be inserted in the *Ciborium*, the lidded, cup-like vessel that contains the consecrated hosts distributed to the congregation during communion. Several unconsecrated hosts would be placed on one side of the divider, and all the consecrated hosts would be on the other side. When a girl Father Dominic knew to be Jewish came to receive communion, he would place an unconsecrated host on her tongue. If he were not sure the girl was Jewish or Catholic, he would offer her an unconsecrated wafer. I made an additional suggestion to cut a small nick in the unconsecrated hosts to insure there would be no accidental mixing of consecrated and unconsecrated hosts.

The problem of the Jewish girls going to confession was more easily solved. It would not be a sacrilege for an unbaptised Jewish girl to enter the confessional and tell her sins to a priest. She need not tell the priest she is unbaptised or that she is Jewish. The priest may not have the power to actually absolve her sins in the eyes of God because she is unbaptised, but no one's immortal soul is in danger. No harm would be done, and it would help protect the lives of our Jewish students.

We taught the Jewish girls the ritualistic words for making a confession, and every week they joined the line of Catholic students at the confessional.[7]

Over the next months, several more Jewish girls joined our community. They were usually escorted by Father Joseph, a Benedictine monk, or a member of the Resistance group, Committee for the Defence of Jews. Sister Ursula would designate a sister as mentor for each one to help them make the transition to life in a Catholic boarding school.

Like the first three Jewish girls they adapted quickly, and their transition was almost seamless. They took their turns working in the kitchen, laundry, and the garden. They did not complain about having only a small basin of warm water with which to wash in the evening.

Sister Monica suggested they "wash like a cat." To tease Sister Monica, some of the girls would "meow" while washing their faces. The order and predictability of convent life buffered the girls from the chaos and brutality just outside the walls. Being assigned tasks like the other girls was not seen as a burden but as providing a sense of purpose, making them feel a part of the community.

One of the biggest logistical challenges was having more children to feed. Our convent was already feeding two-dozen undocumented refugees. The farm provided us with some additional food, but most foodstuffs were only available with ration cards or bought on the black market. The Jewish girls had been given forged ration cards that could be used to qualify for ration stamps. Of course, presenting themselves to a CNAA (*Corporation Nationale de l'Agriculture de l'Alimentation*) agent was a risk to be avoided if possible.

Sister Ursula took on herself the mission of getting monthly ration stamps issued for every sister and student. She collected the sisters' and students' ration cards, arranged them in alphabetical order, and carried them to the local CNAA office, where she piled them on the agent's desk. She would not budge until he had issued the appropriate number of stamps for each ration card. If the agent had any objections or quibbles about the ration cards, he never mentioned them to the imposing nun looming over his desk.

Assuming the agent did have the temerity to niggle, Sister Ursula would have patiently explained to him in her most authoritative voice that he had the option of her marching 150 sisters and students into his office every month. Given that option, the CNAA agent opted to give the ration stamps to Sister Ursula. As the months passed, Sister Ursula need only appear in front of the CNAA agent's desk, and he would quickly count the cards and issue the correct number of stamps. [8]

Although Sister Ursula had warned us about getting too attached to any one girl, it was impossible for me to remain aloof with Andree.

She was charming, witty, inquisitive, and instinctively kind. It was not entirely surprising that she was drawn to me as a surrogate for her mother. Andree had not heard from her mother since she came to us. She felt comfortable confiding in me.

Despite our closer relationship, I was determined not to show her any favouritism. My intent was tested three months after

Andree's arrival. She asked me if I could arrange to have her baptised. I had to disappoint her, explaining she could only be baptised with her parents' consent. I think Andree understood, and my refusal did not hurt our friendship.[9]

Except for one occasion, the Jewish girls were good at responding only to their adopted Christian names and not telling any other student about being Jewish. We had built a delicate house of cards based on complete silence, and it would entirely collapse if the *Abwehr* heard we were knowingly sheltering even one Jewish girl. A mere rumour could trigger a full-scale invasion of the convent and school by *Abwehr* agents.

Consequently, when one of the later-arriving Jewish girls, Esther, revealed to her best Catholic friend that she was Jewish, Sister Ursula immediately acted to limit the potential harm caused by Esther's admission.

Sadly, Sister Ursula's remedy could only be described as cruel. Sister Ursula assembled all the sisters and students in the chapel. Sister Ursula began by describing how God hates lying. She then focused her attention on Esther. She accused Esther of being a brazen liar for saying she was Jewish. Sister Ursula considered Esther's lie as an attempt to mock Jews and said such behaviour would not be tolerated in our school.

Esther was devastated. She broke down in sobs. Yet Esther had the presence of mind to suspect Sister Ursula's pitiless attack was meant to protect her and the other Jewish girls. Esther stood up with tears streaming down her face and admitted lying. She begged everyone to forgive her. Although I knew why Sister Ursula had to make an example of Esther, I could not hold back my own tears, tears of pity and tears of esteem for the incredible courage Esther had shown.[10]

The urgency to accept more Jewish girls into our school increased considerably in 1943. Up to that point in time most Belgians accepted the German explanation for the transportation of Belgian Jews to Germany. The program was called *Arbeitseinsatz*. It was ostensibly designed to recruit workers for German factories. The German radio lauded the generosity of *Arbeitseinsatz* for allowing everyone in the worker's family to join the worker in Germany, where the family would be resettled in comfortable housing. There were rumours that all the trains filled with Jews were destined for death camps, but the thought that the Germans were intending to massacre thousands of men, women, and children was too monstrous to contemplate.

However, in early 1943, Belgian Jews were forced to accept the probability that all of them were fated to die at the hands of the Germans. The Resistance organisation *Front de l'Independence* sent a spy to discover the final destinations of the deportation trains. The agent managed to locate what he described as a death camp in Poland with large crematoriums where bodies were burned.

When the spy returned to Belgium, the news of what he discovered circulated among the Jewish communities. There was no dilemma about what to do. Only one option was available for Belgian Jews. They had to disappear and go underground, either by joining the Resistance or by finding a safe place to hide. Although it forced the break-up of families, our school in Saint-Hubert, due to its remote location, was one of the safer places for parents to send their young daughters.

Sadly, Father Joseph, who was instrumental in placing Jewish girls in our school, was arrested in June of 1943. He was executed at Liége Citadel a short time later. We do not know if Father Joseph was tortured; if so, he did not tell the *Abwehr* anything about the organisation for hiding Jews. No Resistance agents were arrested, and there were no raids on our convent and school.

In a brief bizarre demonstration of humane behaviour, the Germans transported Father Joseph's body to the Benedictine Monastery for a Christian burial, illustrating the odd duality of the German psyche—ruthless, with flashes of civilised humane behaviour. On the other hand, if the *Abwehr* was hoping to send a message to the Benedictines about the risks of cooperating with the Resistance, they failed. Benedictine Father Reynders continued his tireless efforts to find safe havens for Jewish children.

Knowing the destinations of the transport trains were death camps compelled Resistance groups and Jews to attempt more desperate measures to save Jewish deportees. On April 19, 1943, five young members of the Belgian Resistance, with only one pistol among them, used a lantern covered in red paper to stop a transport train between the villages of Boortmeerbeek and Haacht. During the brief stop they managed to open the door of one boxcar, allowing the prisoners to escape. That was only the beginning, however.

Over the next twenty miles the train engineer often slowed the train to a crawl or came to a complete stop, enabling scores of prisoners to jump off the train without injury. Some of the escapees were quickly recaptured, but most of them found members of the Resistance who led them to safe houses. Two of the escapees were brought to our convent. They stayed a week and then left to become active members of the Resistance.[11]

It was a sad occasion when another member of our community had to leave us. The tiny piglet given to the convent the prior year had grown into a 250-pound boar, and it was time for him to be butchered.[12]

Once a pig reaches full size, he stops putting on weight, so it is not efficient farming practice to keep feeding a grown pig, unless it is a sow producing more piglets. We all knew from the outset that eventually the pig would need to be butchered, which was why he was not given a name. On my father's farm, he would allow us to give names to animals like horses, dogs, and cats, but not cattle or pigs.

The problem was who was going to butcher the pig. If we took it to the local butcher, he would take a third of the meat for doing the work. In addition to not having to share the meat with the butcher, I thought learning to butcher a hog would be good for our students in the Agricultural School. It would help them understand the process and appreciate the sacrifices animals make for us to have meat products on our tables. On our Ohio farm, I had to help butcher the livestock, although my brothers and father did the bloody work. I decided our senior agricultural students and I would do the butchering. I found in the convent library a helpful book describing how to properly do the job.

The first thing we did, of course, was to put on full-length aprons to protect our clothes. Then, a major challenge was deciding how to humanely kill the pig. My father would shoot the pig in the forehead with a rifle, but we had no firearms in the convent. In the end, I chose to use the sledgehammer side of the wood maul.

First, however, we had to erect a high scaffold with a pulley in the centre of the crossbar through which a rope would run. The carcass of the pig would be hoisted up to the crossbar by its hind legs. This would allow the pig's blood to drain. The scaffold was also necessary to lower the pig's body into a vat of hot water. When the scaffold and the vat were ready, we tied several ropes around the neck of the pig to keep his head steady. The rope running through the pulley was tied to the pig's rear legs.

My task of killing the pig was made more difficult by the pig's docility. He allowed us to attach the ropes while looking at us with such trusting eyes. Once the pig was immobilised, I quickly raised the maul and hit him in the forehead. The pig dropped to the ground, dead or stunned. I grabbed the large butcher knife and cut the artery in his neck. The blood gushed out in pulses, which meant the pig's heart was still beating. Several girls vomited, and I cannot say I blamed them. I shouted at the six girls holding the hoisting rope to pull, and the pig's carcass, still streaming blood, was hauled up to the crossbar.

The details of the butchering are unnecessary for this narrative, but I must say how proud I was of our students who pitched in and did much of the messy work, including skinning. Our pig yielded 110 pounds of good meat and 20 pounds of fat. We had no means of preserving the meat without large amounts of precious salt and sugar, so Sister Louise cooked the pork as soon as it was ready. She added the meat to large pots of stew that the residents of the convent and school ate over the next several days. The fat I set aside for making soap.

Making soap is not difficult. A crucial ingredient is lye, but lye can be extracted from the ashes of burned hardwood, like oak; we had that in abundance. When ashes are boiled in a pot, lye solution will rise to the top and can be skimmed off. A similar process of cooking the fat produces clean grease rising to the top, which can also be skimmed off. The grease is slowly mixed with the boiling lye solution until it has the consistency of thick porridge. Herbs like wild mint can be added to the mix to create a more pleasant-smelling bar of soap. The concoction is poured into a shallow wooden box and cooled for several days until it is a hard slab. For convenience, the slab is cut up into square hand-size bars of soap. Some of the students were sceptical about using our homemade soap until I explained how the oil in the soap would be good for their complexions.

For washing sheets and other white linens, I suggested a method we used on the farm, one that does not require soap of any kind. If you boil the sheets in a solution of wood ash and water, they will come out perfectly white no matter what kinds of stains the sheets had originally. They are so clean that a hospital could use them on patients' beds.

Our cows, Beatrice and Rosalind, could have met the same fate as our pig since their milk had run dry several months earlier. Dairy cows will lactate for no more than 300 days after the birth of their calves. When they stop giving milk they must be bred again and will not produce milk until they give birth to another calf. Unfortunately, no bull was available for Beatrice and Rosalind, so milking came to a stop. One could say they began living a life of leisure, grazing on grass and roaming around the convent lawn. We could not butcher Beatrice and Rosalind, however. They were only on loan to the convent for the duration of the war. Besides, many of the girls treated them as pets, almost family, demonstrating why farmers do not give names to their animals.

CHAPTER ELEVEN

WAITING FOR LIBERATION

Saint-Hubert and Namur, January 1944

IT SOUNDS BIZARRE TO DESCRIBE THE LIFE OF OUR CONVENT DURING the months preceding the Allied landing in Normandy on June 6, 1944, as routine. After all, we were in the middle of a cataclysmic war, and Belgium was occupied by thousands of German soldiers. We struggled to find enough food to live on. We lived in buildings riddled with concealed passageways leading to secret mysterious rooms. We could be arrested—even executed—at any time for sheltering refugees, Jewish children, and enemy airmen.

Yet, looking back on that time compared with the previous years and later events, it seemed mundane. Every day, wood had to be chopped, classes taught, food cooked, floors scrubbed, clothes washed, Mass attended, prayers said, and hymns sung. It felt normal when Resistance fighters appeared in the middle of the night escorting Jewish children or American pilots who needed to be hidden from the *Abwehr*.

It was the nightly BBC broadcast that reminded us that the world outside our convent walls was anything but normal. The BBC program would always begin with the calm, confident sound of Big Ben tolling the hour in London. We would then hear how the Russians had pushed the German army out of Russia, how American and British armies had captured Sicily and landed troops south of Naples, how Italy had surrendered, and how German towns and cities were being systematically destroyed by thousands of Allied bombers. It was clear that Germany was losing the war and was ultimately doomed. We also knew that it would soon be Belgium's turn to become a battleground with a million soldiers locked in combat. The realisation of what was to come made our lives in Saint-Hubert seem almost bucolic.

Although everything appeared calm and safe for the moment, Sister Ursula never let us become complacent. She knew the slightest misstep or casual unguarded comment could trigger a raid by dozens of storm troopers and Gestapo agents. Sister Ursula was constantly thinking of ways of improving the security of the convent.

One tactic she devised was for the sisters and the students to demonstrate sympathy for the plight of wounded German soldiers. During the Christmas season, she arranged for small groups of our older girls to visit German hospitals and sing Christmas carols to the soldiers. She suggested the hospital visits be arranged at the same time Sister Clare and I made our weekly visit to the *Kommandantur* in Namur.[1]

I decided the best way to recruit ten of our older students for the choir was to ask for volunteers. To draft senior girls for the choir seemed unwise. The reluctant students would resent being forced into a potentially uncomfortable situation in which they had to pretend to have sympathy for the very people who had invaded and occupied their country. I feared their resentment might come out during our visits to the hospitals, undermining Sister Ursula's whole purpose for arranging the concerts. Not all students were hesitant, however; some welcomed the opportunity for an excursion outside the convent walls.

Andree was one the most eager to join the choir. I was very surprised. As a Jew, I thought she would be the last person to willingly entertain the same German soldiers who were transporting thousands of Jews, perhaps her own parents, to death camps. I told Andree it was not a good idea, explaining how traumatic it might be for her, plus there was a risk her true identity would be discovered. Nevertheless, she begged to go. I then realised the love I felt for Andree was not unlike the love a mother feels for her child. I could not reject her heartfelt plea; Andree joined the choir.

They rehearsed a few Christmas carols, and the next time Sister Clare and I made our train trip to Namur to report to the German Military Authority, the girls came with us. Sister Ursula suggested the choir should enter the *Kommandantur* building with us and be introduced to the *Kreiskommandant*, Major Hess, explaining to him our hope to sing Christmas carols to wounded German soldiers. The students were under strict orders to say nothing, but if asked they could give their names. From the pleased expression on the *Kommandantur's* face, it was apparent Sister Ursula's hope of neutralising some of the *Abwehr's* suspicions about convent activities was successful.

Sister Ursula had arranged for us to visit Hospital Saint Elisabeth on the Place Louise Godin. The director of the hospital, Dr. Kuntz, took us to Ward A. The wounded men were mostly airmen from the Luftwaffe who had been sent on essentially suicide missions by Hitler, ordered to hold back the tide of thousands of British and American planes. The Allied air forces knew the German air defence was so puny that they forewarned the targeted cities of an imminent bombing by dropping leaflets in advance of their attack.

The other patients in the ward were soldiers injured by British and American bombs. The choir sang three songs: "*L'est né divi enfant*" (He is Born, the Divine Child), the French version of

"*O Tannenbaum*," and "*Douce Nuit*" (Silent Night). At the end of the brief concert, all the girls as a choir wished the soldiers "*Joyeux Noël.*"

Then a hospital orderly pushed in a cart bearing dozens of *speculaas*, a thin, crispy, spicy cookie shaped like a windmill. The *speculaa* were handed out to the choir and the wounded in the Ward. The girls could not contain their enthusiasm. There was an explosion of giggles. They had not seen such treats in years, yet they managed to rein in their craving for sweets and took just one *speculaa* apiece.

I am not sure why Dr. Kuntz indulged us with cookies. Was he just being a gracious host, or was he trying to show us the war was not going so badly for the Germans because bakers could still create such sugar-filled luxuries? In the end, treating us to the *speculaas* was a vivid reminder of the disparity between the lives of the German occupiers and the Belgians: They feasted while we starved.

While the girls were enjoying the cookies, I sat at the bedside of one pilot and struck up a conversation in German, which surprised him. I asked him the usual questions about his home, about how his family was faring, and did he have a girlfriend.

The last question almost always results in a soldier eagerly pulling out a photo of his girl back home. Somehow, showing a picture of his sweetheart to a total stranger seems to strengthen the invisible threads that bind them to each other and gives a soldier a touch of hope he will see her again.

I asked the pilot how he came to be injured. His answer probably would not have pleased his commanding officer. He told me he was trying to attack a squadron of American bombers. He said he could not get within two miles of the bombers before he was attacked by three American escort fighters and shot down. He managed to safely get out of the cockpit and bail out, but he broke both legs when he hit the ground.

While speaking with the pilot I noticed Andree watching me and listening to our conversation. It was not apparent to me what she was contemplating until we moved on to Ward B.

The same carols were sung, ending with the girls wishing the wounded men *"Joyeux Noël."* There was a slight delay in leaving Ward B for the next and last ward, so I decided to chat with the nearest soldier.

I noticed Andree was approaching a wounded soldier, and hollowness opened up in the pit of my stomach. There was nothing I could do to stop her without raising dangerous suspicions. The gauze bandage wrapped around the soldier's head covered both eyes, so he could not see Andree approaching and leaning close to his ear. I could tell she was speaking German, but could not hear what she was saying. When the soldier smiled, a sense of relief swept over me. No one questioned why this Belgian girl could speak such fluent German. When our escort said we should move on to Ward C, Andree stood up and in a much louder voice wished the blind soldier *"Joyeux Noel"* in French.

In the hallway, before we reached Ward C, I edged up to Andree and whispered in her ear, "Don't ever do that again! You put us at great risk." She nodded and gave me a rueful smile. The remainder of our visit to the hospital was anticlimactic in comparison. The carols were sung and were appreciated by the soldiers. We left Ward C and caught the next train to Saint-Hubert.

On the train, Andree tried to explain why she talked with the German soldier. Andree thought she would hate the German soldier for what he and soldiers like him did to her family and her community. She said she wanted to hate him. She couldn't. Andree admitted the opposite had occurred. She felt sorry for the young man who may have lost his eyesight and probably wished he could have stayed in his small village on the Wollbach River with his family. I told Andree that although I was not happy about what she did, I was pleased she had gained a fundamental insight. When hate fills the mind it empties the soul.

If there were ever any doubts that the Germans were losing the war, those doubts disappeared when German soldiers began removing bells from church steeples; this meant German war factories were running short of metals like copper and tin.

The order to confiscate the bells demonstrated once again the duality of the German psyche, ruthlessness combined with impractical romanticism. The German edict made an exception for ancient bells that were cast before 1850. With German precision, bells were graded "A" through "D" based on their historical and cultural value. "A" bells were cast between 1850 and 1944, "B" bells from 1790 to 1850, "C" bells from 1700 to 1790, and "D" bells before 1740.

Thousands of "A" bells were immediately seized and shipped to Germany. "B" bells were in the process of being removed in mid-1944 when the liberation of Belgium saved most of them. Usually, one small bell would be left in the bell tower to ring in case of an emergency.

If the Germans hoped to sooth Belgian anger by preserving their more ancient bells, they were sadly mistaken. Every Sunday the silence of their bell towers reminded the Belgians of the German theft. That a neighbouring town was able to keep their bells only made them angrier. At the same time, the German romanticism motivating them to spare ancient bells deprived the German war machine of valuable non-ferrous metals they so desperately needed.

The relative lull of early 1944 ended for the Sisters of Our Lady on the Monday after Easter, April 10. Sister Clare and I were in Namur to report to the *Kommandantur* to fulfill our twice-monthly requirement. Massive numbers of leaflets were dropped on Namur, warning that an Allied air attack would take place within the hour. Citizens were told to take shelter immediately, and that they should keep away from major roads, railways, and bridges and especially the large German supply station on the outskirts of the town. It was good advice, but belied reality. When bombs were falling, they could be miles off target.

This was certainly the case on Easter Monday. Our school and convent were over a mile from the supply station, but our neighbourhood was not spared. Many bombs fell on the nearby property of the Sisters of Salzinnes, cracking walls and breaking windows. The orphanage across the road was set on fire, and huge craters were made in the highway leading to Brussels. For a week after April 10, the damage to the railroads prevented Sister Clare and me from returning to Saint-Hubert.

During that week, the air raids were incessant, with hundreds of bombers coming day and night. Air raid sirens could sound at any hour, during a meal, a Mass, or in the middle of the night. We hurried to the cellar, where we would spend long hours praying the bombs would spare the Motherhouse.

Huddling in the cellar and hearing the bomb blasts reminded me of the times on the farm when we would take shelter in the middle of our house as violent summer lightning storms approached. We could hear the thunder and see lightning getting closer and closer, counting the time between the flash and the thunder to estimate how far away the storm was. The delay got shorter and shorter until there was barely a second between the flash and the crash of thunder. We held our breath, knowing the next bolt would be very close. Then there would be a brilliant burst of light and an instantaneous crack of thunder that shook the house. If the lightning hit our lightning rod, there was a crackling, sizzling sound and the smell of ozone. Oddly, smiles would light up our faces. We understood the worst was over and the quick-moving storm would move on, the lightning bolts getting farther away.

Bombs arrived in much the same pattern, with one big difference: there was no lightning rod ever invented that would protect us from a direct hit.

The railway trains and tracks were often targets for the bombers, so train service was very erratic. Only soldiers and those with urgent business would take the risk of travelling by train. Reports came in every day about the great loss of life and property. It was remarkable the Belgian people did not hate the Allied air forces for the devastation they were spreading across their country. However, they understood their suffering was the price they had to pay for liberation. The growing intensity of the bombing meant their day of deliverance was getting closer.

When we heard the BBC broadcast on June 5, 1944, we knew the Allies were poised to invade somewhere along the coasts of Belgium or France. The broadcaster announced that a new phase of the Allied air offensive had begun. The new phase would especially impact people living near the coast. The Supreme Allied Commander promised that whenever possible, the people living in the towns targeted for intense bombing would be given a one-hour advance notice of the attack by the dropping of leaflets.

People within twenty-five miles of the coast, however, should not wait for the dropping of leaflets. They should evacuate the towns immediately, but not on the main roads. They should seek places of refuge in the countryside, at least a mile from the edge of any town. The evacuees were advised to take nothing they could not carry on their persons and to avoid congregating in large groups. Surely the Allies would not be asking hundreds of thousands of people to leave their homes along a thousand miles of shoreline unless the invasion was imminent.

Sister Angela wondered out loud why the Allies would announce to the Germans the start of the invasion. Sister Ursula, who seemed to understand military strategy better than many soldiers, replied that the warning would not be much help to the Germans.

They still had no idea on which beach along the thousand-mile coastline the Allies would land their troops. Alternatively, Sister Ursula said the warning could be just the first of numerous phony alerts, intended to wear down German military units, forcing them to mobilise and then to demobilise every few days.[2]

The next afternoon at 1:00 p.m. on June 6, we knew for certain the warning was genuine. As soon as the first words of the BBC broadcast were uttered, I began furiously writing down every word of the announcement so it could be repeated exactly to everyone in Saint-Hubert, stoking the tiny flame of hope we had been nurturing for four long years. "D-Day has come. Allied troops were landed under strong naval and air cover on the coast of Normandy early this morning. The Prime Minister has told the Commons that the Commanding Officers have reported everything going to plan so far, with beach landings still going on at midday and mass airborne landings successfully made behind enemy lines. More than four thousand ships, with several thousand smaller craft have crossed the Channel; and some eleven-thousand first-line aircraft can be drawn upon for the battle."

For the next two months, time slowed to a crawl; we were like children waiting for Christmas. Liberation could not come soon enough. Sister Ursula made sure at least one sister was tuning in to the BBC all day long so no tidbit of information would be missed. Leaving the radio out in the refectory for hours at a time was probably reckless, but the Germans were so preoccupied with more serious matters that we assumed they would not be spending precious time tracking down clandestine radios.

It was a roller coaster ride. Although the broadcasts were designed to be upbeat, we became adept at reading the bad news between the lines. A month after D-Day, the Allied army was still bottled up on the Normandy peninsula. We cheered when Cherbourg was captured, but nearly wept when a touted Allied army offensive failed to break out of Normandy. Even if the Allies managed to escape the Normandy bottle, Normandy seemed so far from Saint-Hubert. We assumed it would be 1945 before Belgium could be liberated.

I do not know how Sister Ursula, with a lifetime of living in a convent, managed to know so much about military tactics, but she kept assuring us that once cut loose from Normandy, the Allied forces would move much faster. She was right, of course.

On July 18, St. Lo was taken, and the cork was out of the Normandy bottle. In August, the British, American, and Canadian armies swept out of Normandy in an encircling arc. By August 15, the Allies nearly trapped the entire German army in the Falaise pocket. Tens of thousands of German soldiers were killed or captured, and the remainder of the German army escaped across the Seine River. On the same day, Allied armies stormed ashore in southern France in Operation Dragoon.

In addition to the bombing, there was also danger from the increasingly desperate *Rexist* Party. The original ideology of *Rexists* called for a "moral renewal" of corrupt Belgian society. Marxism and capitalism were both seen by *Rexists* as attacks on what had made Belgium strong before the Great War. The Party demanded an end to liberal democracy and the reestablishment of a dominant role for the Catholic Church. The Catholic Church in Belgium wanted nothing to do with the *Rexists*. The Archbishop of Mechelen, Josef-Ernest Cardinal van Roey, denounced the *Rexist* Party, calling it a danger to the country and the Church. After the German invasion, the Party aligned itself with the Nazis and adopted anti-Semitism as one of its core beliefs.

If the *Rexists* suspected the Saint-Hubert Convent was hiding Jews, its so-called beliefs in Catholic values would not have deterred them from denouncing us to the SD and Gestapo.

By January 1944, it was becoming obvious to everyone except the diehard Nazis and *Rexists* that Germany was going to lose the war. The Resistance groups, especially the Communists, increased their attacks on members of the *Rexist* Party. After the Normandy Invasion, attacks on the *Rexists* doubled. The brother of the *Rexist* leader, Leon Degrelle, was assassinated two days after the Normandy landings. The *Rexists* did not know exactly who members of the Resistance were or where to find them, so they took their revenge, like the SD and Gestapo, by killing innocent civilians.

The worst atrocity took place in Courcelles, a village just outside Charleroi, not far from Namur. The *Rexist* mayor of Charleroi was killed on August 17, 1944. The next night a hundred *Rexists* descended on Courcelles. Twenty hostages, men and women, were rounded up, including policemen, doctors, architects, lawyers, and civil officials. One of the twenty was Canon Pierre Harmignies, the *Doyen* of Charleroi. They were locked up in the cellar of a house. During the night, Canon Harmignies tried to comfort his companions with prayer and kindness. It is said his last words were, "I die and we all die so that peace reigns in the world, and that men love one another."

At dawn the next day, the twenty hostages were lined up against a wall. Other villagers were ordered out of their homes to watch. All twenty hostages were shot and killed one at a time.

On August 18, Sister Clare and I made what turned out to be our last weekly trip to Namur to report to the *Kommandantur.* We managed to catch one of the few trains still running between Saint-Hubert and Namur. We were tempted to skip the tedious trip with the Germans on the run in France and train service practically non-existent.

Nevertheless, Sister Ursula told us we should report as usual. Although the Germans were probably reeling from their recent defeats, our not showing up at the appointed hour could still trigger a knee-jerk bureaucratic response. A German squad of SD and Gestapo might be ordered to make a surprise raid on the Saint-Hubert convent. When we did arrive at Headquarters, we were virtually ignored. Dozens of soldiers were scurrying around loading filing cabinets on trucks or throwing documents on a blaze in the inner courtyard. Major Hess was nowhere to be found. A young lieutenant shooed us out of the building. The one train to Saint-Hubert was no longer running, so we decided to spend the night at the rebuilt Motherhouse and school in Namur.[4]

On August 18, 1944, at a little after six o'clock the next evening, we were shocked when a whistling bomb fell directly in front of the Motherhouse. There had been no warning leaflets or flares dropped on Namur by the American bombers, and sirens had not wailed. The walls of the chapel buckled from the explosion.

Thirteen sisters in the chapel saying the rosary were trapped in a cascade of wood and concrete when the roof of the chapel collapsed. Six sisters were killed immediately, and four managed to crawl out of the debris with only scrapes and bruises. Three sisters were buried for several hours before they could be dug out. Two of them had miraculously been flung by the blast under the choir loft, which came down with the ceiling. The loft sagged under the weight of the roof but did not cave in, creating a tiny safe cave under the wreckage. The third buried sister had been in the doorway, protected by its arch when the bomb hit. She was covered with dust but was not knocked unconscious, probably saving her life. Her moans quickly guided rescuers to her location. They could uncover her head, but it still took two more hours to safely dig her out.

Ten or more bombs intended for the nearby railroad bridge fell on the Motherhouse and its grounds. Nothing was spared. One wing of the convent was completely destroyed, and more than half of the refectory building fell in. All the other sisters and I were in the half that was spared. We escaped, covered in dust, with bruises and minor cuts requiring only a few stitches. The two school buildings that had been repaired were rendered uninhabitable. The little chapel in the garden was badly damaged, and the walls of the public chapel were so fissured with cracks that it had to be torn down. The grotto at the end of the garden and the tennis court disappeared completely, without a trace.

Once again, we were homeless. Dear Mother began her quest to find us shelter almost before the bombs had stopped falling. She threaded her way through streets clogged with the brick and mortar remains of destroyed buildings. Fortunately, the Sisters of Saint Marie and the Ursuline Sisters were happy to offer us shelter. We split into two groups, and I was with the group housed by the Ursulines. I had hoped Sister Clare and I would return to Saint-Hubert, but the entire Belgium train system was in shambles. The sisters who died in the bombing were buried in the Motherhouse cemetery. We knew they would be with God and Sister Julie in heaven.

For the next two weeks, we practically lived in the convent's cellars. The radio was still working, so we were able to follow the rapid advance of the Americans. Paris was liberated on August 25. The wanton destruction of Paris threatened by the Germans did not happen. The Allied armies crossed into Belgium on September 2. Brussels was liberated on September 4, and Antwerp on September 5.

The entire civilian population of Namur spent the night of September 5 in their cellars. Rumours ran rampant. The Germans vowed to destroy Namur before withdrawing. German reinforcements had arrived, and the Wehrmacht seemed prepared to contest Namur street-by-street. We would be caught in the cross-fire, just as likely to be killed by American bombs, bullets, and artillery shells as by German. Explosions shook the city throughout the night. The Germans were demolishing all the bridges the American air force had been so eager to destroy. Now the Americans wanted the bridges intact and the Germans wanted them obliterated.

The huge dynamite charges used by the Germans were so powerful that whole rows of houses near the bridges collapsed from the explosive force, burying anyone who was hiding in the cellars.

By morning all the bridges were down, and the explosions ceased. Only the occasional burst of machine gun fire was heard, and then—silence. The quiet was almost as shocking as the bursting of artillery shells.

Suddenly the Americans were there, filling the streets, and the Germans were gone. We were free!

Ever since the news of the D-Day landings, the citizens of Namur were preparing for liberation day by scrounging every scrap of red, white, black, yellow, or blue cloth to make into Belgian, American, and British flags. Several of our sisters made at least a dozen flags. The moment the citizens of Namur were assured the approaching boots pounding out a rhythm on the cobblestone streets were worn by American soldiers, the hidden flags blossomed from hundreds of windows. Sister Helene rushed back to the Motherhouse to hang an enormous Stars and Stripes flag on the wall of our ruined convent. She had stitched it together from a hundred bits of cloth. The people of Namur were wild with delight. They filled the street to cheer our liberators as they passed on foot, in jeeps and trucks, or hitching rides on huge tanks and halftracks. Spontaneous dancing broke out. The joy was so infectious I could not resist the temptation to join the spinning circles of dancers, my flapping habit adding a whirling dervish effect.

The buildings recently vacated by the retreating Germans were quickly commandeered by the Americans. The *Kommandantur* where Sister Clare and I reported every week became the Army headquarters for the Americans with a Town Major now in charge of governing Namur. It was ironic that dear Mother ordered me to report regularly to the Town Major to keep informed about the Allies' relief efforts in Namur and convey our own requests for assistance.

CHAPTER TWELVE

LIBERATION AND AMERICAN LARGESSE

Namur, August 1944

WITH THE ARRIVAL OF THE AMERICANS, IT MIGHT HAVE BEEN possible for me to return to Saint-Hubert, but dear Mother asked Sister Clare and me to stay in Namur for at least a month. She thought our English language skills and our being Americans would be helpful in dealing with the American military.

The first test of my negotiating skills occurred when Sister Rosine, the Sister Superior Provincial, and I travelled to Brussels to collect money being held for the Sisters of Our Lady at the newly reopened American Embassy. When our dear American sisters heard about the liberation of Belgium, especially Namur, they wasted no time in gathering donations from Sisters of Our Lady convents and from schools all over America.

The money was forwarded to the US State Department, which sent it on to Brussels. To collect the donations, however, a properly authorised representative of our order had to personally appear at the embassy and fill out the required paperwork. Dear Mother sent Sister Rosine and me. Since it was our first trip to Brussels in years, we planned to make a day of it.[1]

Sister Rosine and I left Namur at 6:00 a.m. and did not arrive in Brussels until after 9:00 a.m. It was not a comfortable trip, more like riding in our farm cart back in Ohio. There was only one train a day, so it was a milk run, stopping to pick up passengers at every tiny station along the route, with additional stops for the engine to catch its breath.

The Germans had taken or destroyed all the locomotives that were worth anything. Those remaining engines were poor, wheezy relics that seemed on the verge of expiring with every puff. Some passengers said they felt so sorry for the "Little Engine That Couldn't," they were inclined to get out and push a bit.

Eventually the train pulled into what remained of the Brussels North train station. It took an hour at the embassy to sign all the paperwork. The documents were all in English; I read them and surprised the attaché with a few questions. He did not expect to find an American nun in Belgium.

I explained the gist of the papers to Sister Rosine, and she signed them. The attaché then handed us several bound stacks of 1,000-franc notes, newly issued by the Allies as part of its *"Operation Gutt"* to replace the debased currency printed by the Germans.

I had never seen so much cash. We received forty-three francs for every dollar sent to the embassy by our American Sisters. The total was 215,000 francs. We stuffed the bills into our leather satchel and left the embassy feeling a bit like the bank robbers one sees in American movies.

We were anxious to reach our Convent, Ixelles, and not be robbed ourselves. Of course, when carrying a lot of money, one always assumes everyone on the street knows it and is waiting for an opportunity to steal the cash. The reality was, we were two nuns in well-worn habits toting a tattered leather bag, hardly targets for thieves.

The Ixelles sisters gave us a warm welcome, inviting us to share their dinner. Sister St. Rosaire, who is almost blind, treated me to her French accented version of "Yankee Doodle." Up until the arrival of the American Army, they had all been sleeping in the cellars. The bombing by the Allies did not score any direct hits on Ixelles, but like most of our Belgian Houses, countless windows were missing, and doors were askew. Anyone who wanted to make a fortune in Belgium after the war needed only to arrive with a boat full of windowpanes and putty. Not an ounce of putty could be had.

It was sad to see so many houses in such a dilapidated state. I wondered how the sisters escaped catching colds, influenza, and pneumonia. There was only cardboard, if available, to close up the windows and the big cracks in the walls. In the Ixelles Convent, the first thing we noticed when we walked through the front door was a whole series of Bible history charts: Adam and Eve, mixed up with Noah, Isaac, Jacob, and the souls in Purgatory. They were being used to replace the missing windowpanes. Sister Julia felt it was appropriate that the Old Testament was doing works of charity.

Everything was calm and peaceful when we went back to Namur. The town itself seemed to be exuding a collective sigh of relief. People were gradually returning from the country, some only to the ruins of their homes. Plans were made to reopen schools as soon as possible. Part of the Nazareth building at the Motherhouse was still standing, so the habitable part was used to house some of the sisters. Other sisters were living at a home in the country and often had to walk two miles into town when the tram was not running. The primary grades of our school were to be installed in the parlours of our good neighbours, the Ursuline sisters. Those of us living in Nazareth building were soon evicted by rising floodwaters. All the destroyed bridges on the Meuse and Sambre rivers were like dams, causing the rivers to overflow their banks. For the tenth time, we moved furniture from the ground floor up to the next floor. Dear Mother declared that continuing to consider any part of Nazareth remotely habitable would be to perpetuate a lie.

Our prayers were answered by the Father Rector of the College of Our Lady de la Paix. He proposed to let us use the country house of the Jesuits at La Plante.

The day after Father Rector's generous offer, dear Mother and I set out to inspect the Jesuit retreat. The central tram lines were not working, so we walked for over an hour along the boulevard running parallel to the River Meuse. On the way, we passed a substantial edifice occupied by American soldiers. The flags of all the Allied countries, including Russia, flew from the windows. The splendour of the scene was enhanced for me by seeing dozens of American soldiers washing their clothes on the wide veranda in front of the grand building. Doing laundry trumps pageantry.

When we finally arrived at the Jesuit retreat-house we were met by Father John, who was our guide. The country house was a two-storey brick structure with a mansard roof, sited halfway up a steep hill that was part of the ridge of hills surrounding Namur.

The Germans had occupied the house for several months. Although the house was structurally sound, the Germans had removed all the white stucco, making it less of a target at night. The Germans left all their huge comfortable armchairs, spacious beds, divans, desks, lockers, and mirrors. It was a luxurious lifestyle—not the norm for either the Jesuits or the Sisters of Our Lady. With a twinkle in her eye and the slightest hint of a smile on her lips, dear Mother said, "We will just have to get used to it."

The tour of the house showed it could be quickly converted into a convent for the Sisters of Our Lady. On the first floor was a diminutive kitchen, a large room that would be our refectory, two small parlours, and a pretty chapel. On the second floor, there were twenty small rooms for dormitory space.

The German furniture was technically the property of the City of Namur, which had paid for the furniture at the "request" of the German occupiers. The city fathers, however, agreed we could keep whatever furniture we wanted. When Mother General asked the good Father Rector about the rent, he set the price at three Hail Marys a day from each sister living in the house. The Jesuit priests from the nearby seminary offered to act as chaplains so we could have Mass said every morning.

After a few days of robust cleaning, all traces of the German occupation were removed. Cleanliness and simplicity reigned from attic to cellar. The house became a real convent—bright, airy, and religious.

The house was perched high above the level of the river and the road. Unlike our previous residence, there was no chance we would be forced by a rising river to shift our possessions to higher floors. From the porch, there was a wonderful panoramic view of the Meuse River and Namur off in the distance. The picturesque setting was some compensation for the house being so far from Namur. For the first two months, no trams to the central city were available—all the tracks, wires, and bridges having been destroyed. The teachers had to walk four miles in rain or snow to our schools. Their courage never flagged, and their health may have been improved by the exercise. Of course, it was easy for me to assume the benefits of their trek, since I ended up not having to reside in the Jesuit house.

Our dear Mother was ever ready to bear any burden, but even she had to admit her inability to hike into Namur every day. Mother General and the sisters helping her administer the affairs of the order needed to be centrally located. Easy access to intercity rail transportation was essential. Not only did dear Mother need to pay periodic visits to our far-flung convents and schools, she often was required to travel to Brussels to confer or negotiate with Belgian bureaucrats and the Allied occupational authority about logistical problems arising from unstable financial conditions and the need to begin the rebuilding of destroyed schools and convents.

The problem was partially solved when the Reverend Mother of the Sisters of the Congregation of the Filles du Coeur de Jesus offered the second floor of their residence, Salzinnes Abbey, as a refuge for us. The Sisters of the Filles du Coeur de Jesus are cloistered nuns. Before any Sisters of Our Lady would be permitted to live in the monastery, Monseigneur Charue first had to give his permission for a suspension of the normal rules governing a cloistered community. As cloistered nuns, the Sisters of the Filles du Coeur de Jesus live behind high walls. They are strictly separated from the world outside those walls, never leaving without the permission of Reverend Mother. Inside the convent there is nearly total silence except for an hour in the evening. Theirs is a life devoted solely to prayer and contemplation.

Dear Mother, however, did not immediately accept Reverend Mother's kind offer. She asked me to first visit the Salzinnes Abbey and determine if the accommodations would be adequate for her and seven other sisters.

The day after Reverend Mother's offer was the first day of sunshine following several days of rain. Temporary bridges had been thrown across the Sambre and Meuse rivers. I picked the bridge that seemed to require less agility to cross. Unfortunately, it led to a road with no sidewalks. Walking muddy roads is never pleasant, and the road to the Abbey had been churned into a glutinous batter by a continuous stream of American jeeps and trucks on their way to Liege.

It was the custom in those early days of the liberation for sisters to exchange salutes with the soldiers. The soldiers might wave at civilians, but rarely salute them. For some reason, they enjoyed trading salutes with sisters and nuns. When a sister was spotted on the road by one of the soldiers in a truck, he would alert his comrades to be ready to salute. So I was not surprised when I heard a boyish voice call out, "Hello, Sister!"

Some of the boys attempted to say, "*Bon jour!*" I may have been standing ankle deep in muck, but such an inconvenience is nothing compared to the joy one feels when twenty American soldiers snap to attention and salute you as if you were a general. In return, I tried to duplicate their crisp, military salute and offered a prayer for their safety. Although the young men seemed so carefree, they were not on their way to a picnic; I knew the dangers they would soon be facing.

At last, the road turned away from the Sambre River, and I was relieved to find a paved sidewalk on the Avenue Reine Astrid. I crossed the Place Wiertz and climbed the ten steps up to the massive wood and iron door that guarded the entry to the Salzinnes Abbey. A few moments after ringing the bell, there was a loud click and the huge door silently swung inward. There was no human in sight. I assumed the door was controlled by some ingenious mechanism on the inside that kept the sisters isolated from any visitors.

As I entered the gloomy vestibule, the door silently closed behind me, giving rise to a strong sensation of claustrophobia. All I could see was a little hole in one wall covered by a screen. There was another click and the sound of a sliding panel, followed by a soft voice coming from behind the screen bidding me "*bon jour*" and asking how she could help. I explained my mission.

The ethereal voice said, "Oh! The Sisters of Our Lady! Our Reverend Mother is expecting you. I am the portress for the Abbey. Will you please enter the parlour on the right?" I could see almost nothing in the dim light, but managed to find a doorknob to turn, except it didn't. Once again, the disembodied voice encouraged me to go straight ahead. I thought I would run into a blank wall. There was another click, and a door soundlessly swung open.

I entered another parlour, dimly lit by a window with ground-glass panes, rejecting more light than it let through. The floor was covered with brown oilcloth, and the room was divided in half by a brown wooden grille. The furniture consisted of only four rush-bottomed chairs. Before I had time to sit in one of the chairs, there was another click, and a door opened behind the grille. A slender figure, all in white, glided into the room with a gentle, smiling face and words of greeting.

She was Sister Bernardine, Mother Superior of the Salzinnes Abbey. Sister Bernardine was the one of the few members of the abbey allowed to speak directly to outsiders. She took a chair on the opposite side of the grille from my chair, and we continued our conversation through the face-hiding grille.

I explained our plight to Sister Bernardine. She expressed her sympathy for our predicament, and said she hoped she had a solution to our housing challenges. Although permitted to talk, Sister Bernardine still kept our conversation to an absolute mini-mum. She used hand gestures rather than words. She guided me through the door she had just used to enter the room with a slight nod of her head. The door led into a very stiff, austere, and dim parlour. I felt like Alice stepping through the looking glass. On the far end of the parlour was another door leading to a barely lit, tightly twisted spiral staircase. Sister Bernardine told me it was the doctor's stairway to the infirmary.

Before ascending the staircase, Sister Bernardine pointed to two pairs of slippers lying on the first step. At first, I did not under-stand what she was trying to tell me—without telling me. When she took off her shoes and put on one pair of slippers, I knew I was to follow her example. I assumed the shedding of shoes was required for visitors before ascending the stairs because the stair-case was unfinished, cream-coloured wood, easily marred and not so easily cleaned. At the top of the stairs, we put our shoes back on. Should there be more than two visitors, they would probably have to proceed up the stairs in their stockings.

I cautiously ascended the corkscrew stairs. At the top, there was another darkish corridor. Sister Bernardine placed a finger to her lips urging silence, which seemed unnecessary since neither of us were saying anything. I did try to tread more lightly. I later learned the hall was part of the cloister, thus the greater need for quiet. There was another door and twelve descending steps into a wide, airy corridor filled with sunlight streaming in from a wall of windows. It took a moment for my eyes to adjust. The sun-drenched hall ended in a bright, cheery room looking out on a garden filled with fruit trees. The sunny corridor led to the convent's infirmary, meant to be our home until repairs could be completed on the Motherhouse.

The infirmary was divided into four immaculate rooms, each with a large window, whitewashed walls, and white oaken floors that had never been discoloured by wax, varnish, or paint. On entering the infirmary, I could not suppress my enthusiasm. An "Oh, my!" escaped my lips. I quickly explained to Sister Bernardine how enthralled I was by the delightful room and that her generosity in offering it to the Sisters of Our Lady was much appreciated.

Across the width of the building at the end of the corridor was space for our refectory, kitchen, and an attic storeroom. The tiny kitchen had a gas stove (if gas service would ever be reinstalled), a sink, a cupboard, and enough standing room for three people. Since preparing meals in that kitchen would be impossible, I asked Sister Bernardine about meals and whether we would be taking our meals with the Salzinnes sisters. Sister Bernardine's usual serene face was clouded for a moment by a look of consternation. She was probably torn between the need to maintain the order's strict rules of seclusion and the duty of being a gracious host to invited guests. Her solution was a compromise. We would not take our meals with the Salzinnes nuns, but they would be prepared in their convent kitchen. A bell would ring alerting us that our meal had been delivered to us in a type of dumbwaiter, which was usually used to convey laundry and other items between the floors of the cloister. The dumbwaiter was not far from the infirmary, so we could carry the food from it to the infirmary for our meals. Sister Bernardine said she did not expect us to wash the dishes after meals, but to send them back to the kitchen by the dumbwaiter.

I was delighted to see a stairway to the left of the corridor leading down to the sacristy, through which we could pass when going into the church. It was steep, narrow, and precarious. It did have the advantage, however, of allowing us to attend Mass and Benedictions in the chapel without having to pass through the cloister. Confessions were also possible if you did not mind sitting on the stairway and speaking to the chaplain through a hole in the sacristy wall.

I reported to Mother General that the living arrangements at the Salzinnes Abbey would suit us quite well. She told us we would be moving the next day. Dear Mother knew we would not be able to transport all our furniture and other things to the Salzinnes Abbey without help, so when we had gathered together our modest belongings and some furniture, she sent me out to see if I could recruit some American soldiers to assist with the move. I went out into the street and managed to flag down an unloaded Army truck. The sergeant and the driver were probably startled to see a nun waving at them and yelling above the roar of the truck, "Hey, Yanks! Can you lend us a hand?" The sergeant not only agreed to help, he also stopped a passing Army jeep with four soldiers aboard and conscripted them for our relocation.

Many hands did make light work. Everything was loaded into the truck except our valises, which dear Mother said we should carry. The oaken case containing the principal relics of our Foundress, Blessed Mother Julie, was placed in the jeep. It was the fourth journey for our beloved Foundress since 1940. We longed for the day when we could return her remains to our reconstructed Motherhouse.[2]

Our procession to the abbey made an interesting parade: a jeep in the lead with Mother General and three soldiers, followed by a large Army truck, and ending with eight sisters marching behind the truck, each carrying a suitcase.

Ultimately, all our homeless sisters in Namur found shelter with other religious communities. We were spread out around the town, but we thanked the good God for all He had done for our health and comfort.

Many citizens of Namur were forced to live in very crowded conditions in the temporary shelters provided by the city and the American Army.

Our living arrangements in the Infirmary separated us completely from the good Filles du Coeur de Jesus Sisters. At mealtimes the bell would ring, and one of us would walk to the dumbwaiter and return with trays of simple but nourishing food. No sister verbally lamented our inability to wash the dirty dishes before returning them to the dumbwaiter.

We did rue our inability to heat water for our ersatz tea. The gas supply was so tenuous, we had to take the kettle down to the kitchen for hot water. Attempts to use an electric stove proved too dangerous to the sister plugging it into the electrical outlet. Sometimes sparks would leap out, threatening electrocution. Sister Angela suggested we should draw straws to determine who should have the honour of brewing the tea. After blowing so many scarce fuses, dear Mother called a halt to all tea that required the use of the electric stove.

The bell that preceded the arrival of our dinners was also used by Sister Portress to announce the arrival of visitors. She rang the bell three times. When going to meet our visitors, we had to cling tight to the rail of the spiral staircase when descending to the largish parlour Reverend Mother had set aside for our use.

There were three Masses every morning, but we remained in our quarters until the Mass at seven o'clock. Places were reserved for us in the front row outside the grille. Behind the grille the faces of the Sisters Filles du Coeur remained hidden, but their beautiful voices filled the church. I suspected many of the Sisters of Our Lady who were in attendance only joined in the singing pianissimo, afraid to risk adding discordant notes and spoiling the exquisite sound. At five o'clock we attended Benediction. In very cold winter weather, however, some of us listened to Mass from our oratory and only descended into the church for Holy Communion. As Sister Angela said, "There was not the least suspicion of heat in the church." A priest who said one of the Masses remarked how each time he entered the church, he felt he had put on a garment of ice.

The infirmary itself was heated by a separate boiler, making our quarters toasty—if we had coal to put in the furnace. When the supply was low, we conserved what we had by leaving only a tiny pile of coal burning in the furnace, just enough to reignite a larger fire. During those times, we put on extra clothes. I felt like a padded football player.

The Congregation of the Filles du Coeur de Jesus was founded in 1841. Its Foundress was killed by an anarchist in the convent's garden in 1884. They have ten houses, with the Motherhouse in Rome. The three hundred members of the order are divided into two grades of sisters. The choir sisters are dressed all in white and spend ten hours a day in prayer. They pray for priests as one of their special duties. Unlike the Sisters of Our Lady, as cloistered nuns they have no work outside the convent walls.

The sisters who are not choir sisters do most of the cooking, cleaning, and laundry. They wear black with a white veil, except when they are running errands out-of-doors. Then they put on a neat black bonnet with a very short black veil. Although their life in the convent is one of great self-denial, they do not practise severe corporal austerities like some cloistered orders.

The kindness and hospitality of the Filles du Coeur du Jesus community was extraordinary. In so many little ways that count so much, they showed they were glad to have us with them. I suspect they skimped on the use of coal in their own quarters so we could enjoy a bit more warmth. The sisters were very poor and Mother General paying them for our board may have alleviated some of their poverty, but could not begin to compensate them for the spirit in which they took care of the Sisters of Our Lady.

The next challenge was to find accommodations for our school. Since the American military controlled almost everything that happened in Namur, Mother General assigned me, an American, the task of combing the town for a large building fit for habitation and suitable for a school.

Several weary days of searching yielded nothing. All the large buildings had been taken over by Americans or were needed by the city government to replace the town hall that had been accidentally destroyed by American bombs.

Finally, we found a hotel on the edge of town that had been occupied by the Germans. The owner offered to rent us several large community rooms and some smaller rooms for our school. The Germans, however, had left the hotel in shambles. Mother General ordered "all hands on deck" for the cleaning and scrubbing. In two days, we were getting the hotel shipshape when an American colonel arrived in a black limousine. He was surprised to see a crew of nuns slaving away with brooms and scrub brushes. He told us he was especially pleased to see the transformation we had wrought, since American officers would soon be occupying the hotel.

The hotel owner had neglected to tell us the entire hotel had been commandeered by the American Army. Mother General was not pleased. She asked the colonel if he would have his driver take her, with me as a translator, to see the town major. He would have been a brave officer to deny dear Mother's request, so we drove to US Army headquarters in style.

The town major actually had the rank of a brigadier general. He was most gracious. He said he would do everything in his power to find a place for our school, and he would commandeer for us any building we found that met our needs. He summoned Major Martin Thomson to his office and ordered him to serve as our escort for our quest to find an adequate school building. Major Thomson had a jeep and a driver at his disposal that we could use to explore the city. Mother General did not feel up to the rigours of riding in a jeep, so she delegated the task to Sister Clare and me. Major Thomson proved to be a charming and delightful companion. He asked for us to skip calling him major, and to call him Martin.

It was our first ride in a jeep—what a thrill! The weather was mild, with the sun warming our faces. Sister Clare and I rode in the back, with Martin and the driver in the front seats. The ride was bouncy, so we had to hang on with both hands. The wind made our veils stream out behind us. Soldiers would salute the major and us as we passed by. Martin returned the salutes while Sister Clare and I gave them sedate smiles. Some soldiers would shout, "Sisters, can you give us a lift?" Unfortunately, a complete tour of the available buildings yielded nothing adequate for our school. Martin took us back to the Salzinnes Abbey after taking us on a short jaunt in the countryside. He assured us the roads had been cleared of mines, but the thought that there may be lingering danger from them only added to our excitement.[3]

Ultimately, our classes had to be spread out over several locations offered by friends and neighbours. Two families of our pupils offered rooms in their homes, an apartment was rented for the older girls, and the parish school crowded more of its students into its classrooms to free up two rooms for the rest of our students. Martin took complete charge of moving the desks and other equipment to the temporary classrooms. Although Martin had completely satisfied the General's orders, he continued to make his jeep available to us for running errands. With the tram service so spotty, he would often pick us up at the end of the school-day. Martin would drive to free up another seat. I usually rode in the front seat and three other sisters would wedge themselves onto the back bench.

One of the surprises of the liberation was the number of American visitors who called on us at the Abbey. Cardinal Spellman came from New York to visit soon after the arrival of the American Army in Namur. Unfortunately, Mother General was in Brussels at the time. The Cardinal was surprised to find two American sisters in residence. He assumed we would have been interned when America entered the war. After we told him about our bi-weekly trips to the *Kommandantur* and about reporting our observations to the Resistance, he labelled Sister Clare and me "Spy Sisters."[4]

Cardinal Spellman said the Sisters of Our Lady in America had asked him to visit us at Namur and send them news. He took careful note of all we told him and promised to send messages to the sisters overseas. He also brought us news of our religious community in Rome and assured us the sisters in Rome were safe.

Allied liberation also brought the return of mail service to the US. I received the first letter from my family, written by my mother, in over four years. My mother had written numerous letters before, but they had all been returned as undelivered. The family had no idea of what had happened to me, but they had put their faith in the good God and had never given up hope. Sadly, both of my grandparents had died. They had been terribly distraught when the land of their birth once again went to war against the rest of the world. My three brothers had all joined the Marine Corps and were somewhere in the Pacific fighting the Japanese.

The war caused a huge increase in farm prices, so Dad and Mom were comfortably well off. Dad had to hire a fourteen-year-old boy to help with the chores. I wrote back assuring them I was in good health and would be staying in Belgium for the foreseeable future. I promised when I had time, I would give them a more detailed description of what life was like living in German-occupied Belgium. I felt a little guilty about not missing my parents and life on the farm any more than I did. Who would have thought that life in a convent could be so exciting?

The very day we moved into the Abbey, the first soldier visitor appeared. He had made a promise to his sister, a Sister of Our Lady of Namur who lived in Boston, to greet Reverend Mother General, our dear Mother. He did not come empty-handed. He gave dear Mother a solid wooden box he had carried with him ever since the day he landed in Normandy. In his mind the box was a talisman, ensuring he would live to deliver the present. It was tightly packed with needles, safety pins, and pieces of hard candy wrapped in cellophane. From then until the American Army left Belgium, we had a parade of soldiers coming to visit. The Salzinnes Abbey's Reverend Mother gave us permission to use the front parlour for meeting with our guests. I am sure the tread of heavy army boots and the hum of conversation, punctuated with bursts of laughter, disrupted their quiet contemplative life. Some of the soldiers were relatives of sisters or related to former students. A few had themselves been taught by Sisters of Our Lady and were carrying letters of introduction from their old teachers.

Father Joe O'Connell was another frequent visitor. He was a chaplain in the US Army and was stationed near Namur. He was eager to help and made his jeep and driver available to us when not being used on official Army business. Unbeknownst to us, Father Joe had written to many convents in America, suggesting they might like to send food and clothing to Belgium, addressed to him. Then he would make sure they were forwarded to us at the Salzinnes Abbey. He was deluged with hundreds of packages. To deliver them, Father Joe had to scrounge up an Army truck and dragoon a couple of volunteer soldiers to do the heavy lifting.

Father Joe, being a typical impish Irishman, was determined to surprise us. One morning in late October I was told two American soldiers were waiting in the parlour wanting to speak to a sister. Dear Mother had left instructions that when dealing with Americans, Sister Clare and I were to be the designated spokespersons. With wide grins on their faces, the soldiers explained they were on an errand for Father O'Connell, who wanted a few packages delivered to the Abbey.

When we offered to carry the packages into the Abbey, they burst out laughing. "But, sister, you couldn't—this little room can't hold them all." They were nearly right. By the time they had emptied scores of huge mail sacks, a mountain of boxes filled the room. Some of the boxes had broken open when they were dumped from the mailbags onto the parlour floor. A brown fog of cocoa filled the room, perfumed with the delightful scent of soap and tooth powder.

Now of course, we had a logistics problem. We could not impose on the good Salzinnes sisters by commandeering their front parlour for a storeroom. We would have to carry the packages up to the infirmary, negotiating the sinuous spiral stairway in stocking feet. It was a daunting task for just five sisters. Once again, the Salzinnes sisters came to our rescue. Reverend Mother volunteered some of the cloistered nuns to help. She gave them permission to temporarily leave their seclusion to lend a hand shifting the packages.

Twenty Salzinnes nuns, dressed in spotless white habits, silently appeared. It was an odd scene. We Sisters of Our Lady had lived with these sisters in the same building for over a month, and yet they were complete strangers to us, as we were to them. Sister Monica organised a sort of fireman's bucket brigade. The spiral staircase obstacle was resolved by stationing a sister on every third step. Packages were then handed from one sister to the sister on the next highest step until they reached the top of the staircase. All the sisters on the stairs were in their stocking feet, so there was no danger to the unfinished, cream-coloured steps. Packages reaching the top of the stairs were handed to a relay team of sisters who carried them to the infirmary.

The process became even smoother and more efficient once the Filles du Coeur de Jesus Sisters began singing hymns. It was like sailors singing a sea shanty while hauling in the anchor.[5]

The Salzinnes sisters so enjoyed the work, they asked Reverend Mother if they could continue until all the packages were moved to the infirmary. As it turned out, the moving and storing of the packages from America was not a one-time event. Almost every day another truckload would arrive at the Abbey and the sister stevedore team would spring into action. An extra room was made available by Reverend Mother to store the boxes of food and clothes.

Needless to say, it was not dear Mother's intention to stockpile a hoard of articles desperately needed by so many Belgians. So every day an empty army truck arrived, and the team would reverse the flow of goods from the infirmary, down the winding staircase, and out the door until the truck was filled. It was such a joy to share our gifts with our pupils and families impoverished by the war and occupation. On prize day, at the end of the school year, every pupil in our three parish schools at Namur proudly wore a dress or a suit sent by kind friends in the United States. A highlight for me on prize day was the sisters and students joining in a rousing rendition of the "Star Spangled Banner" in English.

The avalanche of packages we were receiving from the US could not have been distributed without the help of Major Thomson; whether Martin adopted the sisters of Our Lady or the Sisters of Our Lady adopted Martin, there was no question that he had become a member of the Sisters of Our Lady family in Namur. Our older students swooned over Major Thomson, thinking he looked like a movie star in his crisp Army uniform. Martin requisitioned Army trucks, drivers, and soldiers with strong backs to deliver packages all around Namur. He was everywhere in his jeep, transporting sisters to the distribution sites and running other errands for Mother General.

Dear Mother used her incredible intelligence network to discover which families were most in need. If she was playing the role of godmother in our familial organisation, I was her consigliere. In the morning, she told me the locations to deliver the goods and specified what kind of items should be included in the packages. She assumed as an American I would be better at negotiating any bureaucratic hurdles the American Army might raise along the way. Our delivery convoy usually consisted of a jeep, driven by Martin with me riding shotgun (an expression I learned from Martin), trailed by a large Army truck loaded with supplies.[6]

During our drives through Namur distributing our wares, Martin and I talked about our homes, our families, and life in America. Martin told me he was a widower, his wife and premature daughter dying during childbirth. I suspected his need for family was partly the reason he had so closely attached himself to our Sisters of Our Lady family. For my part, I talked about what I had been doing in Occupied Belgium during the war.

During one conversation, I asked him if he had killed anyone in battle. I wanted to know if he had a way of dealing with the guilt from taking the life of another human being. Martin said he had fired a lot of bullets in the direction of the enemy. He could not be sure, though, if any of his bullets had actually killed German soldiers. He thought having no proof he had killed anyone made it easier to avoid feeling guilty. I said I did not have the benefit of such doubt. I knew I had been responsible for the death of the three German soldiers who were posing as downed American airmen. If he noticed the tears in my eyes as I described my role in identifying the German imposters for the Resistance, he did not say anything.[7]

Martin was invaluable to the Sisters of Our Lady of Namur and their mission to feed, clothe, and educate as many suffering Belgians as their resources would allow. Perhaps the best way to describe Martin's contribution to the people of Namur is in his own words. Before he was reassigned by the Army and left Namur, he gave me carbon copies of the letters he wrote to the sister superiors of all the Sisters of Our Lady of Namur Houses in America. Here are those letters.[8]

October 10, 1944
Dear Sister Superior,
I am writing at the suggestion of our mutual friend, Sister Superior General Mari-Louise. This is frankly an "ask you" letter. I want you to do something that is guaranteed in advance to make your Christmas a happier one this year. I want you to beg, borrow or steal all the candy (preferably hard candy), chewing gum, and soap that you can for my "Kids" this Christmas. These kids are mostly from poor families, or families made poor by the War. They are suffering to an extent unappreciated by Americans. They also include orphans—the saddest of all—and sick children in institutions.

Some officers and enlisted men and I are planning a children's Christmas Party. Otherwise, Christmas to these unfortunate kids will be Christmas in name only, or just another day. We want to bring at least one bright spot to their lives. We are making arrangements for this party now because it will take time to achieve a Christmas stockpile of candy and soap, the two most wanted articles for our "Kids."

We have made a small start. We are saving our own small candy rations—a few bars of chocolate and a package of chewing gum a week—for the party. I don't think any of us have eaten a piece of candy in a month. Our consciences would hurt us too much if we did. Not that we are soft-hearted, but there is nothing like the light in a little child's eyes when the child is hungry and miserable. It simply tears your heartstrings wide apart.

If you could see these Belgian kids as we see them and appreciate the sadness which is their present lot. The parents, when they have parents, of the overwhelming majority of them are struggling desperately—like drowning men fighting for their lives—to get the bare essentials of life, food, clothing and shelter. Most of these kids, especially those born in the last five or six years, have never tasted candy. You should see the incredulous look on their faces when they bite into a piece of candy for the first time; then the look of utter happiness. It warms your heart more than anything you can describe. You haven't given them a million dollars. You've only given them a small piece of candy of a type that American and British and other kids are accustomed to gobbling up on all occasions. Kids are kids the world over, and these Belgian kids are just as lovable as the kids of any other nation.

I have seen a lot of terrible sights in this war but none as sickening or depressing as to see a hurt, destitute or orphaned child. The real tragedy is that very little can be done in the near future to help these kids. However, with your help, and the help of other relatives and friends, we hope to bring a brief spark of pleasure to as many children as possible this Christmas, God willing. I can only do so, however, with your help. Naturally, it is utterly impossible to buy candy or sweets of any kind in Belgium nowadays. And what passes for soap is a horrible mess that Americans wouldn't scrub their dogs with. That is why I am asking for your assistance.

The postal authorities will permit the unlimited mailing of Christmas parcels to soldiers overseas without specific requests until November 15. After that all that is necessary is to show this letter requesting the candy and soap to be mailed to us. All parcels must conform to certain size and weight specifications which, I believe, are 5 pounds maximum and 100 inches maximum girth (all over size). The parcels should be mailed as quickly as possible to the Army Postal Service so that they will reach me by Christmas.

This is the time of year when the Army Postal Service is swamped with Christmas parcels for men overseas, so please mail early.

I am sure that in the name of the American kids whom God has spared the tragedy and misery of these Belgian kids, you will give me all possible help in this respect. I am sure, too, that the happiness your thoughtfulness will bring to these kids, will be communicated by some supernatural means to you and yours this Christmas. Get your friends to mail me something too. Thank you a million times for whatever candy and soap you can send to me at the address below. I will write you a complete account of our party when it is held. God bless and keep you always.

Respectfully yours,

Major Martin Thomson, US Army

P.S. Please send candy and soap to me at this address:

Major Martin Thomson 280242

306 Ordnance Maintenance Company

A.P.O. 206, Namur, Belgium

c/o Postmaster, New York, New York

P.S. In the meantime, before Christmas, my friends I are having a little party each week or so at different schools, orphanages and other places where there are poor, sick, or orphaned kids. We've already had two parties at schools run by the Sisters of Our Lady of Namur. By dint of much conniving with mess sergeants and bartering cigarettes and other "luxuries" with some of the other soldiers, we managed to scrape enough candy together to give two small gum drops, pieces of hard candy and broken bits of chocolate to each of the 400 children. Their reaction almost made twenty fairly hard-bitten officers and men start to bawl.

Honest, no kidding! – I am currently conducting one of the most unusual raffles ever held. I got a bottle of Jack Daniels from a source I cannot disclose. I am raffling it off at a bar of chocolate or a package of chewing gum a chance. When I get 300 or 400 bars and packs. I will hold a drawing. The candy and gum, of course, are going to my "kids."

P.S. My friends and I have "adopted" the kids at the Sisters of Our Lady of Namur School run by nuns of your Order. They are the ones we are planning the Christmas Party for, and for whom the two parties referred to above were held. In closing, I might add that your Order can be proud of the magnificent accomplishments of Sister Superior General and her band of devoted nuns in establishing, and maintaining under terrific obstacles, a school that would be a credit to any community in the United States. You would be especially proud of the two American Sisters, Sister Clare and Sister Christina, who are in Namur. Their vivacious enthusiasm for helping the needy in Namur is an inspiration to us all. American bombs, I am sorry to say, destroyed much of the convent and school so that the Sisters were required to spread their classes around to several buildings in Namur. What Sister Superior General and her Sisters have accomplished with the students, teaching them to be better Catholics and citizens is truly great.

Sister Superior and her Sisters are well, send their regards, and ask for your prayers.

Yours truly,

Martin Thomson

November 11, 1944:

Reverend Sister Superior,

My recent appeal for candy and soap for my "kids" this Christmas has brought many encouraging replies. In fact, I'm sort of overwhelmed with it all. To date, I have heard from nearly all the relatives and friends I wrote to originally. Their generous response, however, pales in comparison to the response from all the Sisters of Our Lady convents and schools. Every Sisters of Our Lady community in the US has sent packages stuffed with candy and soap. Then—this is the miraculous thing about it—each mail brings letters from total strangers who have heard about my "kids" and who, too, want to help. People in Massachusetts, Ohio, Pennsylvania, Indiana, Washington D.C., and other places have written to say they have mailed candy and soap for our Christmas Party. Now I'm beginning to worry about the Army Postal Service and some of the "brass hats" (high ranking officers to you!).

I'm afraid they might be asking one of these days: "Who in hell is this Major Thomson and what's he doing with all of this stuff?" I'll tell them very honestly that I hoped to get a little candy and soap to brighten up this Christmas for as many needy Belgian children as possible. Good-hearted Americans have been so generous, however, the Sisters of Our Lady and I are laying plans to stage Christmas parties at every orphanage, institution for the blind and crippled kids and in every poor section of the city to the limit of the gifts we receive from America.

This letter, written from the heart, is addressed to all of you folks who have responded so nobly and generously to our appeal. Your generosity has deeply touched the soldiers who are sponsoring this party. It has touched us as nothing else had in our service overseas. Your splendid reaction to our request has made us prouder still of our country and its people—so fittingly represented by you.

The results of your benevolence are twofold. It has made it possible, first of all, for us to plan to give something this Christmas to many, many more needy Belgian kids than our own necessarily limited resources would permit. (We are saving our own small rations of candy for this purpose and getting other soldiers to do the same.) But in a second and larger sense your generosity has had even greater results. To a group of American soldiers—themselves a cross-section of the great Army of the United States—it has demonstrated that love of neighbour and charity and unselfishness shine as bright as ever in the hearts of our home folks. To us, that is where those virtues count the most!

Like all American soldiers serving in foreign lands our hearts and our thoughts constantly turn towards our beloved America. We are fiercely determined to finish the grim job of war successfully so that we can return to our families as soon as possible. At the same time, however, we are terribly homesick. In the midst of our homesickness we keep thinking "Have our people back home kept faith with us in preserving the soul of America in this frightful war?"

We know that our folks in America have sweated and strained to accomplish production miracles in turning our prodigious quantities of armaments, food and other war essentials. We know that you have dug deep into your pockets and have loyally supported every War Bond drive, every Red Cross, USO and other war fund effort. We know that you have left nothing undone to help the Armed Forces of your country in America's time of need.

For all of these things we are proud of you and grateful to you. But they merely reflect the material side of America. What about

America's spiritual side—her soul? We soldiers are primarily interested in this spiritual side because it is the SOUL of a nation that makes it great and keeps it great. We feel, too, that one of the surest ways of testing the soul of any nation is by observing how its citizens practice goodwill, which is merely another way of saying "love thy neighbour."

Yes, what about America's spiritual side—her soul? In contributing, out of the sheer goodness of your hearts, such simple things as candy and soap, to make Christmas brighter for some unhappy children in a foreign land, you folks have given us a large part of the answer. We feel that your spontaneous efforts in this respect have preached a powerful sermon on the Second Commandment. This has been inexpressibly consoling to us. It has reassured us that the soul of America—our country and yours—has been tried in the harsh crucible of war and not found wanting. Thank God for that.

On behalf of our small group, and especially for "our" kids, we are grateful for your generosity and your charity. But we are grateful most of all for your goodwill. For goodwill is the basis of the just peace that Americans are fighting and praying for—to end tyranny, injustice, and persecution of man by man; to spread love of neighbour; and to try to end forever the scourge of war!

We are sure that the prayers of these Belgian kids for you, their benefactors in America, will reward your goodwill in this instance a thousand-fold by making your Christmas more happy and blessed. The only thing we soldiers can add is: "Thanks for what you did for us, too, and God bless all of you always!"

Sincerely yours,

Martin Thomson

Sadly, the Christmas party Martin was so eager to have for the children of Namur never happened. The business of war intervened. Martin and his unit, the 306 Ordnance Maintenance

Company, was ordered to move closer to the front lines to the town of Spa, Belgium, in three days, on December 4, 1944.

We sisters were sad Martin was leaving Namur and that perhaps we would never see him again. The girls in our school were especially distraught. They adored Martin.

Sister Clare and I were also leaving Namur. Dear Mother said we should go back to Saint-Hubert. She knew that with peace returning to Belgium, our school in Saint-Hubert, especially our agricultural school, would be inundated with students in the spring. Dear Mother said we would be needed more in Saint-Hubert than in Namur. We did not know it at the time, but all hopes of Belgium celebrating a "normal" Christmas would be ended two weeks later when the German army launched a massive surprise attack on December 16, 1944.

Although no one was aware of it at the time, the Germans had forewarned us of their planned re-invasion of Belgium. They launched a torrent of V-1 rocket attacks on all the major cities of Belgium, not sparing Namur. The "V" stood for "*Vergeltungswaffen*" (vengeance weapon). It was aptly named. It was much more a weapon for spreading terror than for destroying strategic targets like bridges, railway yards, and military depots. The Belgians called the V-1 a robot since it flew without a human pilot. The Brits called it a "buzz-bomb" or "doodlebug" due to the distinctive "putt-putting" sound of its engine, similar to the drone of a small motorbike. The robot looked like a long gray cigar with a stovepipe attached for a tail. Its primitive guidance system meant it could only be used to terrorise innocent civilians in large cities like London, Brussels, Antwerp, and Namur. The Germans would aim a V-1 in the general direction of a city with just enough fuel to reach its intended target. When the engine died, the V-1 would plunge straight down, taking about ten seconds to hit the ground. The bomb it carried was huge and could cause great damage, if it managed to hit anything. Using a V-1 to destroy a bridge, for example, would be like trying to hit the bullseye on a dartboard while blindfolded.

Soon after D-Day, the Allied invasion of France, thousands of "buzz-bombs" were launched against the city of London from locations along the coast of France and Belgium. Most of the rockets were shot down or exploded harmlessly in farm fields, but they still killed thousands of Londoners. When Allied forces captured the French and Belgium seacoasts, the buzzbombs could no longer reach London. Robots launched from the Rhineland, however, were within easy reach of Belgian cities, especially Namur. On the last Sunday in November, dozens of them fell in and around Namur, causing many deaths and much destruction.

Martin explained to me that the rain of robots was an act of desperation and not a prelude for a major attack by the Wehrmacht.[9]

The complacency of the Allied generals was undisturbed. They assumed the German military machine was so weak it could only operate on the defensive. The robot onslaught confirmed their belief. It meant the depleted Luftwaffe was unable to launch coordinated attacks against strategic targets without the risk of losing the few planes it had left.

Martin's comforting words about the impossibility of the Germans attacking Belgium again, however, did not mean the robots were harmless when it came to the lives of Namur citizens. Those who were not directly harmed by the robots lived in constant fear that they would become the next victims. There was little or no warning of an impending robot attack, so there was no time to seek shelter in deep cellars. The first hint of a raid was usually the putt-puttering sound of the rocket itself, which meant it was very close. At that point, the only defence was hoping and praying the buzzing engine would not stop, because if it did, you were in the target zone.

At first, we continued to live in the Salzinnes infirmary. The row of glass windows made us particularly vulnerable to injury from flying glass shards. The blast from a rocket a hundred yards away could still explode glass windows into a torrent of deadly knives. Dear Mother had some unused tables placed under the windows where we would be the most protected. Many times during meals we dropped our forks and dove under the tables while praying under our breaths, "Please, Sister Julie, don't let the engine stop."

As the number of robots increased, Mother General decided we should just live in the cellar. One cellar room was divided into successive sections—refectory, dormitory, and makeshift chapel. The Salzinnes sisters declined to join us in the cellar; they apparently feared the danger of the robots less than the disruption of their secluded lives of prayer and contemplation if they shared quarters with eight Sisters of Our Lady. In the end the Abbey was spared, with not a window broken. So, while we spent over a week living in a cold, damp, dark cellar, the Salzinnes remained in their cozy, somewhat warmer rooms.

Major Thomson was adamant about distributing as many packages and treats from America as possible before his unit left for Spa. Namur was still under sporadic attack from robots, but Martin dismissed their threat as "statistically improbable." If Martin was willing to accept the improbable risk, I could hardly decline to play my usual part of facilitating communications between the American soldiers and the Belgian children.[10]

The day before I was to return to our House and school in Saint-Hubert, and three days before Martin was to relocate to Spa, we loaded our convoy for a trip to the school in the Temploux district. Martin drove the jeep and I was riding shotgun. We were followed by two soldiers in a truck filled with parcels of food and clothing. While stopped at an intersection, we heard the telltale drone of a robot coming from the east. Martin and I looked at each other. I am sure we were having the same thought, "Please don't stop buzzing." The engine died almost directly overhead. Martin leaped out, grabbed my arm, and roughly pulled me from the jeep. He pushed me into an arched recessed doorway and stood between me and the street. The soldiers in the following truck dove under it. The robot struck a block away, sending up a geyser of dust and debris. We felt little effect from the blast, but within moments we were covered in grey dust.

Our mission to Temploux was over. We joined the throng of people rushing to where the bomb exploded. These kinds of events were now so common that everyone knew the drill. Neighbours would search for the injured and try to locate people buried in the rubble. Time was of the essence. If a voice were heard under a pile of bricks and stone, a line would immediately form, and the debris was passed hand-to-hand and piled in the street. The dead were not immediately moved; rather, some neighbour would usually cover them with a sheet or a blanket.

We reached the scene at the same time as the residents from the neighbouring buildings. The first body I saw was a little girl, about four years old. There were no apparent injuries. Her small lungs were probably not strong enough to withstand the concussive pressure from the blast. My heart seemed to stop beating for a few seconds. I stood staring at that petite body, so much like an angel who fell from heaven; that sweet little face, her jet-black hair peeking out from her soft-shell Belgian cap. Her tiny hands were still clutching her cloth doll. I was frozen in place. Martin tried to gently pull me away, but I refused to move until a young woman covered the tiny body with half a sheet.

The next day, Major Thomson and his driver, Sergeant Kelly, took Sister Clare and me to Saint-Hubert. Martin and his driver occupied the two front seats and Sister Clare and I were wedged on the bench seat along with our two battered suitcases. I knew that as a Sister of Our Lady I should cheerfully obey orders from my superiors, but I must admit to having bittersweet feelings about leaving Namur. There was the ever-present danger from robots, of course, yet at the same time there was the challenge and the excitement of adventure in a big city. By comparison, Saint-Hubert seemed like a dullish backwater. The words of a song, popular after the Great War, came to mind, "How ya gonna keep 'em down on the farm, after they've seen Paree?"

When we reached the front gate of the convent, Sister Clare said her goodbyes to Martin and Sergeant Kelly, then went inside. I lingered for a moment. I was finding it difficult to say goodbye. There was an unexpected ache in my heart, a sense of loss. Martin shook my hand, at first with the brisk efficiency of two soldiers parting, but then he continued to hold my hand more gently. For a brief moment, he looked as if he might kiss me. I cannot say I would not have welcomed it. Martin released my hand and I rushed through the convent's gate without looking back. I never saw Martin again.[11]

CHAPTER THIRTEEN

GERMAN ARMY RETURNS

Saint-Hubert, December 1944

I WAS EAGER TO SEE ANDREE. I WAS CURIOUS TO SEE HOW MUCH SHE had matured during the months I was away in Namur.[1]

She was not in her dormitory room, however. Her roommate Mary told me Andree had left rather suddenly, just two days before, without giving her an explanation. Even after the liberation of Belgium by the Americans, Andree apparently still thought it wiser not to tell anyone, including the roommate of two years, that she was Jewish. Once again, Andree demonstrated the wisdom gained from living at a time when the threat of deportation and death is just one slip of the tongue away. Andree maybe was worried the Germans were not completely defeated and could return. Proclaiming her Jewish identity could still be dangerous to herself and the other Jewish girls in the convent. Andree's sensitivity to Mary's feelings may also have been a motive for her reticence. Mary might have been devastated by the revelation, believing Andree, her best friend, had not trusted her to keep her secret.

Sister Ursula explained Andree's sudden departure. The Jewish Resistance organisation, *Comite de Defense des Jujifs* (CDI), came to the convent and insisted Andree be released into their custody immediately. The CDI was the same organisation that was instrumental in placing Andree in the convent. The CDI had organised another group, the *L'Aide aux Israelites Victims del la Guerre* (AVG), with the mission of reuniting hidden Jews with their families. The CDI agent did not tell Sister Ursula if Andree's parents were still alive.

Sister Ursula told the CDI she would not permit Andree to leave the convent with them unless Andree chose to go. Andree was called to Sister Ursula's office. Wanting to mitigate any undue pressure from the CDI agent, she gave the agent permission to leave the room. Sister Ursula described the circumstances to Andree, emphasising that whether to leave the convent was entirely her choice. In the end, the possibility of being reunited with her family overcame any anxieties she had about leaving the security of the convent. Andree packed her few belongings and left within the hour. Before leaving, however, Andree gave Sister Ursula a sealed envelope with "Sister Christina" written on the outside.

Knowing the letter was from Andree, I took it to my room to read. It was written in French. Here is the rough translation.

Dear Sister Christina,

I am sorry I have no time to write a longer letter to you, but I only have a few minutes before I have to leave the convent on a quest to find my family. Even if I had more time to write, it would be impossible to express in words my deep appreciation for all you have done for me. You saved my life, showered me with kindness and gave me your love when all those I had loved in life were taken from me. I will never forget you.

I love you.

Please pray for me and my family,

Andree

On December 3, 1944, gaps opened in my life. Two friends gone. At the same time, I was so thankful to be a member of the Sisters of Our Lady community. I believed those empty spaces would be filled by the love of God, the love of Blessed Julie, and the love of my fellow sisters.

Life in Saint-Hubert appeared to be returning to normal. Stores and shops were open. Thanks to the largesse of the American Army, and an influx of food and clothing coming from America, no one was going to bed hungry. The winter coats arriving in large boxes were especially appreciated because the weather had turned icebox cold and snowy. People were out on the streets, not cowering in their cellars. Our school was operating at nearly full capacity. I was back teaching agricultural classes, not running around in jeeps. The routine of Mass, prayers, rosary, and evening family time was comforting. We stopped listening to the BBC since Belgian stations were back on the air.

Although the front line was only twenty miles to the east, a sense of complacency filled the air. The tranquillity was shattered on December 6 at 3:00 p.m. with the sounds of V-1 rockets exploding nearby. The first explosions were followed by the terrible sound of silence. One of the rockets exploded near the convent. Several sisters were busy cleaning up after the noon meal. The boarding students were in the sewing room or in the dormitories while the day students were in their classrooms preparing a program for the Feast of St. Catherine. A choking cloud of dust filled the air. The tinkling sound of breaking glass provided an eerie musical background. The furniture waltzed around the room. Clothes closets were toppled, spewing habits, tunics, and veils across the floor.

Sister Clare and I ran through the laundry and across the garden to the girls' dormitory. We were met by a pandemonium of piercing screams. It seemed as if every girl's face was covered in blood. The explosion sent thousands of sharp shards of glass flying through the rooms. One girl had a large piece of glass in her eye. She begged Sister Clare to remove it, which of course Sister Clare could not do without greater risk to the eye.

Sister Clare took charge, trying to wrest some sort of order out of the chaos. The slightly wounded were sent to the upper play- ground while the more serious cases were dispatched to the parlours, where American doctors were arriving. The rumour that the rocket made a direct hit on the school spread like wildfire through Saint-Hubert. Weeping, grieving families besieged the school, looking for their children.

The school building was actually spared the worst damage from the explosion. The V-1 ploughed into the house of Marie Rondeau, just on the other side of the Church of St. Giles rectory. Marie's family, husband, child, and grandfather were all killed instantly.

St. Giles Church absorbed much of the blast that would have otherwise struck our school filled with children. The rectory of the church was in shambles. The dean's woodcutter died in his toolshed. Stunned girls stood in the street. One had a towel draped over one shoulder while holding a comb in her hand, her hair still wet from washing. Another girl must have been shining her shoes. She had a shoe in one hand and a shoe brush in the other.

Except for broken windows, the convent, including our sleeping quarters, the refectory, and the kitchen were largely unscathed. Men carrying stretchers asked to use our kitchen as a private place to identify the bodies. A crowd huddled outside waiting to learn if one of their missing family members were among the dead. The five bodies that were brought into the kitchen were not immediately recognisable. Their scalps, facial skin, and all their clothing had been stripped from their bodies by the force of the explosion. One body was still wearing a single white shoe. It was the shoe that provided the first clue to his identification. A woman had gone to the butcher shop in the morning and saw a man wearing similar white shoes.

A messenger arrived from the Poix stationmaster with good news. The stationmaster would send a special tram to be used in evacuating the pupils, but we had to hurry. It was urgent. Everyone set to work. Again, Sister Clare took charge. The few day students that remained helped the boarders pack their valises with whatever could be salvaged. In less than half an hour the school was empty. Is there a more forlorn feeling than the deafening silence of classrooms devoid of students?

It was only after the safe removal of the children that Sister Ursula had an opportunity to assess the damage. Shattered glass lay everywhere. In the school, not a pane of glass remained in a window frame. All the doors were off their hinges. The convent suffered many broken windows, opening up the interior to the cold wind. Many generous neighbours offered us lodging for the night, but Sister Ursula decided we would not abandon our home, especially with looters on the street, scurrying around the damaged buildings stealing whatever they could. Several looters tried breaking into our cellar, only to meet Sister Brigid, who is six feet tall, holding an impressive cudgel. Armed with hammers, nails, and some hastily found curtains, we covered many of the broken windows in the convent. Planks were nailed over broken doors. It was midnight before the music of hammers on nails ended in the neighbourhood. Although the cold was intense, we slept the sleep of the dead, burrowed under piles of blankets.

As a semblance order was being restored the day after the attack, prayers of gratitude filled our hearts, for not a single one of our students had died in the attack. There could have been scores of students killed if the V-1 had hit fifty yards to the west. Blessed Julie, our Foundress, must have been watching over them. Her intervention might also explain why the Abbot of the nearby monastery arrived the next day with twenty strong young men in tow, including several black-robed brothers. They took on the temporary repair of the classroom building. All the debris of broken glass and fallen plaster was swept up, boards nailed over the windows, and doors rehung on new hinges. One pane of glass was put into each window, and a gap was left in the covering boards to allow some natural light into the classrooms. We actually managed to begin classes the next morning for the day students.

Sister Julie's protection was evident in our *Oratoire*, too. Her statue was the only thing left standing in a room filled with fallen plaster and displaced furniture. Blessed Julie's protection extended to the rooms of the boarding students and the convent. Not one picture of Blessed Julie was damaged.

I am not sure, but Blessed Julie may have had something to do with the convoy of American jeeps and trucks driving up to our front gate in the late afternoon of December 10, 1944.[2]

Hundreds cheering and whistling American soldiers escorted the convoy. Colonel Davis, who was in charge of the convoy, rang the bell. Sister Ursula expected me to be the first person to meet Americans visiting the convent, so I hurried to the front gate.

Colonel Davis asked if the convent could accommodate an important guest for the night, Marlene Dietrich. The Colonel seemed surprised, maybe a little hurt, by my calm reaction to his request. Frankly, at that point in time, I had no idea who Marlene Dietrich was. I assumed by her name that Marlene was a woman. Being in a convent and in a war for most of my life restricted my ability to visit movie houses and keep current on the activities of Hollywood movie stars. The Sisters of Our Lady were hardly in a position to refuse a request by the US Army. It had sacrificed so much liberating Belgium and then supplying us with mountains of food and clothing.

I told Colonel Davis we would do what we could, but that our accommodations were rather spartan. He said Miss Dietrich had endured more rugged lodgings and that the convent was more secure than other locations. In my ignorance, I asked him if she needed protection from the Germans. He laughed. "No, she needs protection from being mobbed by American soldiers." He assumed the convent walls and the presence of us sisters would deter all but the most ardent fans.

Marlene's jeep was obvious. "Marlene Dietrich" was emblazoned on the side. But where was Marlene? There were only three soldiers in the jeep, two large sergeants in the front and a short captain in the back, made to look even smaller next to the large .45 caliber pistol strapped to his hip.

As General Davis and I approached the jeep, the captain stood up and pulled off his helmet, releasing a cascade of blonde hair. The captain was not a "he." A huge cheer burst forth. Never have I seen so many grinning soldiers. That cheer paled in comparison to the roar that followed. It was like a shock wave. Some very loud soldier had yelled, "Show us some leg, Marlene!" With an all-knowing smile, Marlene firmly planted her army boot on the back of the driver's seat and slowly pulled her trouser leg above her knee. Pandemonium reigned. I was amazed at the awesome power a woman could wield over men. Before a riot could break out, the MPs created an escape cordon for Marlene between the jeep and the convent gate.

As soon as we entered the convent, Marlene whispered to me, "I'm exhausted, but I'd give anything for a shower. I haven't had one in two weeks." I told her I had no idea what a shower looked like or how it worked. All bathing in a convent was done in one bathtub. Marlene's look of disappointment motivated me to ask Colonel Davis about the possibility of constructing a shower for Marlene. He asked Captain Mulligan of the Army Corp of Engineers if it could be done.

Captain Mulligan said the "shower head" problem could be easily solved by punching holes in a large food tin and hoisting it over the head of Marlene while she stood in the convent bathtub. The food tin would need to be kept filled with hot water. The tin, however, would only hold five gallons of water, and according to his quick calculations a decent shower, lasting ten minutes, would use at least twenty gallons of water. He assumed Marlene wanted a shower lasting longer than a couple of minutes. The much bigger challenge, Captain Mulligan said, was figuring out how to keep the food tin from running out of hot water in the middle of Marlene's shower. He proposed a Rube Goldberg concoction of pipes and water chutes that would take hours to construct, assuming the materials were readily available, which they weren't.

Sister Clare laughed and told Captain Martin he was "over-engineering" the problem. I had no idea what Sister Clare meant. I had never heard the term before, but Captain Martin acted like he knew the meaning of the phrase. His frown suggested he did not appreciate getting engineering advice from a nun. His frown did not deter Sister Clare. She said the problem was not much different from keeping up a supply of hot water in her family's cold water flat on a Saturday night with six kids taking baths. All you needed were several buckets, a large washtub, and a bathtub.

Sister Clare explained how the one bathtub in our convent was hidden behind a screen in the laundry room. During most of the week the room was used for washing clothes and linen. A stove in the laundry room, burning wood or coal, was used to heat a large twenty-gallon cauldron of water. At the same time, it kept the room cozy, even in the middle of winter. The very hot water was transferred in buckets from the cauldron to even larger washing tubs where the laundry was scrubbed. The only difference in the drill on bath night was that the water in the washtub was periodically poured into the porcelain-covered cast iron bathtub. Used bathtub water was drained through the plug in the bottom of the bathtub after each bath. Therefore, Sister Clare continued, we only had to put the scalding water from the stove in a washtub, cool it a bit with cold water, scoop up the hot water from the washtub in a large bucket and pour it into the perforated food tin. The tricky part of the procedure was someone had to stand on a stepladder to dump the water into the imitation shower head. As an afterthought, Sister Clare suggested it would make the process go more smoothly if one sister was in charge of keeping the temperature of the water in the washtub constant, and another sister scooped the water out of the washtub and handed the bucket to the sister perched on the stepladder.

Besides its simplicity, another advantage of Sister Clare's solution was that it did not require American soldiers entering the more secluded areas of the convent to construct the shower. We sisters could do the job. I used a four-inch spike to hammer holes into the bottom of the food tin and then drove the same spike into the beam above the porcelain bathtub. The food tin shower head was suspended from the spike. The bath was already hidden behind an eight-foot screen, so Marlene had complete privacy while using the shower. While I was fixing up the pseudo shower, several buckets and a tall stepladder were rounded up, and a fire lit in the stove. Sister Brigid began heating the twenty-gallon cauldron.

When the water was hot, but not boiling, Sister Brigid gingerly scooped up several buckets of water and poured them into the washtub. Marlene stepped behind the screen to undress. Sister Clare used cold water to reduce the hot water to a temperature that was toasty warm. She had to make a rough calculation of how much heat the water would lose as it was transferred in cool metal buckets to the food tin shower head and then estimate how much more heat would be lost pouring the water into the food tin. Sister Angela decided to use her hand as a temperature gauge. If she plunged her hand in the water and could not keep it there, it was too hot. Just enough cold water was added to make having her hand in the water tolerable. My task was to stand on the stepladder, lift the bucket over the partition and pour the hot water into the food tin. Sister Brigid would rapidly hand me the full buckets so I could keep the water pouring out of the food tin.

When Marlene said she was ready, I poured in the first bucket and held my breath. Would it be too cold or too hot? When Marlene sighed, *"Wunderbar,"* we knew we had the temperature just right. The hot water lasted about ten minutes. I warned Marlene when I had poured in the last bucket. She said everything was fine and thanked us profusely. Then we left the laundry room.

Fifteen minutes later Marlene stepped into the refectory wearing a crisp freshly laundered army uniform. Her face was still glowing from the warmth of the shower, her lovely, bright, golden hair flowing down to the collar of her uniform. There was a collective gasp from the officers in the room.

Marlene sat in the middle of the long table. The sisters, including Sister Ursula, occupied one end of the table and the soldiers filled in the remaining places. I sat next to Marlene so I could translate what she and the soldiers said into French for the Belgian sisters. Marlene thanked Sister Ursula for her hospitality and the wonderful shower, but quipped that her movie career might be ruined if it ever became known she had spent time in a convent.

The US Army made sure the convent's larder would not be depleted by feeding so many guests. While we were busy arranging the shower for Marlene, an Army truck unloaded enough food for—well, an army.

Army cooks took over the convent kitchen and created a feast. The menu included Virginia cured ham, mashed potatoes, yams, cream corn, green beans, and mounds of fresh bread. Perhaps Blessed Julie played a role in the dessert course, because it seemed like a miracle to us—chocolate ice cream. The same truck also held cases of liquor, wine, and beer. Sister Ursula, however, drew the line with alcohol entering the convent. She was not loath to bend some of Blessed Julie's rules to help the war effort, but she was not going to sanction a complete abandonment of the "no alcohol" decree.

During dinner, Marlene bantered with the soldiers. For every quip they threw at her she returned a jibe that was more astute and more barbed. In the few quieter moments during the dinner, I asked Marlene how she managed to find herself entertaining American soldiers just a few miles from the front line. Her short response was, "*aus Anstand*"—out of decency. She "*verabscheut*" (detested) the Nazis.

In 1937, one of Hitler's minions had invited Marlene back to Germany to make German movies, promising to make her an idol of the German people. As an extra inducement, he hinted the Führer himself was eager for her to return to the Fatherland. Marlene said she had no intention of accepting the offer, but could not resist taunting a Nazi.

She promised to return to Germany on one condition. Her long-time director, Jonas Sternberg, an Austrian-born Jew, must be hired to direct her German movies. After some angry, unintelligible muttering, Hitler's offer was withdrawn.

Marlene said she considered it an honour when her films were subsequently banned in Germany. As the number of Jews and dissidents fleeing Germany after 1937 became a deluge, Marlene raised money to help them escape and find countries that would accept them. She donated her entire salary from her movie *Knight Without Armour* for the resettlement of the refugees.

By 1939, her German citizenship was an emotional burden she could no longer bear. Marlene refused to accept the fiction that the German people bore no responsibility for the Nazi atrocities. She renounced her German citizenship and became a US citizen. When America entered the war after the attack on Pearl Harbor, Marlene threw herself into supporting the war effort. She travelled the country selling war bonds and entertaining troops that were destined for overseas service.

The Office of Strategic Services (OSS) for the United States Army recruited Marlene to help make musical propaganda broadcasts designed to demoralise German soldiers. Songs like "Lili Marlene" reminded German soldiers about missing their homes and forsaken lovers. In 1943, Marlene decided the troops that most needed a boost in morale were those soldiers who were actually on the front line doing most of the fighting and dying. From then on, she focused on entertaining soldiers who were often within range of the German guns.

I imagined the shock of a muddy, exhausted GI hunching in a fox hole when a beautiful, blonde, blue-eyed woman, dressed in an equally muddy army uniform, asked to share his shallow pit in the ground. Marlene seemed oblivious to the danger of being within striking distance of German forces.

I asked her what would happen if she were captured by a German patrol and Hitler had her transported back to Berlin?

Marlene flashed a mischievous smile and replied, "That is a risk Herr Hitler will just have to take."

It became obvious to me that even Marlene's prodigious energy level was ebbing. She was ready for the evening to end. She shouted to the soldiers, "Okay, boys, time for you to go home. I need my beauty rest."

There were moans of disappointment and comments about how Marlene's beauty was eternal, all of which she ignored. There was a plea, however, from Colonel Davis for her to sing "Lili Marlene." Although it was a German song, American soldiers loved its melancholy mood, which never failed to evoke memories of home and the girl left behind. Marlene climbed onto the table and sang "Lili Marlene" *a cappella*. She stopped after each verse so I could translate the words, although I thought my English translation detracted from the beauty of the music.

Outside the barracks, by the corner light I'll always stand and wait for you at night We will create a world for two I'll wait for you the whole night through

For you, Lili Marlene, For you, Lili Marlene, Bugler tonight don't play the call to arms I want another evening with her charms

Then we will say goodbye and part I'll always keep you in my heart With me, Lili Marlene, With me, Lili Marlene

Give me a rose to show how much you care Tie to the stem a lock of golden hair

Surely tomorrow, you'll feel blue But then will come a love that's new For you, Lili Marlene

For you, Lili Marlene

When Marlene stepped down from the table there was a moment of poignant silence, giving time for quite a few soldiers to wipe the tears from their eyes. Then the room filled with cheers and applause. Marlene knew how to make a dramatic exit. She marched out of the refectory like the soldier she was.

The next morning, we were startled when Marlene, dressed in a fresh army uniform, appeared at morning Mass. She obviously knew a lot about Catholic ritual, reciting many of the liturgical Latin responses. The army's continued largesse was evident at breakfast. Marlene joined us for a feast of fresh eggs, bacon, ham, warm bread, canned peaches, and real coffee. Marlene thanked Sister Ursula for her warm hospitality and especially for the hot shower. She told us she would give a performance in the Basilique des Saints-Pierre-et-Paul at noon, and then her convoy would take her to Echternach, a Belgian town near the border with Luxembourg. I could not restrain myself from whispering, "How did you manage to get permission to use the *Basilique* for your show?" Marlene laughed and said she imagined General Gavin of the 101st Airborne Division might have asked the bishop for his blessing. She added that even the Catholic hierarchy would be reluctant to deny a request from the Americans who were shedding their blood to liberate Belgium.

At 11:00 a.m. Marlene was ready to take her jeep the short distance to the *Basilique*. She was still dressed in her US Army captain's uniform. As another example of how being in the middle of a war can induce even Sister Superiors to bend the rules, Sister Ursula gave all of us permission to attend Marlene's performance. In fact, Marlene asked Colonel Davis to reserve two rows of seats in the front of the stage for us. We must have been quite a spectacle walking down the Rue des Pres behind Marlene's jeep like a black-robed phalanx of Praetorian Guards. When the procession reached the Place de l'Abbaye in front of the *Basilique*, Marlene's jeep turned down the Rue de la Teinture, which leads to the rear of the *Basilique*.

Waiting for us was a squad of MPs to escort us into the church. The extraordinary day became stranger still when a sea of soldiers parted as we sisters entered the church and the MPs led us to our front-row seats, all while hundreds of GIs welcomed us with boisterous cheering. A temporary wooden stage had been hastily built overnight by army engineers in the middle of the nave, immediately in front of the high altar. The stage was flanked by two huge sculptures, each surrounded by four Greek columns. A statue of Mary was on the left, looking on with an expression of beatific bemusement. The faces of the saints' statues on the right were frozen either in shock or wide-eyed enthusiasm, not much different than those on the eager animated faces of the soldiers.

Marlene came into the church unseen through the Sacristy door. She emerged from the Sacristy and moved slowly and sinuously up the three steps to the makeshift stage.

Although the December weather made it chilly, Marlene appeared oblivious to the cold in her low-cut sequined gown and high-heeled shoes. She sauntered up to the microphone, temporarily installed by the army engineers, and struck a provocative pose. Her sultry "Hello, boys!" was greeted by a cacophony of cheers and whistles. Marlene was a one-woman vaudeville show, a singer, a comic, a musician, a pin-up girl, and cheerleader.

After a few songs Marlene announced that she had the ability to read minds. She summoned a private in the third row to come on stage. One could not picture a happier man. She leaned her head near the soldier's forehead and told him to focus on whatever he was thinking about, putting all other thoughts out of his mind.

There was a pause of ten-seconds while Marlene, with a knitted brow, hovering near kissing distance of the soldier's cheek, concentrated on reading what was on the soldier's mind. Then she pulled back with a shocked expression, immediately followed by a mischievous smile. With an obvious stage nod toward us sisters in the front row, she told the soldier, "Oh, think of something else. I can't possibly talk about *that*!" We could not help laughing along with the howls of the GIs.

Comedy was followed by serious music, namely "Amazing Grace," except that Marlene provided her rendition of the melody on a crosscut saw. Another advantage, as far as the men were concerned, was that playing the saw required her to hike up her skirt, once again displaying the legs that launched a thousand sighs. The wooden handle of the saw was wedged under her right thigh and the body of the saw was bent over her left leg. With her left hand, Marlene bent up the tip of the saw blade. In her right hand was a bass fiddle bow. She stroked it up and down across the teeth of the saw. She jiggled the saw with her right leg while at the same time increasing or decreasing the bend of the blade. The saw actually produced a sweet melodic tune that sounded like "Amazing Grace"—most of the time. I'm sure the GIs hardly noticed the few sour notes.

The final act was guaranteed to bring the house down. Marlene sang "Lili Marlene" as only she could sing it. The applause, cheers, and whistles were deafening. The show was not quite over, however. Marlene knew how exit a stage. She retired for a few minutes to the Sacristy, returning to the stage in her captain's uniform, carrying her helmet, .45 caliber side-arm, and her Army boots.

She first stuffed her blonde locks into her helmet, then strapped on her side-arm. She sat on the edge of the stage, pulled on the boots by raising her leg high in the air, which obliged her, of course, to display the calves of those famous limbs. Finally, Marlene stood militarily erect on the centre of the stage, gave the soldiers a crisp salute and then hurried off to her jeep, waiting outside the Sacristy door with its motor running.

As we were leaving the *Basilique*, I could not help thinking about all the soldiers in the church who would probably not survive the war. The Latin phrase above the *Basilique's* imposing entrance took on more meaning; *"Amore non Timore"*—"Love not Fear." For a few brief moments Marlene did make love and joy oust fear.

CHAPTER FOURTEEN

LIBERATION REDUX

Saint-Hubert, January 1945

OUR CELEBRATION OF LIBERATION LASTED ONLY A FEW MORE DAYS. On December 16, the German army launched a massive attack against eastern Belgium. The invasion caught the Americans by complete surprise, especially the location of the onslaught.

The US generals thought it impossible for German tanks, troops, and trucks to manoeuvre through the rugged hills and dense forests of the Ardennes Mountains. They were wrong. Two hundred thousand German soldiers quickly broke through the lightly defended American lines. In Saint-Hubert, the onslaught was announced by a barrage of V-1 buzz bombs. There was no warning and no time to take shelter during the first wave of rockets. Hundreds were killed and wounded. For the rest of the day the citizens of Saint-Hubert huddled in their cellars. Some sought the protection of our cellars in the school and convent, probably the deepest in the town.

The very erratic, inaccurate nature of the V-1 buzz rockets terrified us more than typical bombs. Bombs often went "off-target" and fell on houses, schools, and hospitals. The bombs dropped by

British and American bombers unintentionally obliterated wide swaths of our cities and towns, causing far greater destruction than the damage caused by a few V-1 rockets. Somehow, British and American bombs seemed more benign. We assumed Allied bombs falling on us meant liberation was that much closer.

Our assumption that American bombs were dropped with good intent also made us more forgiving when bombs meant for bridges, rail yards, and military targets destroyed a house, an apartment building, or even a school. The only intent behind the rain of unguided V-1s was to kill innocent men, women, and children. If they actually hit a bridge or a rail yard, it was pure accident.

Knowing the Allied airmen were not trying to hit us while we crouched in our cellars made us feel more secure. Not true, of course. Unlike Allied bombers that dropped leaflets warning of bombing raids, the V-1s arrived with only a few seconds' notice. It was not enough time to take shelter. Waiting for the explosion, your terror lasted for an eternity.

The danger from both the V-1s and the bombs loomed bigger every day. All day long a stream of refugees passed our door. There were men, women, and children struggling with bundles too heavy to carry that would soon be abandoned by the side of the road. Most evacuees walked. There were some with bicycles and carts, and rarely an automobile. The exodus mimicked the flight of the Belgians during the first invasion by the Germans in 1940.

One of the V-1s hit very close to the school building being used by the American Army as a hospital. Casualties were light, but the damage to the structure made it unusable as a hospital. General Davis expected the bombardment would only increase, and that if the German advance approached Saint-Hubert, the V-1s would be replaced by more accurate artillery fire. Therefore, he ordered the hospital operations to be moved underground.

Our deep cellars were an obvious location. General Davis could have requisitioned our buildings and cellars for the hospital, requiring all the sisters and others taking refuge to leave. Instead, he asked Sister Ursula for her permission to move the hospital into one wing of the cellar under the school. We sisters would still be able to occupy the other wing. Sister Ursula did not hesitate. She not only agreed to the extraordinary living arrangements of nuns sharing quarters with soldiers, she also volunteered us to care for and feed the wounded.[1]

As the German invasion gathered momentum, the number of wounded increased every day. The soldiers who could be safely transported west were moved farther away from the front in ambulances, trucks, and jeeps. The more seriously wounded cases were kept in Saint-Hubert until they regained enough strength to endure the trek to Brussels.

The GIs were surprised to find an American sister from Ohio tending to their wounds. Our common bond made them eager to talk about home, sweethearts, and sometimes the war. Almost all information about the German attack was censored. Even the reliable BBC provided only vague optimistic descriptions of what was happening in Belgium. German broadcasts, of course, touted the imminent collapse of the Allied armies and the reoccupation of Belgium. Therefore, it was from the soldiers I tried to learn what was happening.

A wounded sergeant described German infiltrators in American uniforms who were roaming through the countryside. I believe he was trying to frighten me just a bit, perhaps thinking I was a sheltered nun who knew little about the dangers of war. I let him have his bit of fun. I did not tell him about the four years we had lived with German soldiers swarming our streets while Gestapo and SD troops invaded our homes, shooting anyone they pleased. When he realised I was impervious to this kind of teasing, he told me there really was not too much to worry about from infiltrators. He said most of them were incompetent spies. Their English was poor, and they might as well have hung signs on themselves saying, "I am not an American soldier."

He described how one group of four phony medical officers in a jeep was stopped at a checkpoint by suspicious MPs. Four officers in a jeep was the first hint something was amiss, since that would be a rare sight. They were not wearing combat boots, but they were wearing side-arms, which medical officers are forbidden to carry. A few questions about baseball quickly unmasked the imposters. After being interrogated, they were imprisoned in a barn. The German officers were entertained in the evening by previously captured German nurses singing German Christmas carols. The next morning, the four officers were shot.[2]

A trickle of optimism began to emerge from the initial surge of gloom when it was rumoured that the German advance was stymied by the resistance of the American soldiers in Bastogne. Our hopefulness evaporated when the next rumour was that the German army was bypassing Bastogne on both sides of the town. It did not take a military genius to conclude that the two arms of the German pincer movement would be aimed directly at Saint-Hubert.

Shortly after the circulation of the latest rumour, a severely wounded soldier, Lieutenant Lowery, asked to speak with me. I did not consider his request unusual at the time. When I sat by Lieutenant Lowry's cot, he appeared especially agitated. He had been shot in his left arm and right leg and was suffering the after-effects of frostbite. He said his wounds were painful, but he had to be evacuated from Saint-Hubert as soon as possible. I assured him he would probably be on his way to Brussels in a few days when his wounds had healed enough to cope with the rough journey in an army truck. He said two days might be too late, and he could not risk being captured by the Germans again. "Again?" I said. The Lieutenant then told me about his capture and escape from the SS near the village of Malmedy. As best as I can remember, I will try to tell Lieutenant Lowry's story in his own words:[3]

"Panzer tanks over-ran our position. We were surrounded, so we emerged from our trenches with our hands up."

German soldiers immediately surrounded us taking our rings, watches, and cigarettes. They were particularly eager to get gloves. SS troopers with burp guns herded about 130 of us into a field sixty feet off the road within sight of the Café Bodarwé. We were packed together in eight rows. I was in the front row. Holding my hands above my head made them very cold.

I assumed we were waiting for trucks to take us to POW camps, and that my Christmas would be spent behind barbed wire. Instead of trucks, a SS officer halted two tanks and ordered them off the road with their guns pointing at us. The same officer shouted an order in German to a SS soldier. The soldier saluted, drew his pistol and shot my jeep driver standing next to me. Men in the front row tried to push themselves out of the line of fire. An American officer ordered them not to move.

Perhaps he believed if we tried to run it would give the Germans an excuse to shoot all of us. No excuse was necessary. The same SS soldier then shot a medic.

There was a shout, *"Machen alle kaput"* and the machine guns on both tanks began firing. I was not hit in the first burst of gunfire. I instinctively buried my face in the mud and tried burrowing under the bodies around me. For what seemed like an eternity the machine guns continued to shoot into our prostrate bodies. I was hit in the leg and the arm. The screams and moans of the wounded eventually stopped.

For two hours those of us who were still alive did not move. From time to time, German soldiers on passing tanks and trucks would fire a few rounds into the mass of bodies and laugh. For a while there was silence, but I still did not move. Then I heard German soldiers approaching, and there were periodic pistol shots. They were intent on finishing off any GIs who managed to survive. One soldier who spoke some English promised medical attention to the wounded. Several soldiers responded and were immediately shot. I tried desperately to control my breathing, hoping when I exhaled no steam could be seen in the freezing air. A soldier stopped nearby, and I heard his boot smash against the head of soldier. The moan from the soldier was followed by a shot from a pistol. The same German soldier stood by my head, reloading his pistol, talking and laughing. I doubted I could take a kick in the head without wincing. Miraculously, the soldier moved on, and then there was another shot.

After an hour of silence, soft whispers began emerging from apparently dead bodies, survivors trying to determine if they were alone. Just the knowledge that others were alive allowed a scrap of hope to lodge in my heart. There was murmured debate about what to do. I urged waiting until dark, but others wanted to make a run for it immediately. The dispute ended abruptly when one soldier stood up and yelled, "Let's go!" There was no choice. Twenty men rose from the dead and attempted a staggering, drunken run. Many of the men sought refuge in the nearby cafe. It promised warmth but not safety. I went into a horse shed and covered myself with straw.

A German soldier must have seen the men go into the cafe. They set fire to the building and then shot the men as they ran out to escape the flames. I waited until dark and wandered in the woods until I saw a farmhouse. There was no choice. I had to risk knocking on the farmhouse door and seek help or freeze to death in the woods. I must have appeared as a blood-soaked maniac to the old man who opened the door. In spite of my looks he took me in and sat me in a chair near the kitchen stove. After a few French words I did not understand, two of his four daughters scurried around getting me some soup and wine, while the other two washed and bandaged my wounds. The warmth revived me; I knew I was not going to die. At about three o'clock in the morning the four sisters practically carried me down a steep hillside into Malmédy where there was an American command post. I was evacuated from Malmedy to the hospital in Saint- Hubert."

When Lieutenant Lowry finished telling me about his near-death experience at the hands of his German captors, I understood why he was so desperate to leave Saint-Hubert.

I quickly sought Sister Ursula's advice. She said she would make inquiries. Within two hours, Sister Ursula told me the army would be evacuating Lieutenant Lowry the next day. When I thanked Sister Ursula for her help, she replied she had nothing to do with the decision. She said the army had already decided to evacuate Lieutenant Lowry as soon as possible. General Hodges had ordered a complete investigation of the massacre and was intending to prosecute the murderers as criminals after the war. He did not want to risk letting one of the few surviving eyewitnesses of the Malmédy massacre to fall into the hands of the German army.

Lieutenant Lowry was evacuated just in time. By December 20, the German army was pressing Saint-Hubert from two directions. V-1 rockets were replaced by artillery shells. It was one of those types of shells that killed Sister Ursula and wounded me in the leg. With the death of Sister Ursula, Sister Nathalie temporarily assumed the role of Sister Superior until such time as Mother General named a new Sister Superior for Saint- Hubert.

In the early evening of December 20, a Canadian officer came to our gate and asked for a place to rest his hundred men for the night. We offered him the classrooms in our school. After inspecting the classrooms, he said it would be a pity to disrupt the order of the rooms by shifting all the desks and chairs, so he would be happy to have his men shelter in the attic. I doubt his men were consulted about the officer's generous offer; the attic was much colder than the classrooms. In the morning, the Canadians left before eating any breakfast; they were obviously in a hurry to march away from the approaching Germans. Just before joining his men on the march, the Canadian officer admitted the Germans had already taken the nearby village of Houffalyse. At the same time, he offered some reassurance, declaring authoritatively, "Bastogne would never surrender!"

At 2:00 a.m. on December 21, two men dressed as monks came to our door seeking shelter. They said they were from the Beau-Plateau Monastery and were fleeing from the rapidly advancing German army. After hearing all the stories about disguised German soldiers infiltrating behind the lines, I was sceptical. My doubt increased when they asked if they could say Mass—in the middle of the night? A few questions in Latin, however, quickly eased my anxiety, and we offered our hospitality. It was obvious to us that the Americans were abandoning Saint-Hubert without a fight. I suppose their decision to escape was justified by military necessity. That rationale, though, did not assuage the fears of the citizens of Saint-Hubert who were left behind. All the local men fled the town and went into hiding, a few making use of the hiding places in our convent where we used to hide fugitives during the earlier German occupation.

The Army's precipitous flight also meant the severely wounded American soldiers, along with the doctor and medics who volunteered to stay and care for them, were abandoned to their fates. The last American I saw was late in the afternoon on December 21. He was racing down Nestor Martin Avenue in a jeep toward the road to Namur. Several minutes later he was walking back up the street with his arms raised above his head, his jeep being driven by a German soldier.

The German army did not arrive in great numbers until after midnight. We could hear the rumble of truck engines, the clanking of tank treads, and we could feel the ground vibrate. Windows in the shops were soon broken by looters. If doors to homes were not immediately opened, they were shattered by heavy blows from rifle butts, followed by soldiers snatching not just food and alcohol, but anything that took their fancy like clothes, pillows, or ceramic figurines.

All the sisters descended into the cellars except Sister Agnes and me. We went to the parlour to wait for the inevitable arrival of the Germans. To calm our nerves, we began reciting the rosary. We were expecting heavy blows on the door by the German soldiers, so we were unprepared, and more alarmed, by the gentle, discreet tapping we heard. We opened the door, and a stocky young man burst into the room pleading for a place to hide. He was incoherent, muttering how the Germans had killed all his friends, but he had escaped. He said his name was Leon Praile from the village of Saint-Ode, ten miles east of Saint-Hubert. We expected German soldiers to appear at any minute, so there was no time for Leon to relate his full story. Sister Clare hurried him down to the cellar. She also supplied him with a new set of clothes.

Shortly after Sister Agnes returned from the cellar, there was a hammer-like pounding on the door, probably the butt end of a rifle. I feigned what I hoped was my most inscrutable expression, slowly opened the door, and asked them in German, "What do you want, gentlemen?" The Germans' fatigued faces showed they desperately wanted food and shelter. Poor exhausted men—just boys, really. They had been marching for five days and nights without stopping. Their uniforms were soaked and muddied up to their hips. They did not look like warriors seeking the mythical glories of war; they might have been happy to swap their weapons for fire, coffee, food, and a dry place to rest. We called the sisters up from the cellar, and we spent the night scurrying to supply them with food and real coffee. As a precaution, I told Major Weber, who seemed to be in charge of the crowd, about the wounded Americans and medical personnel in one part of the cellar. He told three soldiers with burp guns to go with him to the cellar, where he declared the Americans were now prisoners-of-war. German soldiers were posted as sentries.[4]

Ironically, the invasion of the convent by these heavily armed German soldiers lessened the fear of death that had haunted me since Sister Ursula was killed in the cellar, and I was struck down by a piece of hot shrapnel. Seeing these exhausted teenage soldiers sprawling on the floor assured me it was just a matter of time, and a brief time at that, before the American Army would retake Saint-Hubert. Those children masquerading as storm troopers represented the Nazi's last gasp. Of course, there was still danger from American bombs and shells, but we knew the Americans would not intentionally target civilians. Finally, my faith in accepting God's all-seeing plan and that Blessed Julie was extending her protection over the order she founded was rekindled. If my death were foreordained, there was nothing I could do about it.

The next day, Leon Praile had calmed down enough to tell me what happened in Saint-Ode. Leon said he had just emerged from the village's little stone church after Mass when he and most of the men over seventeen years old were rounded up by the SD (Sicherheitsdienst), the security branch of the SS. An officer said they were only doing an identity check, and everybody would be home for dinner. They were then herded into an old sawmill. A German officer grilled Leon about a Resistance group, the Armee Secrete. The SD suspected the Armee had killed several German soldiers not far from the village.

In the gathering dusk, people from the village congregated outside the sawmill with coats and food, not meant for the prisoners, but as bribes for the Germans. The Germans graciously accepted the gifts, but refused to release the men. Leon did manage to exchange a few words with his fiancée before the men were divided into two groups, those over thirty-two and those under thirty-two.

Leon and the other younger men were ordered out of the sawmill and told to line up in three rows. All their pocketbooks, money, rings, watches, and even rosaries were stolen. Leon assumed they were fated to join the ranks of so many other young Belgian men who had been transported into Germany to work in factories. As he and the other young men were marched down the road with their hands on top of their heads, Leon's fiancée called out to him that she loved him.

Once out of sight of the village, the men were ordered to halt beside a burned-out cottage reduced to four walls surrounding a cellar. The SD soldiers pushed the men into three lines with their backs to the house. Then a guard abruptly grabbed the shoulder of the last man in the first row and steered him to the doorway of the house. He was looking down into his own grave. After a shot to the back of the head the man tumbled forward into the cellar. The first man was quickly followed one at a time by a second, third, fourth, and fifth man.

Leon was the eighth man chosen. Leon said he knew the only way any of them would survive would be for all the men to break and run at the same time. They just needed some spark to break their sheep-like thrall. Leon hoped to supply that spark. A sergeant held Leon's shoulder, almost gently guiding him to the doorway. Leon saw tears on the man's face. Leon knew this was the moment. He wrenched himself free of the sergeant's light grip and smashed his fist into the sergeant's face, dropping the German to his knees. During the momentary confusion, Leon sprinted across the road, leaped a hedge, crossed a little stream, and plunged into the gloomy woods with bullets flying around him. His wet clothes froze solid during the night, but he resisted the temptation to leave the protection of the dense woods. By the grace of God, he survived. He could not locate the American lines, so Leon sneaked into Saint-Hubert and knocked on our convent door, assuming correctly we would not turn him away.[5]

Major Weber broke down the doors of the Basilica, saying he wanted to use the bells to warn of air raids by Allied planes. I explained the Basilica's bells had not rung for years, having been confiscated by the German army during their earlier occupation of Saint-Hubert. I smiled and said the bells might even be in some of the cannon they brought with them.

The next day placards in French and Flemish were posted all over the town. "No one will be allowed on the street after 5:00 p.m. without a pass signed by Major Weber." "All the potatoes are ours." The sign "All the livestock are ours" explained why all our chickens had vanished from the hen house. "Tomorrow, all positions at the city hall will be filled by members of the Wehrmacht." When British and American bombs began falling on the city, a new placard went up. "All doors must remain open" to allow soldiers to take cover in the nearest house.

A Panzer tank rammed through the beautiful iron gate leading to our orchard. The fruit trees were uprooted when a dozen camouflaged tanks and half-tracks were parked among the stumps. About fifty soldiers were with the vehicles. Some were tank drivers and gunners. The rest were infantrymen assigned to protect the tanks in battle.

We were surprised the soldiers did not search and loot our convent buildings. Was it once again some vestige of respect for religious orders that deterred Major Weber from treating us like he treated the other citizens of Saint-Hubert? We did not assume, however, such forbearance would last. We moved most of our food supplies, including a large supply of recently baked bread, into the attic. Our flour was poured into buckets, carried to the attic and pushed under the eaves. It all was hidden behind a pile of old broken furniture and what can only be described as junk. The effectiveness of our camouflage was never tested. The Germans did not have the time, energy or inclination to make extensive searches of buildings. They were far too busy trying to defend Saint-Hubert from the counter-attacking American Army and Air Corps.

While moving our food stock into the attic, we could hear the American planes flying close overhead. We could not resist taking turns poking our heads through the skylight to watch them soar by just a few hundred feet above the convent, seemingly oblivious to all the sputtering anti-aircraft guns trying to bring them down. When I took my turn peeking through the skylight, just watching them lifted my spirits. I saw two of the American planes fly by and then circle back. They were so graceful. The pilots were aiming their planes right at me. I was preparing to wave when their machine guns began blazing away at the German tanks in our garden. Some of the bullets ricocheted off our slate roof.

When all the German soldiers ran into the refectory, I knew why they were heading for the safety of the cellar. I pulled my head from the skylight and shouted to the other Sisters, "Drop everything and get to the cellar!" I realised the next time the planes returned to attack the German tanks in the garden, they would be dropping bombs. Before we reached the first landing, bombs were exploding, and there were four flights of stairs to go. Time stood still. Would we ever reach the cellar? How far away it seemed. The building shook, with plaster falling from the ceiling, windows blown apart, and doors coming unhinged. Mercifully, the bombardment stopped shortly after we reached the cellar. We did a quick count, and realised six sisters were missing. I feared the worst, but Blessed Julie was still protecting us. The missing six sisters stumbled into the cellar, covered with dust, but with no serious injuries.

The damage from the bombing to the convent and school was less than expected. No bombs directly hit either building. Many windows and doors were hanging loose. Walls were full of holes where the plaster gave way. The garden was a moonscape with a half-dozen bomb craters. Several German tanks were destroyed or damaged. Houses just outside the garden had been destroyed by errant bombs.

During the first days of the second occupation, we sisters tried living in the refectory, but the frequent bombing raids by the Allies drove us into the cellars many times a day. Sometimes we had to descend into the cellar several times during one meal. It was awkward, though, to find the German soldiers having beaten us to the shelter. Sisters would lie on the floor along one wall, Germans would lie along the opposite wall, and the wounded American prisoners-of-war would occupy another portion of the cellar. The German army could not spare the trucks to move the prisoners to POW camps in Germany.[6]

The only feasible solution was for the sisters to take up permanent residence in the basement shelter. Two trestles and a long plank served as a table. Purified water was available. The fruit cellar was well-stocked with apples. We had our hidden supply of bread, which had been baked originally for the boarding students. For twenty-three days, we and the wounded ate the bread and apples. During a lull in the bombing, the sisters who were cooking would rush up to the kitchen to throw together a skimpy but hot meal. Bed springs and mattresses were placed on the concrete racks that had held our supply of potatoes, long gone. No services were taking place in the chapel, so we had a good supply of candles. They were our only light source, day or night.

Over a few days, a bizarre cellar community developed among the four very disparate groups: German soldiers, American soldiers, nuns, and refugees. In the outside world their fellow citizens might be trying their best to kill each other, but inside the shared shelter, protecting them from the rain of bombs, peace and tranquility reigned. Foes became—not friends, but fellow sufferers. A German sentry guarding the wounded American prisoners might employ his broken English to chat with a GI who would reciprocate the friendly gesture by offering a cigarette. The American doctor would stitch and bandage wounded German soldiers, while a German medic often changed the bandages on wounded Americans.[7]

Although the falling bombs and artillery shells threatened all our lives, they were also messengers of hope for the Belgians and the Americans. The more the bombardment intensified, closer came the day of Saint-Hubert's liberation.

I was able to move freely among the Americans and the Germans in the cellar. The Americans were keen on conversing with an American woman even if she was wearing a nun's habit. I could speak their language. I could speak German, so some of the German soldiers seemed to feel the same.[8]

Since we sisters and the soldiers shared the same cellar during Allied bombardments, there was ample opportunity for me to talk with them. Most soldiers are eager to talk about the same things: home, family, and girlfriends.

The exception was Frantz Neidert, a fifteen-year-old German soldier. Frantz had been slightly wounded by a piece of shrapnel during an American bombing raid. The POW American doctor stitched up and bandaged the wound. Frantz then spent two days convalescing in the American wing of the cellar, surrounded by wounded GIs. Although Frantz was wearing an SS uniform, he was also a frightened child.

When I greeted Frantz in German, it triggered a torrent of words that had been bottled up—for good reason. He presumed the nearby Americans would not understand what he was saying, and his fellow German comrades were too far away to hear. He seemed confident a sister would not divulge anything he said. Sadly, his story about how he had come to be on the front line was not unusual at that stage of the war.

Thousands of children, some as young as twelve years old, had been killed or captured by the advancing Allied forces. Frantz said that when he turned twelve, his parents were ordered to send him to a camp in the country where he would be safe from the American and British bombs. Frantz was just one of the millions of children evacuated from the cities that were being systematically destroyed. Frantz said he did not feel safer in the camp. Life inside a boys' camp was harsh, even brutal. Schoolwork was neglected and was replaced with a dreary routine of roll calls, paramilitary field exercises, hikes, and marching to the cadence of shouted Nazi slogans. The rest of the day was spent singing Hitler Youth songs and Nazi anthems. Boys had to snap to attention at any time of the day or night and obey all orders without question.

Frantz said he was one of the smaller boys in the camp and had trouble making friends. Weakness was despised. Survival of the fittest ruled. An informal caste system grew up in which the youngest and most vulnerable boys were bullied, humiliated, and sometimes sexually abused. His miserable life in the camp was a major reason the siren song of the army recruiters in early 1944 was so enticing.

Recruiters freely distributed chocolate and lollipops while promising a clean, orderly, and disciplined life in the army. Like all the children in Germany, Frantz was thoroughly indoctrinated with Nazi propaganda from the time he could walk. He was programed to be a pure Nazi, eager to fight for the Fatherland, and to consider it an honour to die for Hitler. An added inducement was the promise that he would be a member of an elite SS unit. Frantz and thousands of boys like him volunteered to be part of the 12th SS Panzer Division, *Hitlerjugend* (Hitler Youth).

Sadly, Frantz said that after joining the army, the boys were given ill-fitting SS uniforms and very little training before the 12th SS Panzer Division was sent to France to fight the Allied army pouring into Normandy after D-Day. He spent several hours learning how to fire the *Panzerfaust* (Armor Fist) rocket.

The *Panzerfaust* was the weapon most often given to the smaller boys because it was light and did not require much training to use. The missile fired by the *Panzerfaust* looks like a small flower vase attached to the top of a foot-long wooden stick. The vase is packed with an explosive designed to penetrate armour plate. The rocket launcher is a disposable hollow tube. Using the *Panzerfaust* is like trying to aim a Fourth of July rocket: Accuracy is not one of its strengths. A soldier operating the rocket launcher must get close to a tank, less than a hundred feet, before the missile will have any effect on tank armour. To fire the *Panzerfaust*, the soldier also had to stand erect and hold the launching tube in the crook of his arm.

In essence, a soldier trying to use the *Panzerfaust* against enemy armour was on a suicide mission. He could rarely hide and wait for a tank to come to him. He often had to run toward the tank through a hailstorm of bullets to get within a hundred feet before firing. Assuming he could fire the rocket, the smoke spewing from the backside of the tube alerted every enemy soldier within 200 yards where to aim their weapons. The German army considered the young boys as disposable as the *Panzerfaust* launching tube.

In the Normandy fighting, Frantz had seen many boys bravely leap out of their foxholes cradling a *Panzerfaust* and charge right at a tank. None of them survived, and few tanks were even damaged. Frantz also saw what happened to the boys who hesitated about leaving the protection of their foxholes: An officer would shoot them in the back of the head. Frantz was fortunate in having a more compassionate squad leader. When Frantz panicked and was on the verge of running away, the squad leader grabbed him by the shoulder and held him back.

Frantz whispered to me that he knew the war was lost, and he had lost all faith in the Führer. He asked if I could help him safely surrender to the Americans. He knew that his SS uniform increased his chance of being shot. I pointed out the obvious to him: At the moment, it was the American GIs who were the prisoners of his fellow German soldiers. Nevertheless, I told Frantz it was just a matter of time before the Americans retook Saint-Hubert, and if I could help facilitate his safe surrender, I would try. Frantz's final words to me were a warning to be careful speaking with other boys in his company. Many believed Germany could still win the war. They had absolute faith in the Führer and would willingly die for the Nazi cause. The next day Frantz rejoined his company, and we never spoke again.

Two days later I was passing a group of German soldiers taking shelter in our cellar while American bombs and artillery shells were raining down on Saint-Hubert. Another boy in an SS uniform called out to me in German, asking to talk with me. His name was Klaus. He had heard me speaking German to other soldiers. He also learned I had a German heritage and that my grandparents had immigrated to America. Klaus asked if I was outraged by the destruction of my German homeland by the barbaric American bombing. Surely, he said, as a Catholic and a nun, I must support Germany's effort to stem the tide of the godless communists and Jewish vermin.

My response to Klaus's harangue was my oft-practised enigmatic smile. Debate would serve no purpose. It would not change Klaus's mind, a fanatic declaring he would be proud to die for the Führer. There was also the risk of saying too much. The Germans were becoming desperate occupiers, like grey squirrels trapped in the corner of our barn back home: best left alone. The finale of Klaus's lecture was full of bravado. While huddling in a cellar as more and more American bombs fell on Saint-Hubert, he boasted Germany would win the war when the Führer's powerful secret weapons were unleashed. I doubt he appreciated the irony.

In spite of Klaus's virulent repetition of hateful Nazi propaganda, I could not help feeling sorry for him. He was the unwitting product of a lifetime of exposure to a campaign of indoctrination, and he and his generation would pay the bitter price.

As the bombardment intensified—good news, actually—Sister Nathalie decided it would be wiser not to hold Mass in the chapel, so we erected a little altar in part of the cellar. In the brief calm between the explosion of shells, we hurried to the chapel to get the altar stone, altar cloth, and sacred vessels. A proper Mass could now be celebrated. The saying of the rosary became a twice-daily event. A novena to Blessed Julie asking for her help had begun.

The novena had been in progress for several days when our Foundress, Blessed Julie, gave us a sign she had not forsaken us. On December 27, we heard that the German advance was slowing down and that Bastogne was no longer surrounded. The German army was now in danger of being trapped. Those soldiers still in Saint-Hubert, however, showed no desire to leave. Instead, they were pillaging houses, forcing people at the point of a revolver to give them food and anything else they wanted.

Although the Germans were entrenching themselves in Saint-Hubert, they did remove their tanks and half-tracks from our garden. Once the American pilots had discovered their location, they were like fish in a barrel for bombs and artillery fire. Relocating the tanks meant the tank crews and Panzer grenadiers were moved to safer sites and no longer took refuge in our cellars. Unfortunately, the wounded American soldiers were also moved to the *Basilique* where other American POWs were being held. I missed my daily conversations with the Americans, who continued to be cheerful and humorous despite being held as prisoners. My conversations with the Germans were not so pleasant.

As the American bombardment continued, our convent and school were gradually being reduced to rubble. One shell ripped the roof off the dormitory and descended through every story down to the first floor. Another shell pierced the attic, opening it to the sky. A third shell struck the gallery near the kitchen and opened the entrance to our cellar. Some of the walls were so charred and unsupported that a strong wind could have blown them down. It was the threat to the attic, however, that alarmed Sister Nathalie the most. Most of our food supply was still hidden there under the eaves. Its loss would have been catastrophic. During a lull in the shelling, all the sisters capable of climbing four flights of stairs dashed to the attic and descended to the cellar with as much food as they could carry. After half a dozen trips, most of the food was now stored in the part of the cellar vacated by the Americans.

Life in the cellar alternated between boring and terrifying. Prayer, especially reciting the rosary, was comforting and filled some of our time. As for dealing with the terrifying moments, we found comfort in repeating the prayer "Dear God, what will happen to me today, I know not. I do know that nothing shall come to me but what You have foreseen from all eternity. That is enough for me."

On January 4, a mantle of snow was on the ground, and the temperature dropped below freezing. The ground was as hard as iron. Nothing could stop the cannons, though. They continued day and night. The Americans were close.

No two days were alike. Sometimes there were hours of calm followed by hours of screaming shells and explosions. We were fortunate to have a good supply of food, including twenty-three-day-old bread that still tasted good to us. Sister Angelica and Sister Helen Marie worked miracles in the kitchen. Every day they took great risk ascending to the kitchen, where they cooked root vegetables and prepared vats of soup to keep those of us living in the cellar healthy.

Sister Nathalie was determined that our grim circumstances would not ruin our celebration of the Feast of the Epiphany, or Three Kings Day, on January 6. Mass was held in the cellar, accompanied by *a cappella* singing of many joyous hymns, including the traditional favourite, "We Three Kings of Orient Are." Sister Nathalie secretly (she thought) hid a piece of candy in one apple on a plate of apples as a way of determining which sister would win the first and biggest slice of three kings cake. Sister Angela, however, had seen Sister Nathalie insert the tiny piece of candy in the apple and whispered to us not to choose the apple with the missing stem. When all but one of the apples had been selected, and it was Sister Nathalie's turn to pick, only the stemless apple remained on the plate. Sister Nathalie knew she was the victim of a conspiracy, but she laughed even harder at the joke than the rest of us. Then it was her turn to surprise us. Sister Nathalie gave each of us a small bag of sweets, continuing an old tradition of the Saint-Hubert convent.

Two days later a German army captain pounded on our door. Sister Angela pretended she did not understand German and fetched me. I pulled out a strand of my blonde hair before entering the parlour, forced a smile on my face, made quick eye contact before demurely lowering my gaze, and greeted the German officer. *"Guten tag, Herr Major."*

I had noticed how even stone-faced German officers become more genial when someone mistakenly promotes them to a higher rank. Captain Berger chose not to correct my mistake. Although the captain's iron-fist was concealed in the velvet glove of politeness, his request was no less draconian. He matter-of-factly declared the German army required our buildings, and especially our cellars, to house its soldiers. When I pointed out to him the cellars were already occupied by dozens of sisters and many refugees from the bombing and shelling, he coldly said, "Then all of you will have to leave within two days. We will be making cellars throughout Saint-Hubert into defensive bastions, equipped with lethal flamethrowers." According to the captain, Saint-Hubert would become impregnable.

Captain Berger next insisted on inspecting the cellars. We first showed him the cellar that had been vacated by the wounded American soldiers. He nodded his approval of the space, and then asked to see the cellar where we sisters were living. Sister Angela's calm countenance gave way to a fleeting look of panic. Most of the convent's food was hidden in that part of the cellar. I thought argument would be useless, so I tried a different tack. Once again making eye contact, I told him we would be happy to show him the cellar, but would he please make his inspection as quiet as possible. I explained some of the sisters and all of the children we were sheltering would already be in bed. The captain probably thought he was being gracious when he declined to disturb the sleeping children and sisters, even while ordering all of us to be out of our home in two days.

As I was escorting the captain from the convent, he ordered that we keep our door to the convent open at all times so his men could find immediate shelter in our cellars during Allied bombing.

Sister Nathalie did not believe unlocking the door during the day was a cause for concern, but allowing open access at night was worrisome. Looters were everywhere, looking for opportunities to steal and rob. An unlocked door was an open invitation to raid the convent. Sister Nathalie asked Sister Helen Louise and me to guard the door by spending the night in the nearby parlour. Two large armchairs were our sentry posts. We took turns; one of us tried to sleep in a chair while the other kept watch.

There must be a proverb that a watched door is never opened.

Neither German soldiers nor intruders of any kind came through our convent door the first night. In fact, we never saw Captain Berger again. Best of all, no German officers ever came to force us from our home. The reason soon became obvious. The staccato of machine gunfire in the distance was a stark reminder that the Americans were closing in.

The impregnable town of Saint-Hubert was fast becoming an inescapable trap. The Germans were devoting most of their energies to getting out of Saint-Hubert and stealing as much as they could carry. They were taking the oddest things, considering their hurry to "get out of town." Mattresses, furniture, and linens were hot articles for some reason. Common sense would dictate such heavy, cumbersome items would be readily discarded just a few miles down the road. I doubt many German soldiers had read Tolstoy's description of Napoleon's disastrous retreat from Moscow in *War and Peace*. The muddy road just east of Moscow was littered with chairs, drapery, porcelain chamber pots, plates, and samovars.

Even the French thought better than to try to tote mattresses. The theft of wine and spirits was more logical. They could be immediately consumed and need not be carried for long distances. The quick consumption of alcohol by fleeing soldiers, however, undermined the German army's escape preparations. Soldiers were staggering down the street, and trucks were crashing into lamp posts. Perhaps with enough alcohol they were able to delude themselves for an hour or two that they were not being squeezed increasingly tighter in a vice.

The Germans' mattress quest continued throughout the day. In the afternoon of January 9, a truck pulled up in front of the convent. Three German soldiers emerged from the back, walked through our open door, and were unexpectedly confronted in the parlour by Sister Helen Louise and me.

I knew the flirting nun routine would not deter these soldiers from their intended mission, so in addition to the "black robe" deterrence effect nuns have, we both donned our severest frowns, usually employed to subdue rambunctious teenagers. I took advantage of their momentary hesitancy to say in my harshest German accent, "*Wer auch immer sie sind, bleiben sie sofort stehen!*" (Whoever you are, you stop right there!) I told them they were entering a convent. For good measure, I added that the building had been commandeered by Major Berger the previous day, and he ordered that no furniture was to be removed from the buildings.

Having risked igniting a confrontation, I then offered the "face saving" bait. I suggested they could take the two mattresses in the adjoining parlour that had been used by German soldiers, but they must promise to return them. The negotiations continued with the soldiers trying to squeeze more concessions from us. They demanded the two chairs we had slept in the night before. Not wanting to risk losing our negotiating edge, I told them, "*Nein, wir brauchen sie."* (No, we need them.) Fortunately, they did not argue. They put the two mattresses into the truck and drove away, neither soldiers nor mattresses to be seen again.

As the German troops left, the town was becoming more in the control of looters; sadly, many of them were Belgians. During the night of January 10, we heard footsteps on the floor above the cellar. Sister Nathalie, Sister Terese, and Sister Agnes bravely went up the stairs to confront the intruders. They saw a light moving and called out, "Who is there?" No answer.

We assumed the sound of scurrying feet retreating from the refectory meant the danger was past. Soon after midnight, footsteps were heard again by Sister Agnes. She sounded the alarm, and once again the footsteps fled. In the morning we did a quick inventory and learned they had made off with fifty bags of flour, but they left one of their shoes behind and some broken jars of jelly. To prevent looters from stealing from our convent every night, we nailed the doors shut, and sisters took turns standing watch.

Most of the German soldiers were gone by noon on January 11. In the late afternoon sirens suddenly blared. The first Allied soldiers we saw were French paratroopers riding large horses. Sister Agnes cried out, *"Vive la France!"* The paratroopers replied, *"Vive la Belgique!"*

Hundreds of American soldiers were soon filling the streets. Scores of captured German soldiers marched by with their hands on top of their heads. Some of them were actually smiling. They had managed to successfully negotiate the fine line of fighting vigorously enough not to be shot by their own officers for cowardice, while minimising their chance of being killed by the Americans. Then they picked the right time to throw up their arms and surrender. One of the prisoners was permitted to step out of line. He pointed to where, unknown to us, eight anti-tank mines had been buried outside the wall of the convent. Perhaps it was another example of Blessed Julie's protective embrace. The constant shelling and bombing kept us as virtual prisoners in the convent cellars, but it had also prevented us from walking through a minefield.

After the great deluge in the Book of Genesis, God gave Noah a sign in the form of a rainbow, promising, "No more water, the fire next time." For the Sisters of Our Lady in Saint-Hubert, it was just the opposite.

We had survived weeks of explosions and fire only to be inundated by a flood. The intense cold had frozen the water in the convent's downspouts. Ordinarily those pipes channel rain and snowmelt away from the building. With the pipes clogged with ice, however, water from the melting snow had no escape route except to back-up through the slate roof, pour through the ceilings, and flood the front parlours of the convent.

Six of us grabbed brooms and mops in an attempt to divert the flowing water out the door as it leaked in. We were so busy stemming the tide that we did not notice we were pushing the wave of water toward the feet of Sister Pauline de la Sainte Famille, the American General Councillor, who was standing just outside the door. Sister Pauline did not have time to avoid the rush of water and keep her feet dry. She calmly picked up the hem of her robe and sloshed through the pool of water while giving us a cheery greeting. Water could not dampen her joy at finding us alive and well after we had been caught in the middle of what later was called The Battle of the Bulge.

Sister Pauline was at the Motherhouse in Namur when Saint-Hubert was cut off and occupied by the German army. She had no information about what was happening to us and feared the worst. When she heard Saint-Hubert had been liberated, Sister Pauline hitched a ride in an American ambulance going from Namur to Neufchateau. The driver was willing to make a slight detour to Saint-Hubert and promised to come back the next day for the return trip to Namur. It didn't. After several days, Sister Pauline was increasingly anxious about being needed back at the Motherhouse, so she visited the American headquarters to enquire about catching a ride on another Army vehicle going to Namur.

With her American-issued identity card and her black habit, Sister Pauline breezed by the multiple levels of security guards and knocked on the major's door. Major Arnoff was delighted to see her. Sister Pauline explained her dilemma. Unfortunately, the major told her there were no vehicles scheduled for the trip to Namur. He added, however, the next day he would personally arrange a trip to Mons for himself and deliver Sister Pauline to the Motherhouse on the way to Mons. The next morning an open jeep with Major Arnoff and a driver pulled up in front of the convent. Knowing jeeps and the state of the roads between Saint-Hubert and Namur, I told Sister Pauline she would be in for an exciting ride.

Apparently, that proved to be the case. We received a brief note from Sister Pauline a week later thanking us for our hospitality and describing her trek back to Namur. The road to Namur was a rugged trial with crisscrossing ruts skirting deep water-filled holes. When she arrived at the Motherhouse, she was covered with mud and dirty water. Sister Gertrude, on door duty, would not permit Sister Pauline to place one foot on the light-wood flooring until she had changed her shoes and robe. Sister Pauline closed her letter saying the jeep ride to Namur would be one of the highlights of her life.

The focus of the war was moving eastward. Long columns of tanks, jeeps, trucks, and soldiers streamed through Saint-Hubert as part of the immense military build-up for launching the invasion of Germany. Most of the American soldiers, including the company of military police, had left the village. The only Americans left behind were a dozen combat engineers removing the last of the German mines. The mayor of Saint-Hubert was ostensibly in charge, but his police force, never large, was decimated during the two German occupations of the town.

Now there was a power vacuum that the long-repressed Resistance groups were only too eager to fill. Many of the Resistance bands were controlled by the communists. They resolved to root out and kill any Belgians who had, or appeared to have, collaborated with the Germans. Other Resistance forces saw the absence of effective governmental authority as an opportunity to seek revenge for long-remembered personal vendettas that continued to simmer during the German occupation. Finally, there were rogue groups with no other purpose than to enrich themselves by looting the homes of their fellow citizens while claiming to be maintaining law and order.

The danger from the roaming Resistance factions came to the convent the night the Americans left Saint-Hubert. There was a frantic pounding on the door. It was Jean Vondermeer, a Flemish man who helped out on our farm. He had heard that members of the Communist Partisans Arme were accusing him of being a collaborator, and he needed somewhere to hide. Jean acknowledged talking with German soldiers during the reinvasion and, from time to time, giving them a few potatoes from the farm's fall harvest, but he insisted he was not collaborator.

Sister Nathalie had thought our role of providing sanctuary for hunted refugees was over. She was mistaken. Less than an hour after Mr. Vondermeer's arrival, Marian de Smit quietly tapped on our door and entreated us to hide her from the Resistance. She admitted having a relationship with a German sergeant who had supplied her with food that she shared with her brothers and sisters. Although it might appear Sister Nathalie was switching her allegiance, she asked Sister Angela to take Jean and Marian to the false room in the cellar.[9]

The next morning three armed members of the *Partisans Arme* rapped on the convent door.[10]

When Sister Angela slid open the small speakeasy door, their leader insisted on speaking with Sister Superior. Sister Angela followed the same routine Sister Ursula had established before her death to deal with unexpected visits by the Germans. She invited the men to wait in one of the two entry parlours while she went to find Sister Nathalie. Before leaving the entryway, Sister Angela made sure the interior door to the convent was locked behind her.

Following her usual pattern when dealing with insistent intruders, Sister Nathalie made them wait for ten minutes before she made her appearance. Then, donning her no-nonsense expression, Sister Nathalie unlocked the inner door, and with sure deliberate steps, descended the short flight of stairs to the parlour. She recognised one of the men immediately and used that knowledge to her advantage.

Addressing the partisan leader like a miscreant schoolboy, she asked, "Louis, what are you doing here?" After a moment's hesitation, Louis loudly demanded that Sister Nathalie turn over Jean Vondermeer and Marian de Smit. As Louis's voice got louder, Sister Nathalie's voice got softer and steelier, telling the men she would only turn over Jean and Marian to proper civil authorities.

Louis touched his machine pistol and gave his best imitation of a menacing growl. "We can take them if we want." Sister Nathalie knew Louis was bluffing, then, and coolly replied, "Louis, I doubt you are going to knock down two sisters and go rampaging through a convent looking for people you will not find." Louis muttered a few more empty threats and quietly left through the door Sister Angela was holding open for them. Still a schoolboy.

I remember reading an ancient proverb that says, "The enemy of my enemy is my friend." I believe there must be a corollary, however, that is seldom quoted: "When my enemy ceases to be my enemy, does my friend cease to be my friend?" Both phrases captured the situation in Belgium during and after the occupation. When the Germans were the enemy, the Flemish Belgians, the Walloon Belgians, and a multitude of other factions, including

233

the communists, acted like the best of friends. Once the Germans were finally expelled from Belgium, however, there was a general falling out among the faux friends.

Belgian radio reported that the growing conflict among these intense adversaries was not limited to occasional drunken street brawls finishing with dozens of black eyes, bruised knuckles, and split lips. The rival groups had held on to the rifles and pistols they had used against the Germans during the occupation, so fights easily escalated into exchanges of gunfire. There was a communist-inspired riot in Brussels in which almost a hundred people suffered bullet wounds. Sister Nathalie said the last thing the Allies needed while slugging it out with the Germans on the Siegfried Line was to deploy precious troops to keep the Belgians from engaging in pitched battles among themselves. Ultimately, the order came from General Eisenhower himself that all Resistance groups must turn in their guns. A few guns were surrendered; most were hidden for another day, which hopefully would never come. Ike's order at least had the salutary effect of keeping ex-Resistance fighters from strutting around the streets fingering their pistols.

It became clear that one of the fundamental issues dividing Belgians was the question of what to do with King Leopold. Should the King be invited back to resume his role as constitutional monarch? Or should he be deposed in favour of his younger brother, Prince Charles, who was already serving as regent? Should Belgium evolve into a pure republic like the United States? Of course, this was a solution that I naturally favoured.

Many felt strongly that the King had betrayed Belgium when he surrendered the Belgian army and the country to the Germans and should not return to the throne. Even in Saint-Hubert there was a spate of marches, demonstrations, counter-demonstrations, and protests by the opposing factions, which often ended in violence. These civil disturbances forced the Allied army command to clamp down and regulations were issued. Groups of four or more people were prohibited from gathering on the street. Marches and parades celebrating national holidays were forbidden. Excessive displays of Belgium's flag were discouraged. I thought it ironic that many of the Allies' restrictions were similar to those imposed by the Germans during their occupation. Unlike the German ban on listening to the BBC, however, we were still permitted to listen to Radio Berlin, if we chose to do so. The increasingly fantastic rants by Nazi propaganda minister Joseph Goebbels were actually diverting.

Saturday, January 20th began as an unusually beautiful day for Belgium in the midst of winter, with not a cloud in the sky. The sun appeared extra bright after weeks of dull grey, frigid weather. It was a January thaw, when Mother Nature tricks you into thinking spring is in the offing. In the afternoon I found a delightful, south-facing corner of the garden that trapped the warmth of the sun, my black habit providing even more welcome warmth; a perfect spot for prayer and meditation. When Sister Angela entered the garden, walking toward me, looking distraught, my warmth ebbed, and a slight shiver went through me. Her hands were hidden beneath her tunic. When they emerged, Sister Angela was holding a letter. She said she had been sorting the mail and noticed the letter addressed to me. The return address indicated it was from Sergeant Kelly, Major Martin's jeep driver. She thought I might prefer reading it in a quiet secluded spot.[11]

In the envelope were only a few lines scrawled on a sheet of paper torn from a notebook.

Dear Sister Christina,

I am sorry to inform you that Major Thomson was killed by a sniper last week near Aachen, Germany. I thought you would want to know. I am including a picture of the Major and you standing in front of his jeep. The photo was found among his personal effects. I am sure he would want you to have it.

Please accept my deepest sympathy, Sergeant Kelly

My hand was shaking when I handed the note to Sister Angela to read. My legs felt weak, and tears trickled down my cheeks. I felt like I was losing a piece of myself, a piece I did not even know I had. I probably would have fainted, but Sister Angela wrapped me in her arms and hugged me. With my head resting on her shoulder, she led me into the partially destroyed chapel and sat me down on a pew.

Sister Angela continued to hold me, although she knew such physical contact between sisters was strictly forbidden. At that moment, I understood the feelings I had for Martin were unlike what I had ever felt for anyone else. I had been deceiving myself about the importance of Martin in my life, but could no longer cling to that fiction. Must I ask forgiveness for the forbidden attraction I just discovered I had for him? How can it be a sin to love another human being, even if the "other" is a man? I could not recall ever having any sinful thoughts about Martin, yet guilt still lingered on the periphery of my conscience.

After a minute or two the initial feeling of faintness passed. I asked Sister Angela if she would leave me alone in the chapel to pray and meditate. She removed her arm from around my shoulder. Both of us were slightly embarrassed by our display of affection toward each other. I felt guilty that my emotional reaction to the death of Major Martin tempted Sister Angela to violate one of the cardinal rules of the order, touching a fellow sister in an affectionate way. At the same time, I was enormously grateful for the comfort her touch of tenderness gave me. Sitting alone in the cold half-destroyed chapel gave me the time I needed to reflect and pray. I decided I would not tell anyone about my newly discovered feelings for Major Martin. He was dead. Any potential dangers to my vows in the future vanished with his death. What would not disappear soon, if ever, was the pain and the empty space in my heart. It was Blessed Julie's advice that gave me a sense of direction.

"To be a true Sister of Our Lady one must possess the virtue of abandonment to its fullest extent. We must abandon ourselves for life and for death, for consolation and for desolation, for honour and for contempt. We must abandon ourselves for our charges, for all the employments that holy obedience assigns us, here to-day, tomorrow elsewhere; the whole earth is the Lord's, and everything ought to be the same to Sisters of Our Lady, who have the happiness of walking in the footsteps of the apostles, according to the spirit of our holy Institute."

I would abandon myself to the work of rebuilding the convent and the school. I would enthusiastically embrace my role as a teacher of young girls. I would seek solace in the love of God, Blessed Julie, and my fellow Sisters of Our Lady. In time, I hoped to feel whole again.

CHAPTER FIFTEEN

END OF THE WAR

Saint-Hubert, January 1945

ONCE SAINT-HUBERT WAS LIBERATED AGAIN FROM THE GERMANS, the floodgates opened for a tidal wave of foodstuffs, clothing, and money flowing into our convent. The entire Sisters of Our Lady of Namur network in America was mobilised to bring relief to those in need. Thousands of dollars were raised to support our rebuilding effort, which started almost as soon as the last German soldier passed the city limit, slinking his way back to Germany. In fact, Sister Nathalie requested food shipments be curtailed. Between the American Army and other relief agencies, putting good food on the table was the least of our worries. Besides, it cost a lot to ship bulk food, and it was better to send hard currency as long as the currency limit imposed by the newly installed Belgium government was not breached.

In order to deter speculators and manipulators of currency, there was a limit on the number of dollars a person in Belgium could receive every month. Money could not be transferred by cable, and it was naive to think cash in an envelope sent through the regular mail would ever reach its intended destination. The partial solution was to have money raised in the US be deposited with the US Treasury. The Department of Treasury would then send it to the US Embassy in Brussels, where recipients could collect the cash.

There was a per-person $1,500 monthly limit, and donations over the limit would be returned. Mr. Blake at the embassy suggested a solution. The four Sisters of Our Lady of Namur Provinces in the US would take turns sending $1,500: March—Cincinnati, April–Waltham, June—California, and July—Ilchester. Mr. Blake hoped and expected the currency restrictions to be lifted before July came around.

The crates of clothes, shoes, and other sundry items were more than welcome. They contained the kind of goods that were not available on the open market at any reasonable price. Even the black-market supply was limited. The metal bands on the crates were cut with a can opener. Each crate contained dozens of individually wrapped parcels. One might have expected our opening of the packages would resemble a Christmas scene, like expectant children ripping open presents as fast as they can. Our unwrapping process was the exact opposite. One sister would exclaim, "Oh!" Every other sister in the room would stop their own unwrapping to admire the discovered treasure. Lovely girls' dresses and boys' suits were passed from hand to hand so that each sister could feel a fabric they had not seen or touched in four years. The texture of silk was a special thrill.

The discovery of a package filled with hundreds of toothbrushes was greeted with as much excitement as if it were a pirate's chest filled with gold doubloons. During the occupation toothbrushes were as rare as hen's teeth. The light-hearted mood turned to laughter when Sister Anthony suggested swapping some of the extra toothbrushes for a puppy, obviously not thinking about what our community would do with a puppy.

Many people might think sisters and nuns are not fashion conscious; they are wrong. When the crates containing wool serge habits and veils, along with stockings were opened, spontaneous Hosannas broke out, followed by thanks being offered to God and Blessed Julie. For years we had fashioned habits out of whatever material was available, mostly cotton. They were coloured with a black dye that bled profusely every time they were washed, leaving the habits more grey than black. We were as happy as if a shipment had arrived from a Paris fashion house.

While our black clothes were getting more grey, our whites were getting duller. During the occupation, you could obtain beef steaks on the black market easier than you could get good laundry starch. Many pieces of our habit needed to be starched so they would be crisp and wrinkle-free when ironed. Ideally, the front of our white capes or wimples are starched so much they become as stiff as cardboard. An essential ingredient of laundry starch is cornstarch, but before the war almost all of Belgium's corn had come from the US.

Laundry starch made from potatoes stiffens the fabric, but also discolours it. When the last crate was opened, and boxes of starch spilled out, Sister Delores, who is in charge of the Saint-Hubert laundry, let out a whoop of joy. She said we could finally start looking like Sisters of Our Lady again and not like a ragged gaggle of itinerant monks.

With clothes and food no longer being in short supply, the main concern of Sister Superior Nathalie was the reconstruction of the destroyed and damaged buildings. Funds began flowing in from the United States, but reliable contractors were needed to do the work. In March, Blessed Julie again answered our prayers. I was returning from a visit to the *Basilique* when I saw a middle-aged man standing outside the convent's door. Shuffling back and forth on his feet would be a better description. He was hesitant, like a man trying to decide whether to knock or not. He almost jumped when I asked if I could be of service. He had a slight stammer and introduced himself as a Gaston Joris. He pointed to the ruins of the

Oratoire and said he might be of some service in reconstructing it, and asked if he could look inside the ruins.[1]

I told Monsieur Joris I would be delighted to show him the Oratoire, explaining it was the exact spot where, in 1809, our Foundress, Blessed Mother Julie, had made her plans for opening the house of the Sisters of Our Lady in Saint-Hubert. The damage to the *Oratoire* from a V-1 rocket was extensive. Windows and doors were broken, ceilings and walls had collapsed, and furniture was in pieces, but in the midst of all the destruction stood the statue of Blessed Mother Julie, upright on its pedestal, untouched. At first Monsieur Joris was sceptical when I described how the statue had survived the devastation unscathed. His doubt was erased when I tilted the statue slightly backward. While everything else in the Oratoire was covered in grey dust, underneath the base of the statue was a square space perfectly dust-free. Monsieur Joris was stunned. He grasped immediately that the statue could not have been placed on the pedestal after the bombing, but had actually survived the attack that destroyed the Oratoire.

After I reset Blessed Julie's statue, Monsieur Joris told me he was a contractor and that he would be happy to rebuild the *Oratoire* for the Sisters of Our Lady. When he added that he would do the work for only the cost of the materials and labour if the sisters would regularly include him in their prayers, I quickly ushered him into Sister Nathalie's office. Sister Nathalie said she wanted to check Monsieur Joris's references before she agreed to the contract, but ultimately Gaston Joris was hired to rebuild the Oratoire. He commenced work as soon as the weather permitted. Sister Nathalie helped lay the foundation stone and Reverend Dean Davot asked God to bless the work.[2]

In the spring of 1945, it was obvious from me listening to the radio reports that the German army was being beaten on all fronts. I heard how, after the Battle of the Bulge, the Allied armies captured Cologne and crossed the Rhine River into the heart of the German homeland. German soldiers were surrendering in droves, but some SS units continued to fight on.

In April, we learned that the Russians had entered Berlin, and, while in Italy, Mussolini had been captured by Italian partisans and hung. Finally, it was announced that on April 30, Hitler committed suicide in his Berlin bunker, but his body was not found. On May 7 came the news we had all been praying for: the German government and army surrendered unconditionally. The war in Europe was declared officially over on May 8, 1945. Spontaneous celebrations erupted all over Belgium.

It was strange, but I did not feel the same sense of euphoria that I did when the Allied armies had first liberated Namur. Then, like so many others, I danced in the streets. In part, it was the sobering news leaking out about the Nazi death camps at Auschwitz, Buchenwald, and Dachau describing unimaginable atrocities committed by the Germans in their attempt to kill every Jew in Europe. My thoughts turned to Andree. Did her family survive, and if so, was she able to find them? Why did she never try to contact me after her abrupt departure from Saint-Hubert?

Instead of smiles and cheerfulness, I suffered headaches and bouts of tears for no apparent reason. I was agitated, irritable, and I could not sleep. I was constantly tired, with little appetite. The future looked empty and meaningless to me. I now understood what my Uncle Lewis meant when he said that the best years of his life were when he was a soldier in the First World War.

I wondered how being in a filthy trench surrounded by death and destruction could induce any kind of happiness or contentment. He said you cannot imagine the adrenaline rush you get from facing the prospect of immediate death and then eluding the grim reaper. Plus, there are the friendships forged while machine guns are spraying bullets over your head and artillery shells are exploding all around you. The bonds between comrades who face death together and shed their blood for each other are stronger than any ties arising from the accident of birth. All that ends, however, with the silencing of the guns and the disbanding of the army.

Comrades swear solemn oaths not to lose touch and to reunite regularly sometime in the future. Uncle Lewis said it rarely happened, though, and even when reunions did occur, the conditions that forged the friendships could not be recreated. For myself, how could anything I might do in the future ever match the intensity and excitement of the last four years? The routine of convent life that had been so comforting before the war loomed like a prison sentence. At least I had the consolation that my comrades-in-arms, my fellow sisters, would be there for me. But would the pain I felt from my loss of Sister Ursula, Andree, and Martin ever ease?

After VE day, Mother General decided to lead a pilgrimage to the cemetery in Rocogne, just outside Bastogne, where a memorial service was to be held on May 30 (Memorial Day in America). The cemetery had been created in February, after the Battle of the Bulge, to be a temporary resting place for the thousands of soldiers, both American and German, who had died during the battle. Eventually the American soldiers would be moved to the Ardennes American Cemetery and Memorial in Neupre, Belgium. The German dead would be relocated to another site. Our pilgrimage was made in the name of the families, parents, children, and wives, of all who lay in the cemetery under the American flag—soldiers who had died in December and January defending Belgium. We would also represent all the American Sisters of Our Lady of Namur who could not show their heartfelt affection for the dead in person. Finally, we would pray for the souls of all who had died in the battle.

Uncharacteristically, Mother General, dear Mother, did not select the sisters who would make the pilgrimage to the cemetery; instead, she asked for volunteers. I did not hesitate; I requested to be one of the pilgrims. In addition to honouring the dead, I had another strong motive for making the pilgrimage. I knew Martin was buried in the Ardennes Cemetery. I hoped if I stood over his grave and prayed for him that the pain in my heart would begin to lessen and I could bring closure to those Namur memories.[3]

Sister Angela and I joined Mother General and thirty other sisters on the three-mile walk from Bastogne to Rocogne. Although the cemetery was meant to be only a temporary resting place, it was beautifully laid out with long rows of wooden crosses and Stars of David covering acres of lush green grass, separated by well-groomed gravel walks. The entrance was flanked by two simple stone columns. Just inside of the entrance was a small structure containing two grave registry volumes, one for American soldiers and one for German soldiers. The names of the soldiers were in alphabetical order. It was easy for me to get the precise locations of the grave of the German child soldier, Frantz Neidert, and the grave of Major Martin Thomson. The only difference between the American side of the cemetery and the German side was that each American soldier had an individual marker at the head of his grave, while there was only one wooden marker for a grave enclosing six German soldiers.

The memorial service began with several patriotic speeches. The most haunting remarks for me were delivered by a general quoting a Memorial Day speech given by Oliver Wendell Holmes, Jr.[4]

But grief is not the end of all. I seem to hear the funeral march become a paean. I see beyond the forest the moving banners of a hidden column. Our dead brothers still live for us, and bid us think of life, not death—of life to which in their youth they lent the passion and joy of the spring. As I listen, the great chorus of life and joy begins again, and amid the awful orchestra of seen and unseen powers and destinies of good and evil our trumpets sound once more a note of daring, hope, and will.

An American Army band played several musical selections. The ones I remember were "Eternal Father," and "Battle Hymn of the Republic," during which a few members of the audience began singing the lyrics, quickly joined by the entire crowd.

When the stanza "As He died to make men holy, let us die to make men free" was sung, there was not a dry eye anywhere in the cemetery. Finally, of course, there was the singing of the National Anthem. The most moving part of the ceremony was how it ended. There were no speeches or prayers, just three minutes of total silence, followed by the poignant playing of "Taps." As the crowd dispersed there was not a sound except the whisper of shoes and boots shuffling through the grass.

The religious services for the Memorial program were held in separate locations on the cemetery grounds. The Catholics gathered near the entrance, where a temporary altar was erected on a four-foot wooden platform. The Protestants erected a pulpit on the north side of the cemetery, while the Jews placed their pulpit, called an *almemar,* on the south side. Four Catholic Army chaplains said Mass and distributed communion. The Mass ended by the singing of *"Non Nobis Domine"* by the sisters, brothers, and priests. *"Non nobis, Domine, non nobis, sed nomini tuo da gloriam"* (Not unto us, O Lord, not unto us, but to thy name give the glory.)

After the Mass, Sister Angela and I found Frantz's grave in the German portion of the cemetery, or at least his name was on the wooden placard. He died a poor frightened child who so wanted to live. We knelt by his grave and prayed for his soul. I hesitated before going to the American section. My resolve to stand and pray over Martin's grave was weakening. Sister Angela took me by the arm and encouraged me to find Martin's grave, saying I would never forgive myself if I did not visit Martin's last resting place and bring closure to that part of my life.

Martin's grave was in row F, five down from the central walk dividing the German and American sections of the cemetery. We passed dear Mother talking to two Jesuit priests. She looked at me and slightly nodded her head. I wondered at the time if she knew what I was going to do, and her nod indicated tacit approval. I stood at the foot of Martin's grave staring at the slightly mounded earth for a few moments, gathering the courage to look at the name on the white wooden cross. Seeing Major Martin Thomson written in black on the crossbar released a flood of pent-up emotions. I began sobbing uncontrollably, I couldn't breathe, and I was gasping for breath between sobs. Only Sister Angela holding my arm kept me from collapsing at the foot of Martin's grave. Mother General and several other sisters rushed over to me, but that is all I remember until I woke up in my cot back in the convent.

Sister Angela was at my side, trying to feed me soup. The next day, Sister Superior Nathalie came into my room and sat in a chair beside me. She explained that I was suffering from a kind of shell shock, similar to that experienced by soldiers who have been in combat for too long. It was understandable, she added, that after four years of occupation and war I was experiencing combat fatigue.

I was grateful Sister Nathalie did not mention Martin or any possible feelings I had for him. She did say, however, that dear Mother had decided it was time for Sister Clare and me to return to the United States for rest, reflection, and prayer. Two weeks later we were on a ship sailing to America.

EPILOGUE

LIFE AFTER WAR

Cincinnati, Ohio, August 1945

I ARRIVED AT THE SISTERS OF OUR LADY OF NAMUR CONVENT IN Cincinnati on June 30, 1945, still emotionally fragile, but stronger for having a better understanding of myself and how my years in Belgium had fundamentally changed me— for the better, I hope. Since coming to Cincinnati, I have been surrounded by the love and caring of my fellow sisters. At first, I was depressed; there is no other way of putting it. It seemed like I was being put on the shelf, destined to live a quiet, routine-driven life in the convent.

Dear Mother and Sister Nathalie must have known I needed something to look forward to. I was told by the Cincinnati Provincial that in January of 1946 I would become principal of Cuvilly High School in Dayton, Ohio. The news lifted my spirits immediately. Although becoming a principal for a large girls' high school was intimidating, I asked myself whether anything I faced during the rest of my life could be more daunting than having a squad of gun-toting SD troops bursting into a room. My family would also be close, the family farm being less than fifty miles from Dayton. I now had a mission: learning how to be a principal. I could focus on the task ahead, problems that needed solutions, decisions to be made—by me. I knew I was on the road to recovery.

Another important element of my healing process was completing this history of the Sisters of Our Lady of Namur during the German occupation. My initial incentive for writing the narrative was to suppress my fear of death. My motivation for finishing the story was to bring closure to that exciting and traumatic part of my life. I did not want to be like Uncle Lewis. He fought in World War I but could not leave it behind, although he lived for fifty more years. He, however, did not have the support of belonging to a religious order of sisters with strong traditions linking them to the past while dedicating their lives to making the future better.

Finally, after months of meditation and prayer, I may have gained a deeper understanding of what it means to love God. Perhaps before I could obtain a firm grasp of the elusive love of God, I first had to experience the love among companions who share a common danger; the love of a mother for her child; the love of a special friend; and the love of a man. Last week a young postulant told me that when I talked to her about the love of God the expression on my face suggested I had some special inside knowledge of God's love. Do I?

AFTERWORD

In my opening Preface I described how I came into possession of the letters and other materials Sister Kim Dalgarn discovered in the back of a file drawer while she was organising the Cincinnati Archives for the Sisters of Notre Dame de Namur, and, how I offered, perhaps, to actually write a book based on content of that file drawer. The day after that conversation, however, I was beginning to have "morning after" reservations. There were two big problems lurking out there. First, I had never written a book. I understood that writing law review articles, a trial skills book, and columns for a newspaper was probably inadequate training for writing a book. Second, I am an atheist. How could someone who doesn't believe in the existence of God write about an order of Catholic sisters whose entire lives are oriented around their belief in an almighty deity?

Writing a book based in part on historical events usually requires the author to comb through thousands of pages of original documents and read dozens of books before penning a single paragraph. This presents a significant challenge, for I am an impatient and slothful person. The thought of spending countless hours searching for a single factual nugget I could actually use was daunting. Thanks to Sister Kim, however, I did not need to dig through a mountain of paper. Hundreds of pages filled with delicious pertinent facts were dropped into my lap. There were many other books to read, but I only needed to glean those facts that were relevant to the story I wanted to tell. The sisters' own letters and journals told the tale in graphic detail; any additional research would be focused primarily on supplying a larger context to the events. Acquiring that larger picture became significantly easier when Lady Luck dropped a stack of chips onto my research pile in the form of a recently published book by Jean-Michel Veranneman, *Belgium in the Second World War*. This extremely well researched, thoughtful, beautifully written book supplied a cornucopia of context and individual stories that could be easily woven into my narrative. Another book that deserves special mention is *Hidden Children of the Holocaust* by Suzanne Vromen. It provided a thorough and insightful description of what life was like for Jewish children being hidden in Catholic convents.

Another big hurdle for me was my deficient foreign language skills. I passed the foreign language requirement in college, but I suspect the grade was due in part to my playing tennis with my French professor. While he regaled the class with racy French jokes, my face would be an image of incomprehension. I was too embarrassed to ask other students to explain the Gallic humour. This was more than a roadblock; it was an insurmountable stone wall. The sisters' letters were originally written in French or English.

I knew it was portentous when Sister Kim explained that the translation of the French documents would not be a problem. In the era before emails, tweets, and Siri, the sisters had a brilliant way to facilitate the exchange of news among their worldwide network of schools and convents. Whenever a sister at one house received a letter from a sister located at another house anywhere in the world, that letter, if written in French, would be translated into English, typed, mimeographed, and ultimately mailed to all the

Sisters of Notre Dame de Namur houses in Europe, Asia, Africa, and the Americas. Not only could I dodge the translation bullet, I would not have to decipher handwritten letters.

Finally, I also had my ace, Sister Kim. She would allow me access to any archival material she had at the Notre Dame Museum in Cincinnati. Most importantly, she offered to help me navigate my way through the documents and artifacts. Plus, entrée to Sister Kim's encyclopedic memory bank would be like having my own personal Wikipedia just a phone call or email away.

Thus, my initial trepidations about the burden of extensive and time-consuming research bumping up against my innate slothfulness were alleviated. My book writing stars seemed to be aligned. If I were ever to attempt writing a book, this was an opportunity not to be missed.

The second hurdle that had to be cleared was more philosophical than practical. I am an atheist, and I am ambivalent on the issue of whether organised religions over the millennia have caused more pain and suffering in the world than healing. My sixteen years of Roman Catholic education started with eight years of catechism classes at my grade school, Immaculate Conception in Dayton, Ohio, run by the Sisters of Notre Dame. That was followed by four years of religion classes at Chaminade High School in Dayton. Finally, I graduated from Georgetown University in Washington, DC, with a minor in Theology. All the religious training I received only reinforced my belief in the absence of God. Could I be fair to the sisters, or would my own prejudices skew their story?

A visit to the Sisters of Notre Dame Museum in Cincinnati made me realise my prejudice pool was shallower than I had thought. I was browsing through the memorabilia in one of the display cases, and I spotted three samples of the dreaded "clickers" the Sisters of Notre Dame de Namur used in my grade school. The sisters used the clickers to organise every aspect of our classroom lives. The clicker was also an instrument of dispensing discipline. From a young student's perspective, the clicker was the equivalent of the swagger sticks carried by drill instructors in the military.

Clickers appear relatively benign. They are made of a hardwood, like maple, about eight inches long, as thick as the handle of a fishing rod. They fit comfortably in the hand. In the middle of the clicker is the most intimidating feature, a hard, round knob that can serve as a miniature cudgel. A rap on the wrist or a gentle tap on the head was enough to encourage the unruliest student to cooperate with a sister's request.

The clickers, however, also had another important role in our lives. Attached to the clicker by a rubber band was a thin strip of wood. When a sister pushed down on the wooden strip with her thumb and released it, the strip smacked the body of the cudgel, generating a loud crack/click that resonated through a classroom. Everything we did as a class was in response to that sound. Sister would click and we would all immediately stand up. Another click would tell the first row of students to walk quietly out of the classroom. The next click would be the signal for the second row to exit, and so forth. In church, the click told us when to genuflect and when to kneel. To this day, if I hear a similar sounding click, I have to suppress the urge to stand at attention.

The irony was that seeing those clickers did not send shivers down my back, but invoked a sense of nostalgia. I realised I had received a good education at Immaculate Conception School, and the clickers had been important tools in fostering a favourable learning atmosphere. Otherwise, with over forty students in each class, chaos would have reigned.

Visiting the museum helped me see the positive side of organised religion and appreciate the contributions made by the Sisters of Notre Dame in educating children. Sister Kim showed me a book listing the names of all my teachers at Immaculate Conception School. I doubt there is a boy anywhere in the country that attended a Catholic grade school in the 1950s who cannot tell tales of how sisters terrified them. My standard tale is about my penmanship teacher, Sister Mary Margaret. She loomed over me while was I was unsuccessfully trying to copy her perfect script on the blackboard. In my memory, the more she loomed, the worse my writing became. Unfairly perhaps, I often blame her for my abominable cursive handwriting.

When I checked the names of my other teachers who taught me at Immaculate Conception School, however, I realised I actually liked most of them. They nurtured my love for reading, maths, and history. In the seventh grade, Sister Bernadette probably bent the rules a bit when she allowed me to take home stacks of Hardy Boys mystery books, expediting my quest to read all of the series before the end of the school year. Seeing Sister Bernadette's name also reminded me I may have had a teenager's crush on her. The austere habit she wore could not disguise the fine features of an attractive young woman. She was so genuinely kind, how could any schoolboy not be slightly in love with her? With these fresh images in mind, my predisposition about the evils of established religions was moderating.

What ultimately undermined my anti-religion biases was recalling my experience with the Sisters of Notre Dame de Namur as teachers at Chaminade-Julienne High School in Dayton, Ohio. All three of our children graduated from CJ, and my wife, Kathy, also taught Science there for thirteen years. For four years I coached the school's mock trial team. The sisters there were less like the authoritarian figures I remembered from grade school and more like friends and colleagues. Make no mistake, the sisters at CJ were strong-minded and not to be "crossed" lightly. It was obvious, however, they were totally dedicated to their teaching profession and inspired to teach by a love for their students.

It is not unusual for truly committed teachers to love their pupils, but what makes the Sisters of Notre Dame de Namur special is their love for their fellow sisters. They live in a community that is literally an "all for one and one for all" society. The sisters have a better phrase: "Where one of us are, all of us are." Families related by marriage and DNA could not be closer than the Sisters of Notre Dame family. When they take their final vows, the sisters include a vow of poverty and all of their earthly possessions become the property of the community. If sisters earn any money from their work or from gifts, it all goes into the community treasury. A large portion of those sums is used to support the order's charitable work.

The sisters live in small rooms furnished with a narrow bed, a dresser, a desk, a chair, and a small closet. The sisters are no longer required to wear the traditional habit, although some of the older sisters may still wear a veil. All the sisters wear a distinctive SNDdeN cross on a chain around their necks. Meals are taken together unless a sister is away from the residence or too ill to get to the dining room. One gets the sense that if ten sisters had only one loaf of bread and an apple in the communal larder, then they would be divided into ten equal pieces and the sister who had the greatest need for food would be encouraged to choose first. Sisters care for each other when they are sick or disabled. Younger sisters go out of their way to help the older, less mobile sisters. The Mount Notre Dame Health Center in Cincinnati is a convent, an assisted living facility, and a nursing home all in one. Sisters who are at the end of their lives are able to die surrounded by their loving family.

The sisters we know are also fun. They taught my family how to play a cut-throat game of dominoes. They are no different from other competitive game players—they like to win, and they hate losing. They do not curse, however, when they lose. Sisters sometimes surprise you with their antics. Sister Damiemme Grismer, for example, once agreed to be part of a fundraising event for CJ. It was a contest with bumper boats racing around a pool at a Beavercreek, Ohio, amusement park. Sister Damiemme donned parts of a traditional nun's habit and raced around the course with her veil streaming behind her. I do not remember if she won, but she certainly was the star of the show.

Although the Sisters of Notre Dame de Namur are motivated by their love of God and a firm belief that the Catholic Church is a force for good in the world, they are not oppressively indoctrinated. They are quite tolerant of other belief systems, do not proselytise non-Catholics, and perhaps they add a slight pinch of salt before digesting official church doctrine. The sisters do not use religious beliefs for dividing people into "us" and "them." To the Sisters of Notre Dame, "we are all we." Their readiness to respect the beliefs of other people and their reluctance to chastise others for their beliefs has sometimes made them the target of Vatican doctrinal purists. Under Pope Benedict XVI, the Vatican's dogma watchdogs, the "Congregation for the Doctrine of the Faith" launched an extensive investigation of the Sisters of Notre Dame de Namur, along with other women's religious orders that were members of The Leadership Conference of Women Religious. The Vatican wanted to determine if the sisters were deviating from official Catholic policy.

Cardinal Gerhard Mueller said:

The sisters were focusing too much on social justice issues, such as caring for the poor and advocating for immigrants, and were too active in promoting health care reform. It said the LCWR members should spend more time advancing church teachings on sexuality and abortion.

Why would the Catholic Church want to harass and intimidate the Catholic religious groups that were doing so much to further the mission of the Church by educating children and caring for the less fortunate? Apparently, Pope Francis had the same question after he was chosen. He thanked the Congregation for its report and then ignored it.

Unlike many of us, Sisters of Notre Dame do not ease into retirement at sixty-five years of age. They continue to work well into their seventies and eighties. Their motivation is due in part to their love of service and the opportunity to continue practising the vocation that motivated them to join the order many years ago. They also need the money they earn to contribute to the support of the community. They receive no financial support from the Catholic Church. With the order rapidly shrinking and aging, there are fewer young sisters to support more elderly sisters. So, older sisters continue to work if they can. Their vow of poverty prevents them from having personal pension funds. Any inheritance or gifts from family members are turned over to the order and the sisters give up any use of the inheritance. The challenge for the sisters with their vow of poverty is to have enough resources so they do not starve or become homeless, but not so many worldly goods that they slip into the too-comfortable middle class.

In contrast, many priests do not take a vow of poverty, so they can invest in a pension fund that is supplemented by contributions from the Church. They can inherit and accumulate wealth through investments and may even be permitted by the Church to do such things as buy houses for resale or rental. Yes, a priest can be a landlord.

Nothing better illustrates the Sisters of Notre Dame de Namur's strict adherence to their vow of poverty than the saga of the Treasure Hugo d'Oignies. The Treasure is considered one of the seven most valuable art collections of Belgium. It is a collection of thirteenth-century gold reliquaries, monstrances, and other religious objects. The collection is worth millions of dollars.

During the 1789 French Revolution, the Priory of Oignies owned the Treasure. Rather than let the priceless works of art fall into the hands of the French revolutionaries, the last Prior of Oignies had the Treasure buried on a farm in Falisolle, fifteen miles west of Namur. When the farmer died in 1818, the Treasure was turned over to the Sisters of Notre Dame de Namur for safekeeping. The Priory of Oignies and the order that founded the Priory was disbanded in the nineteenth century. Of course, the farmer's family had no rights to the artifacts. For nearly two hundred years the Sisters of Notre Dame kept the Treasure safe.

By the twenty-first century, however, the Sisters of Notre Dame were experiencing severe financial difficulties. The number of sisters had declined precipitously. Some schools and convents could not be maintained and had to be closed. The cost of caring for aging sisters was soaring. In addition, the expense of keeping the Treasure secure was prohibitive, even while its value was skyrocketing.

One would think the obvious solution for the order would be to sell the collection to the highest bidder. There was no one with better title to the Treasure. No one had ever claimed a legal interest in any of artifacts. In fact, there was no person or organisation that could legitimately claim a scintilla of ownership rights. In the case of the Treasure, the two hundred years of possession constituted substantially more than the proverbial nine-tenths of the law. Although the law would likely regard the Sisters of Notre Dame de Namur as the rightful owners of the Treasure, the sisters themselves still only considered themselves temporary guardians. To sell the Treasure would be a violation of trust, like the breaking of a vow. Therefore, in 2010, although the order desperately needed money, the sisters donated the Treasure to the Museum of Ancient Arts in Namur, where it is now on display.

The donation was a remarkable display of integrity, so how can anyone, even an atheist, not admire the Sisters of Notre Dame? The sisters may be motivated in large part by the love of a God I do not believe exists, but they represent the best qualities of organised religion in general and the Catholic Church in particular. They live their beliefs. The Sisters of Notre Dame are not like those who proclaim that their religious principles guide their lives, except when those principles require significant sacrifices like replacing an SUV with a Smart car. The sisters accept the harder path rather than the easy path. They are a force for good. I believe in their mission. The fact that I do not accept their God reinforces my admiration for what they accomplished during the Nazi occupation of Belgium in World War II.

I believe this brief history of my experiences with the Sisters of Notre Dame de Namur gets me over the second hurdle: how a committed atheist can tell the story of a Catholic order of nuns without letting my personal lack of belief seep into the narrative. It is often tempting for agnostics and atheists to seize on incongruous and inconsistent aspects of theological dogmas and assumptions with the goal of demystifying them. This book, however, is not about that. It is a book about good people doing brave things at a very dangerous time in our history. It is about the Catholic sisters sometimes risking their lives to aid the victims of war. Part of their motivation for their valour may have been their belief in a Supreme Being, the values espoused by the Gospels, and the tenets of Catholic Church doctrine, but I think a large part their motivation was driven by their empathy and love for people. It was a story that needed to be told.

I would be remiss if I did not mention the influence another religious order had on my ability to reconcile my atheism with a strong belief in the religious missions of some sisters, priests, and brothers. The official name of the order is The Society of Mary, but its members are usually called Marianists. It is an order comprised of brothers and priests dedicated to teaching young men and women. The Marianists differ from many Catholic orders in that there is no distinction made between the status of priests and brothers. In some male religious communities, the brothers do much of the manual labour like cooking and cleaning, and the priests are free to engage in more spiritual, intellectual pursuits. Furthermore, a brother in those communities could never aspire to be the Provincial of the Order. By contrast, a Marianist brother can be the provincial or can be president of one of the Marianist universities.

I attended a Marianist high school in Dayton Ohio—Chaminade—but it was not until I began teaching at the Marianist University of Dayton in 1974 that my appreciation for the Marianists grew from respect to profound admiration. They live very simply. Most of them reside in communal houses where they share the domestic chores. A favourite part of my tours of the campus for prospective faculty and deans was to drive by the house on campus where the brothers and priests lived. They were amazed when I told them that the President of the University of Dayton, Brother Fitz, lived there in a modest room, sharing a house with other Marianists, and he had dish duty like everyone else in the house.

The characteristic of the Marianist priests and brothers that most impressed me, however, was their acceptance of the diverse religious beliefs of faculty and students. Although they are totally committed to their own theological beliefs, and the University of Dayton is a Catholic institution, the Marianists not only tolerated a professor like me who espoused atheism, but welcomed me. Religious institutions' tolerance levels for deviating theological beliefs range from "believe or be gone" to "believe anything you like." On one end of the spectrum is a school like Bryan College in Dayton, Tennessee. It requires all its professors, including its science professors, to promise to adhere in their teaching to the school's official doctrine: "We believe that all humanity is descended from Adam and Eve. They are historical persons created by God in a special formative act, and not from previously existing life forms." There is no question that the University of Dayton is on the opposite end of the spectrum from Bryan College. It is a fundamental tenet of the Marianist teaching philosophy to inspire its students and professors to engage in careful, critical examination of all facets of knowledge. For them, no topics are immune from rigorous analysis, including Catholic doctrine. The Marianists' philosophy and commitment to teaching young people how to think critically is why I know I have a home at the University of Dayton and why I have been accepted as a member of the Marianist family.

Another challenge for me in trying to tell the history of the Sisters of Notre Dame during World War II was describing the events in a coherent and logical narrative. The letters by the sisters are often eloquent with vivid descriptions of their lives while living in occupied Belgium and Italy, but the incidents took place in many different convents in different locations. Furthermore, the sisters who participated in the events and the sisters who authored the letters are a diverse group of nuns who were eyewitnesses only to the incidents that took place at their particular convent. My solution to the multiple voices and stories dilemma is to create a fictional order of nuns, The Sisters of Our Lady of Namur, and a fictional sister, Sister Christina, who was living in Belgium during the War and who had first-hand knowledge of many of the events, or at least an opportunity to hear about them from people who witnessed them. Sister Christina narrates the quasi-fictional story of the Sisters of Our Lady of Namur in the form of a memoir. Some of the events described in the memoir as taking place in Belgium may have actually occurred in Italy. Some of them are my creation. The identities of the sisters are often difficult to determine from the letters, so I provided fictional names. Some incidents included in the memoir did not actually involve any Sisters of Notre Dame de Namur, but I wove them into the memoir as if the main protagonists were Sisters of Our Lady. Finally, some scenes are entirely of my own imagination. I attempted to make them realistic and compatible with the main storyline. I like to think they could have happened.

This a book that can best be described as imaginative nonfiction or a fictional memoir of actual historical events involving a fictional order of sisters, the Sisters of Our Lady of Namur. It is inspired by the letters of the Sisters of Notre Dame de Namur describing life in German-occupied Belgium and Italy during World War II. The memoir is based, in large part, on the eyewitness accounts appearing in the letters, but the story is told by a fictional participant in the story. Original sources are cited in the endnotes and bibliography. When I moved the characters and locations, or described entirely fictional scenes not based on any original documentation, I included endnotes explaining the modifications.

AUTHOR'S REFLECTIONS

If I were more religious, and believed that God and the saints periodically intervened in affairs of the world, I could make a good case for Saint Julie Billiart being the invisible hand directing the writing and publishing of this book. So many fortuitous and coincidental events occurred over the past twenty months to push this slothful author forward. It was like driving down a busy street and having all the traffic lights turn green as you approach each intersection. Whenever I was feeling a little discouraged, or suffering from a bout of writer's block, some total stranger would pop into my life and motivate me to keep writing.

I described in the Preface how Sister Kim Dalgarn dropped the Sisters of Notre Dame de Namur's letters on me like manna from heaven. A more apt analogy might be like rain in the desert, because it came at a time in my life when I was wandering in a wilderness of depression caused by the antics of the 2016 election. I could not believe what was happening to the country I loved. The land of tolerance and diversity was descending into a maelstrom of hatred and racism. Every story I read in the paper or watched unfold on television gave me spasms of psychic pain.

I wasn't sleeping, and it was increasingly difficult to concentrate on other aspects of my life. My solution was to take the pledge and totally swear off reading newspapers, watching TV news, and surfing online media. I changed from a news-junkie to a news-abstainer. Writing the book was like a drug. For three to five hours a day I was on a trip, oblivious to what was happening in the real world. The twilight zone effect lasted even longer. Throughout the day my thoughts would wander back to the book, drafting the next paragraph in my mind, planning plots. Even my insomnia subsided because thinking about the structure of a sentence is a great sleep inducer.

As luck—or Saint Julie—would have it, my first Amazon search for resource books found a book published in 2015 that was the definitive work on the German invasion and occupation of Belgium: *Belgium in the Second World War*, by Jean-Michel Veranneman. Ambassador Veranneman is an internationally respected diplomat. He has served in embassies in Germany, at the United Nations in New York, at the European Union, and at NATO in Brussels. He had been the Belgium Ambassador to Mozambique, Portugal, Israel, Brazil, and the United Kingdom. I was so impressed with the quality of his book, I wrote to Ambassador Veranneman to thank him for writing such an excellent account of the German occupation of Belgium. I explained in the letter how important his book was to the writing of my book. I sent the letter in care of his publisher, Pen and Sword, in Great Britain. Locating the book could be attributed to marvellous Amazon algorithms, but what happened next was beyond belief. I received an email from Ambassador Veranneman, thanking me for my letter and expressing interest in reading my book. Our exchange of emails blossomed into a real friendship with the dropping of titles and surnames and sharing stories and photos of our families. Jean-Michel invited Kathy and me to have dinner with him and his wife, Maria, when we came to Belgium to do on-the-ground research for the book. I invited them to visit with us at our cottage in Michigan. In addition to giving me some excellent advice about one of my scenes in the book, he asked his publisher to consider my book for publication. Finally, Jean-Michel agreed to read the completed manuscript and write a review. Was it coincidence or the influence of…?

In February of 2017, another piece of good luck occurred during a dinner at Jay's Seafood Restaurant in Dayton. I was playing host to a British High Court Judge, Sir John Royce, who spent a week at the University of Dayton School of Law as its Jurist-in-Residence. The former Dayton city manager had been invited but was unable to attend, so Patricia Mayer, whom I did not know personally, came instead. During the dinner conversation, I described my book. After dinner, while leaving Jay's, Pat mentioned that I might want to interview a friend of hers in nearby Yellow Springs, Ohio, Andree Bognar, who had spent four years under German occupation in Belgium during WWII. This amazing piece of luck (?) was curiously enhanced by the fact that one of the major characters in my book was named Andree.

Kathy and I arranged to have lunch with Andree the next week at the Mill House in Yellow Springs. Andree was charming and witty. After describing for us in detail what life was like for a child in occupied Belgium, she asked if during our upcoming trip to Belgium in June we intended to visit her hometown of Louvain. If we did, she added, we could meet her two sisters who were still living there. More "luck"? This was another opportunity not to be missed, so through Andree lunch was arranged with Therese Vandermotte and Mimi Wolfss in Louvain for June 2, 2017.

I was still basking in the glow of my good fortune when another piece of luck literally popped up in front of me in the visage of Sam Lauber. Sam was one of my students in a class (*Where Would You Like to be Arrested?*) that I taught in the University of Dayton's Osher Lifelong Learning Program. The course compared the American criminal justice system with the criminal justice systems of several European countries. Sam sat in the first row immediately in front of the lectern. During one class I mentioned the book I was writing and how Belgian convents were hiding Jewish children in their schools during the German occupation. Sam almost jumped out of his chair and announced, "I was one of those hidden children!" Over lunch, Sam told me his story, which I incorporated into the book. Coincidence or providence?

In June 2017, Kathy and I spent a week in Belgium doing research for the book. We travelled to many of the sites where Sister Christina's story takes place. Although the train fares in Belgium are established by Belgian Rail, our fares seemed miracle-like to us. Since we were over sixty, we could travel from one end of Belgium and back on fast comfortable trains for $6.50 each, less than the cost of a lunch.

On June 2, we travelled to Louvain to meet Andree Bognar's sisters, Therese and Mimi. I wanted to get their perspectives on what life was like during the German occupation. Therese and Mimi were just as enjoyable company as Andree. Before lunch they showed us where their father's shoe store was located— that is, before it was reduced to rubble by American bombs in 1944. During lunch we were transfixed by their stories, especially how their family fled across Belgium on their bikes to escape the invading Germans, only to ride their bikes back across the country after Belgium surrendered.

I included some of their saga in the book, but more importantly, Therese and Mimi provided me with a deep appreciation of what life was like in occupied Belgium, something I could never have gleaned from cold print. More Turner luck, or something else? Our next train trip was to Saint-Hubert, the town at the heart of Sister Christina's story. I was wandering around the town taking pictures of the Basilica, the town hall, and Main Square, but I was having trouble locating the Sisters of Notre Dame convent and school.

Finally, I found a person who could decipher my atrocious French and give me directions to the convent. I had just about finished taking pictures of the buildings and garden when I noticed a man putting an envelope in the convent's mailbox. I floundered through a question about whether he knew the sisters who lived in the convent, and he graciously asked if I would prefer carrying on the conversation in English.

His name was Guy Joris. When I told him why I was in Saint-Hubert, he pointed to the convent's chapel, the *Oratoire*, and told me it was his grandfather, Gaston, who had rebuilt the *Oratoire* after the war. It had been completely destroyed by American bombs. As if this was not "coincidence" enough, Guy told me he had pictures of his grandfather helping lay the cornerstone of the new *Oratoire* and that he would be happy to scan the photos and forward them to me. It seemed preordained that I should incorporate Gaston's story into the book.

Another remarkable "coincidence" occurred in July 2017. Kathy and I spend our summers near Traverse City, Michigan, and I row a shell on Lake Leelanau. A shell is a twenty-foot-long boat the width of a telephone pole, propelled by nine-foot oars. I met Chris Gordon one morning about dawn near the boat rack. Chris is a rower, too. In an attempt to keep me drier, he offered to let me row his shell, which is more forgiving to capsize-prone rowers like me. Over the course of Chris's two-week visit to Michigan, I talked to him about the book. As fate would have it, Chris was a pro at editing, and he kindly offered to complete a detailed edit of my book for free. My only cost would be the bruised ego I would have from his tough, rigorous proofreading. It was a price I happily agreed to pay. Destiny?

Finally, the last in the series of improbable events happened shortly before my book was going to press. Cheryl Keggan, a student I taught at the University of Dayton law school, came across my Facebook page and informed me about an anecdote her father, a WWII bomber pilot, told her about another American pilot who had been shot down in Europe and was hidden for a while in a convent. As an Evidence professor I am naturally cautious about hearsay evidence, but I did not want to bet against my run of good luck. I stopped the presses and included her father's tale in the book.

So, in light of all the marvellous, miracle-like occurrences I have experienced from the very beginning of my book-writing saga, have I altered my atheistic beliefs? The short answer is "No."

First, it would be arrogant in the extreme to believe that some supreme being would deign to manipulate worldly events to facilitate some unknown writer's quest to write a book. Second, it would utterly offend my sense of justice to think a supreme being would allow millions of people to die in concentration camps in World War II, but would give me help in writing a piece of imaginative non-fiction.

That is not the kind of god I could ever believe in. At the same time, however, researching and writing this book has moderated my perception of how sincere religious beliefs may impact societies for the better. Those beliefs may motivate them to "do good" and ultimately make the world a better place. I also have a better understanding how the religious beliefs of individuals help them cope with the travails of day-to-day living. I have never been an evangelical atheist, but writing this book has made it far less likely that I will ever be one. If theological principles motivate people to help their fellow human beings and increase their own happiness at the same time, why would I want to urge them to abandon those principles?

Father Jim Heft, a Marianist priest and president of the Institute for Advanced Catholic Studies, may have the best argument for religious beliefs incentivising people to "do good." He describes how his theology impacts on his willingness to put aside self-interest for the benefit of others.

"Could people who don't believe in God lay down their lives for others, speak truth to power and dedicate themselves to the poor? Of course. But in all honesty, left to my own devices, I am not that good. I need all the help I can get. My understanding of God helps me to be a bit more courageous than I think I would be otherwise. Jesus sets the bar pretty high. I still have a long way to go. I'm not confident that I could be good in this way without a God who pushes me beyond my comfort zone."

ACKNOWLEDGEMENTS

I have often seen authors of books acknowledging the invaluable contributions their spouses or partners have made to the final written product, sometimes even dedicating the book to them. I must admit I often regarded those comments with a trial lawyer's sceptical eye; thinking such effusive praise for a spouse or partner in boldface print was tainted by the author's self-interest in helping foster domestic bliss. As writing this book altered some of my perception of religious institutions, my views on an author's lavish praise of a domestic partner has also changed. I now understand why such tribute is entirely justified. When my wife, Kathy, agreed to help me on my book writing rollercoaster ride she had no idea what thrills and chills lay ahead, and of course, neither did I. This book would never have been written without Kathy's total support. She reminded me at the top of the hills, when my hubris was peaking, that sharp drops were likely to follow, and at the bottom of the dips she assured me confidence would return.

In addition to providing encouragement, Kathy and I spent hours discussing plot and character development. Kathy did not reject my crazy ideas with the curt laugh they deserved, but she gently guided them into the dustbin of discarded fantasies. Finally, Kathy went through the book line by line completing a detailed edit of the manuscript, which may have even pried a compliment loose from H.L. Menken. Thank-you, Kathy.

In addition to Kathy, I am also deeply indebted to our children, Sonya, Michael, and Caroline, as first readers, and to many other people who have provided invaluable help in getting *Sisters of the Resistance* published. Sister Kim Dalgarn SNDdeN has to be near the top of the list. I have described Sister Kim in the Preface to this book, so rather than repeat that ode, I will just say that without Sister Kim there would be no book. She was the catalyst, the spark, from which everything else followed.

How can I ever give adequate thanks to the Sisters of Notre Dame de Namur who wrote about their experiences coping with the German occupations of Italy and Belgium in World War Two, and their intrepid efforts to save the lives of people seeking refuge in their convents and schools? But for their letters they would have remained completely unsung heroes and this book unwritten.

Then there is Jean-Michel Veranneman who in 2015 wrote a unique history of World War Two that focused almost entirely on the impact of the war on Belgium. His book provided me with a context and a description of events that could be easily woven into the tapestry of Sister Christina's narrative. And, as a special bonus, Jean-Michel and I became friends, although we are living on opposite sides of the Atlantic Ocean. Thank you, Jean-Michel.

I forgive Brad Hoicowitz, Sales Manager for *Cincy Magazine*, for beating me regularly on the tennis court, and instead I want to thank him for his invaluable help in promoting and marketing my book. Kudus must also be awarded to Brad for introducing me to my marvellous publisher, Sue Ann Painter, who took me by the hand and guided me through the Byzantine world of book publishing.

Constructive criticism is an art form, and I was most fortunate to have two consummate editorial artists read and critique my early drafts of the book. They were Don Lystra and Chris Gordon. Their suggestions improved the book immeasurably. But, I am most grateful that they undertook their arduous tasks out of friendship. How lucky is that?

Finally, there are all those people mentioned in Reflections who magically appeared and told me their stories about life in occupied Belgium in World War Two—stories I could include as part of Sister Christina's narrative. Therefore, I want to extend special thanks to the three sisters, Andree Bognar, Therese Vandermotte, and Mimi Wolfss, and to Sam Lauber and Guy Joris.

I was spellbound as the three sisters described how they rode their bikes back and forth across Belgium during the first German invasion.

Perhaps more importantly, however, their description of life living with the German occupiers provided a rich context for my book, which would have been impossible to find from cold historical documents. Plus, their remembrances were shared with such warmth and charm.

Sam Lauber's tale of his life as a "Hidden Child" in Belgium during the German occupation provided me with personal insights into the myriad of contradictory feelings a "Hidden Child" has about his or her life trying to pass as a Christian. The fact that for a while Sam was hidden by Catholic nuns made his story fit seamlessly into Sister Christina's story.

Finally, I am so grateful to Guy Joris who, during our trip to Belgium, materialised on the street outside the Sisters of Notre Dame de Namur convent in Saint-Hubert. He told me about how his grandfather, Gaston Joris, had rebuilt the convent's Oratoire after the end of World War Two. Guy even dug out old black-and-white photographs showing his grandfather at the dedication of the Oratoire; he scanned the photos, and then mailed them to my home in Dayton, Ohio. The photos and Gaston Joris's story were perfect additions to my book.

It is inevitable that the Acknowledgements portion of a book falls short. Inarticulate expressions of gratitude and the omission of people who have helped the author along the way may give rise to disappointment. If that is the case with this attempt to express my appreciation, please forgive me. I think Saint Julie would support my plea.

WHO IS DENNIS TURNER?

Dennis Turner graduated from Georgetown University in 1967 with a degree in History. He received his Juris Doctorate degree from Georgetown University Law School in 1970. He has served as an Assistant County Prosecutor and as a Magistrate-Judge. Since 1974, he has been a Professor of Law at the University Of Dayton School Of Law. During his tenure at the University of Dayton he has served as Assistant Dean, Acting Dean, Director of the Law Clinic and Director of the Legal Profession Program. The University of Dayton has awarded him its highest award for teaching, The Faculty Teaching Award. He has also received numerous Teacher of the Year Awards from the students at the University Of Dayton School Of Law and was chosen to be one of the Master Teaching Fellows for the University. He has been a visiting professor for the University of Notre Dame London Law Program. He also has extensive experience with the British criminal justice system through his association with the barrister firm, Pump Court Chambers, in Winchester, England.

Dennis Turner is the author of many law review articles and a law textbook, *Steele v. Kitchener Case File*. For two years, he also wrote a bi-weekly column for the *Dayton Daily News* entitled, "On the River."

Dennis Turner lives in Dayton, Ohio, with his wife Kathleen. They have been married over forty-eight years which suggests that their original blind-date to the Trinity College Junior Prom in Washington, D.C. was a success. They have three children, Sonya, Michael and Caroline; and two grandsons, Lucas and Max.

Dennis became an avid sailor at the age of twelve in a land-locked Ohio county as a result of reading a book that changed his life, and the lives of his family. The book was by a British author titled *We Didn't Mean to Go to Sea*. It described the sailing adventures of four kids about Dennis' age. After reading the book twice, Dennis just knew he had to have a sailboat even though there was not a lot of water around Dayton suitable for sailing. He built his first sailboat which was actually a raft with a muslin sail. At least it floated. If clipper ships had still been crisscrossing the oceans, Dennis might have signed on as a member of the crew.

Lessons for life learned from sailing.

Enjoy the journey. Destinations often prove disappointing.

The pessimist complains about the wind. The optimist expects it to change. The realist adjusts the sails.

NOTES

CHAPTER 1

1. This event with Sister Superior being killed by a shell fragment while praying in the cellar chapel did occur, but the location was the convent in Bastogne. The author inserted Sister Christina and her injury into the scene.

CHAPTER 2

1. The author added the back story for Sister Christina. Her reasons for joining the Sisters of Our Lady of Namur were rather typical of young girls who wanted to become nuns. The description of the education and training Sister Christina received is also typical.

CHAPTER 3

1. The description of the two sisters travelling from the US to Belgium is from a letter by a sister. The author changed the names to Sister Clare and Sister Christina.

CHAPTER 5

1. The evacuation of the children is described in the letters. The author added Sister Christina to the story and created the dialogue.

2. The author added the dialogue to the description in the letters.
3. The exodus from Namur is well described in the letters. The author added the dialogue between Sister Superior Provincial and Sister Christina.
4. This whole scene with Sister Christina and the refugees on the road trying to board the truck is not in the letters and is totally the author's creation.
5. The following description of the sisters' journey into France is closely based on the letters. Where there is dialogue, however, it is the author's addition to the story.
6. Mimi and her two sisters, Andree and Terese, are still living. They were part of the Vandermotte family. Mimi and Terese were interviewed by the author and his wife, Kathleen, in Leuven, Belgium. Andree was interviewed in Yellow Springs, Ohio.
7. This scene with the French officer interrogating Sister Christina is entirely the author's invention. However, in the letters a French officer does question the sisters. He ultimately releases them, concluding they are truly sisters and not German parachutists. It is not unreasonable to assume that some kind of definitive proof was offered that convinced him the sisters were women.

CHAPTER 6

1. The essence of this story is true and appears in *Belgium in the Second World War*, by Jean-Michel Veranneman. The author, however, created the fictional brother, Albert, so he could tell the story to Sister Christina.
2. The author added this conversation. The dialogue with the German general is captured in the letters.
3. The author added this conversation. The dialogue with the German general is captured in the letters.

4. The transferring of Sister Christina to Saint-Hubert convent and her description of her duties there were added by the author.
5. Author's assumption of what Sister Superior would have said.
6. *Belgium in the Second World War*, by Jean-Michel Veranneman.
7. Story appears in *Belgium in the Second World War*, but the author connected the story to the convent by having Madam Varley relate the story to Sister Agnes.
8. *The Brass Saxophone* by Josef Škvorecký was the source for this information.

CHAPTER 7
1. This scene is not mentioned in any of the letters, but the dialogue is consistent with the active role of the Sisters of Notre Dame de Namur in resisting the German occupation.
2. The author assumed that in light of the sisters' actions in resisting the occupation that there would be significant contact between the convent and the Resistance.
3. There are no original documents describing in detail Sister Christina's or any other sisters' collaboration with the Resistance. The author assumed some kind of regular contact was maintained with the Resistance and the method for exchanging information is standard spy-craft.
4. This process may have been used by other religious orders. The letters do not say the Sisters of Notre Dame de Namur engaged in such practices but do describe how people were often searched to determine if they were carrying contraband food.
5. This is a true story about the Van Daelen-Speckaert family, which appeared in *Belgium in the Second World War*, but their connection to Sister Christina was added by the author.
6. This scene has been completely invented by the author.

7. The conversation with Sister Superior is not found in any original documents.

8. Secret hiding places were constructed in Sisters of Notre Dame de Namur convents, but the letters do not say such rooms were constructed in the Saint-Hubert convent. The descriptions of the various hiding places were taken from other sources and incorporated by the author into the Saint-Hubert story.

CHAPTER 8

1. This meeting with the Kommandantur took place, but the dialogue was added by the author.

2. This scene is totally the creation of the author.

3. The description of the ways the Germans tried to detect clandestine radios is supported by original documentation. The author assumed the techniques would have been used in Saint-Hubert, but there are no original documents to support that assumption.

4. The alarm system was installed in a Sisters of Notre Dame Convent, but there is no mention in the letters that a similar system was installed in the Saint-Hubert convent. The author assumed there had to be security drills if the alarm system was to be effective, but there is no mention of security drills in the letters.

5. In the letters, when the alarm system is explained, there is also a description of a strategy of delaying any Germans who came to the convent to search for refugees and Jews. A young Swiss sister was designated as the person to engage in a stalling tactic. There is little explanation of how the young Swiss sister was to delay the Germans, but it is reasonable she would employ some feminine wiles to distract them. The author has Sister Christina hone her distracting skills to accomplish a similar effect sought by the young Swiss sister.

CHAPTER 9

1. German soldiers did come to convents to search for refugees periodically. The scene is the author's description of how a raid may have been carried out.
2. Four sisters were detained by the Gestapo. The dialogue after their release was added by the author.
3. This is a true story appearing in *Belgium in the Second World War*, but the author connected participants to the Saint-Hubert convent.
4. Story appears in the letters, but takes place at another Sisters of Notre Dame convent.
5. Anecdote added by the author.
6. Sisters often had to burn wood and had to use their trees. Wood chopping scene was added by the author.
7. Cows and a pig were given to a Sisters of Notre Dame convent, but not the Saint-Hubert convent.
8. Description of farming, milking, and similar practices were added by the author.
9. This incident was described in the letters, but it took place near a Sisters of Notre Dame convent in Italy.

CHAPTER 10

1. Incident is described in the letters, but took place near another Sisters of Notre Dame convent.
2. The Comet line was an effective organisation in getting downed pilots through France into Spain and eventually to Portugal. The documents suggest religious institutions were stops on what was essentially an underground railroad. There is nothing in the letters that suggests a Sisters of Notre Dame de Namur convent was one of the stops. The author made the Saint-Hubert convent one of the stops and added the scene with Sister Christina interrogating purported American pilots. It is well documented that the Germans tried to infiltrate the

Comet organisation by having American-speaking German soldiers pose as downed American pilots. The Colonel Sam Niven anecdote was told to the author by Cheryl Keggan, a graduate of the University Of Dayton School Of law. Cheryl happened to see the author's Facebook page which motivated her to tell the author an amazing story that her father, a WWII pilot, told her about a fellow pilot who was shot down, escaped from a POW camp, and was hidden in a convent. Reportedly the nuns taught the pilot how to play bridge, but try as he might the author could not incorporate that scene into the book.

3. There is much original documentation confirming the role of Catholic sisters concealing Jewish children in their schools, including Sisters of Notre Dame du Namur. It is reasonable to assume the sisters in Saint-Hubert concealed some young Jewish girls in their boarding school. See Vromen, Suzanne, *Hidden Children of the Holocaust.*

4. This particular dialogue did not specifically appear in the letters, but was adapted from other sources describing the lives of hidden Jewish children, especially those being hidden in Catholic religious institutions. See Vromen, Suzanne, *Hidden Children of the Holocaust.*

5. Sam's story does not appear in the letters, but was adapted from Sam Lauber's memoir. Mr. Lauber was a student in a class taught by the author in the University of Dayton's Osher Life-Long Learning Institute. The coincidence was another example of the author's luck in getting access to wonderful stories without lifting a finger. Full story: Lauber, Sam, "A Hidden Child's Story," *The Dayton Jewish Observer,* May 2008.

6. This dialogue does not appear in the letters, but is included in other documents about the hidden children. See Vromen, Suzanne, *Hidden Children of the Holocaust.*

7. This scene was added by the author and does not appear in any original sources.
8. This is an elaboration by the author of the ration card process described in the letters.
9. Adapted from what happened at another convent that was hiding young Jewish girls.
10. This incident took place at another convent and was added by the author.
11. Author's addition.
12. The letters do tell about a Sisters of Notre Dame convent, not Saint-Hubert, getting two cows and a piglet from a local farmer. The description of the care and feeding of the animals, and the butchering of the pig, was added by the author.

CHAPTER 11

1. There is nothing in the letters that suggests that the concert ever occurred, or could have occurred. The scene is completely a product of the author's imagination.
2. Dialogue added by author.
3. Transcription of a BBC broadcast on June 6.
4. This scene is not described in the letters, but was added by the author.

CHAPTER 12

1. Description of trip described in the letters, but author inserted Sister Christina into the scene.
2. This scene with the soldiers was added by the author. Everything else is described in the letters.
3. The jeep ride in the countryside was added by the author.
4. Dialogue added by author.
5. The reference to the singing of hymns was added by the author.

6. The American Army did provide logistical help, but many of the details of the distribution system and the role of Major Thomson were added by the author.
7. All conversations between Major Martin and Sister Christina were added by the author.
8. The letters were originally written by Major John Hinkle and describe the events at another Sisters of Notre Dame de Namur convent and school.
9. Dialogue added by author.
10. This entire scene was added by the author.
11. The entire farewell scene was added by the author and no hint of such a scene appears in the letters.

CHAPTER 13

1. The description of Sister Christina's search for Andree and the conversation with Sister Superior were added by the author.
2. The Marlene Dietrich scene is a compilation of actual events during Marlene's visit to Belgium just before the Battle of the Bulge. At the outset of that battle, Marlene was almost captured by the German army. The author collapsed the events into one incident and set the scene in Saint-Hubert. The manufacturing of the shower device for Marlene was done by an American army unit in the Ardennes. Marlene's conversations with the sisters were added by the author, although Marlene's description of being courted by a Hitler henchman and her work entertaining troops is based on original documents. The description of Marlene's show in the *Basilique* is based on numerous written accounts of her performances for Allied soldiers.

CHAPTER 14

1. These events took place in Bastogne. The author changed the location to Saint-Hubert.

2. The events described by the sergeant occurred during the Battle of the Bulge, but the dialogue was added by the author. MacDonald, Charles, *A Time for Trumpets: The Untold Story of the Battle of the Bulge*.

3. The description by the lieutenant is well documented. The conversation with Sister Christina was added by the author. MacDonald, Charles, *A Time for Trumpets: The Untold Story of the Battle of the Bulge*.

4. His sharing of a cellar by German and American soldiers is based on an incident that occurred in a Sisters of Notre Dame convent in Italy.

5. The massacre is well documented. The dialogue with Sister Christina was added by the author.

6. This odd sharing of space by German and American soldiers did not take place in Saint-Hubert but did occur in another convent. In Saint-Hubert, the German soldiers and the sisters did occupy two separate wings of the cellar.

7. The sharing of cigarettes and the caring for the enemy wounded is not mentioned in the original documents, but was added by the author as something that very possibly could have occurred.

8. The conversations between Sister Christina and the German soldiers were added by the author. The substance of what was told to Sister Christina by the two soldiers is well documented.

9. These incidents occurred at another Sisters of Notre Dame convent in Italy.

10. This scene and dialogue were added by the author.

11. This scene and dialogue were added by the author.

CHAPTER 15

1. This scene is based on a conversation the author had with the grandson of Guy Joris in Saint-Hubert. While taking pictures of the convent in Saint-Hubert, the author saw a gentleman

putting an envelope in the convent's mail slot. Starting in French, but quickly switching to English, the gentleman told the author his name, Guy Joris, and explained how it was his grandfather, Gaston Joris, who rebuilt the Oratoire. The next day, he emailed pictures of the ceremony for the laying of the foundation stone.

2. The description of the damage to the Oratoire appears in the original documents. Also included in the original papers was a description of how the statue of Blessed Julie was completely undamaged and still on its pedestal after the destruction of the Oratoire. The dialogue with Gaston Joris was added by the author.

3. Sister Christina's thoughts and dialogue were added by the author.

4. The detailed description of the ceremony did not appear in the letters, but was based on accounts of similar Memorial Day ceremonies that took place at the World War II cemeteries in Europe.

BIBLIOGRAPHY

Ambrose, Steven, *Americans at War*, Berkley Books: New York, 1998.

Ambrose, Steven, *Citizen Soldiers*, Simon & Schuster: New York, 1997.

Ambrose, Steven, *Comrades, Brothers, Fathers, Heroes, Sons, Pals*, Simon & Schuster: New York, 2000.

Ambrose, Steven, *The Supreme Commander*, Anchor: Sioux City, Iowa, 2012.

Armstrong, Karen, *Through the Narrow Gate*, St. Martin's Griffin: New York, 1981.

Astor, Gerald, *June 6, 1944*, Random House: New York, 1998.

Boll, Heinrich, *A Soldier's Legacy*, Knopf: New York, 1985.

Boll, Heinrich, *The Casualty*, Farrar, Straus and Giroux: New York, 1987.

Boll, Heinrich, *The Train Was on Time*, Melville House: New York, 2011.

Boll, Heinrich, *Where Were You, Adam*, Northwestern University Press; Translated edition: Chicago, 1994.

Brofen, Elizabeth (2010, January). *A Diva's War: Marlene Dietrich's glamorous female soldier.*

Brokaw, Tom, *The Greatest Generation*, Random House: New York, 1998.

Deighton, Len, *Blitzkrieg*, Jonathan Cape: London, 1979.

Dietrich, Marlene, *Some Facts About Myself,* Avon Books: New York, 1990.

Hastings, Max, *Overlord,* Vintage: New York, 1984.

Keegan, John, *A History of Warfare*, Vintage: New York, 1993.

Keegan, John, *Guderian,* Ballantine Books: New York, 1973.

Keegan, John, *Soldiers,* Konecky & Konecky: Connecticut, 1997.

Keegan, John, *The Second World War*, Penguin Books: London, 1990.

Knappe, Seigfried, *Soldat,* Dell Publishing: New York, 1993.

Lucks, Guenther and Stutte, Harald, *Hitler's Forgotten Kids' Army*, Rowohlt Verlag: Reinbeck, Germany, 2014.

MacDonald, Charles, *A Time for Trumpets: The Untold Story of the Battle of the Bulge*, Quill / William Morrow & Co: New York, 1985.

McDonough, Sister Julie, *A People Remembers: St. Julie Billiart and her Oratory, St. Hubert, Belgium,* Sisters of Notre Dame de Namur Publishing: Maryland Province, USA, 1995.

Moore, Don (2012, November 9). *Making Marlene Dietrich's Wish Come True.*

Murdock, Sister Thérèse Marguerite, *In His Service: The Roman Mission of Notre Dame 1931–1946,* Sisters of Notre Dame Publishing: Ipswich, Massachusetts Province, 1982.

Pace, Edward Aloysius, *The Catholic Encyclopedia: An International Work of Reference on the Constitution, Doctrine, Discipline, and History of the Catholic Church,* Encyclopedia Press: New York, 1922.

Parker, Ken, *Civilian at War,* Horizon Books: New York, 1985.

Sisters of Notre Dame de Namur, *Letters 1931–1946,* Archives, Ohio Unit, Sisters of Notre Dame de Namur: Cincinnati, Ohio.

Škvorecký, Josef, *The Brass Saxophone*, Ecco Press: New York, 1999.

Standifer, Leon, *Not in Vain (A Rifleman Remembers World War II),* LSU Press: Louisiana, 1992.

Stillwell, Paul, *Assault on Normandy*, Naval Institute Press: Annapolis, Maryland, 1994.

Van Creveld, Martin, *Technology and War*, Touchstone: Austin, 1991.

Vaughan, Edwin, *Some Desperate Glory*, Pen and Sword: Barnsley, England, 2010.

Veranneman, Jean-Michel, *Belgium in the Second World War*, Pen and Sword Military: Barnsley, UK, 2014.

Von Luck, Hans, *Panzer Commander*, Dell Publishing: New York, 1991.

Vromen, Suzanne, *Hidden Children of the Holocaust*, Oxford University Press: UK, 2008.

Yaros, Ester (2013, November 20). *Jewish Children Hiding in Convents*. Publisher: Musee de l'Holocauste Montreal.